Killing Physicians

Killing Physicians

Shakespeare's Blind Heroes and Reformation Saints

John J. Norton

An imprint of 1517 the Legacy Project

Killing Physicians: Shakespeare's Blind Heroes and Reformation Saints

Published by:
New Reformation Publications
PO Box 54032
Irvine, CA 92619-4032

Printed in the United States of America

Publisher's Cataloging-In-Publication Data
(Prepared by The Donohue Group, Inc.)

Names: Norton, John J., 1971–
Title: Killing physicians : Shakespeare's blind heroes and Reformation saints / by John J. Norton.
Description: Irvine, CA : NRP Books, an imprint of 1517 the Legacy Project, [2017] | Includes bibliographical references and index.
Identifiers: ISBN 978-1-945978-50-0 (hardcover) | ISBN 978-1-945978-49-4 (softcover) | ISBN 978-1-945978-51-7 (ebook)
Subjects: LCSH: Shakespeare, William, 1564–1616—Criticism and interpretation. | Reformation in literature.
Classification: LCC PR3011 .N67 2017 (print) | LCC PR3011 (ebook) | DDC 822.3/3—dc23

NRP Books, an imprint of New Reformation Publications is committed to packaging and promoting the finest content for fueling a new Lutheran Reformation. We promote the defense of the Christian faith, confessional Lutheran theology, vocation and civil courage.

Contents

Introduction

This book will examine humiliation as a redemptive agent in Shakespearean drama. In the tragedies and late plays in particular, Shakespeare's protagonists face humiliating circumstances that serve to lift them to a higher level of emotional and psychological stability. Following their humiliation, these characters achieve a greater sense of discernment as it pertains to the human condition and a clearer sense of who they are in relation to the world around them. This book will offer a close reading of Shakespearean plays wherein humiliation and the resultant redemption of the protagonists occur. As part of this close reading, I will examine Shakespeare's chief inspiration for a humiliation that lifts and ultimately redeems. This kind of humiliation is found in great abundance in the writings of the Protestant Reformers of the fifteenth and sixteenth centuries. The Reformers I deal with in this book, because of their voluminous contribution to the formation of the early Protestant church, are Martin Luther, John Calvin, and Richard Hooker.[1] These theologians claimed that humiliation was employed by God in the lives of men and women to save them from damning pride.[2] This pride, according to the Reformers, prohibited men and women from recognizing their depraved state and their accompanying need for a redeemer.

Whether Shakespeare embraced or rejected the teachings of the Reformation—or of Roman Catholicism for that matter—is not debated in my work here. Of course, Richard Wilson, Richard Dutton, Alison Findlay, and others claim that biographically Shakespeare was a Roman Catholic.[3] This claim is dependent on the controversial "Spiritual Will and Testament" of John Shakespeare, which was supposedly found in the rafters of his home in 1757.[4] A gentleman named John Jordan submitted a transcript of the will for publication in "The Gentleman's Magazine" in 1784, but it was refused for unknown reasons.[5] Further support from circles that support the idea that Shakespeare was a Roman Catholic look to the will of Sir Alexander Hogton, which appears to place a "William Shakeshafte" in extremely Catholic circles in Lancashire in 1581.[6] Both of these claims are deeply problematic, as Robert Bearman has argued.[7] Biographically, it is not in fact safe to make the assumption that Richard Wilson does, saying that Shakespeare was "all through his life . . . writing just a wall away from the secret cell of Catholic extremism."[8] Of course, even if he were, it would not invalidate the argument of this book that Shakespeare's works partake of Lutheran theology. Dennis Taylor strikes a middle ground in his work *Shakespeare and the Reformation*, in which he takes a position that I hope to build on in my work here. Taylor's position is one that embraces the great complexity of religious thought in Shakespeare's England. Taylor writes, "Shakespeare's works are full of the culture of Catholicism mixed with the elements of the new culture of Protestantism. It is between these two mindsets that he is negotiating, trying to imagine how the Protestant horse can be put back into the Catholic barn, or conversely, how English Catholics can ride into a Protestant future."[9] Roland Frye's work is also important for its recognition of the complexity of religious thought in the period: "[Shakespeare] may have been essentially a pagan, or he may have been a deeply committed Christian, or he may have occupied some intermediate position. This much, however, we do know: it was in a culture shaped by the ideas that we have discussed [namely, the Reformation theology proposed by Luther, Calvin, and Hooker] that Shakespeare lived and wrote. It was also in terms of this culture that he expected to be understood. His was an age of great theological excitement."[10] More recently, Huston Diehl has written in a very similar way, describing the rich theological climate in which Shakespeare lived: "Because [Shakespeare] wrote for the commercial theater, his livelihood depended on his ability to appeal to the interests and tastes of London's citizens . . . The degree to which Shakespearean drama is a product of that evolving religious culture is often underestimated in our more secular age."[11] Claire McEachern, in her introduction to *Religion and Culture in Renaissance England*, recognizes "the massive centrality of religion to this period's cultural imagination and production."[12]

One component of what McEachern describes as the very popular religious discourse of Shakespeare's England involved a reaction to the controversial writings of Martin Luther. Considered the father of the Reformation, Luther exerted a profound influence on the Protestant church during his lifetime and long after his death. The source of Shakespeare's understanding of redemptive humiliation can be clearly attributed to the influence of Martin Luther on English spirituality. An important figure in Anglican Church history, on whom Martin Luther had a significant impact, was Archbishop Cranmer. When commissioned to create the articles of the Anglican Church in 1538, Cranmer met with Lutheran theologians and agreed on thirteen of the articles from the Confession of Augsburg. The Thirty-nine Articles of the Anglican Church, which received royal assent on June 12, 1553, have a clear Protestant flavor and use strong Lutheran language. Cranmer, a great supporter of Martin Luther, also employed much of Luther's works, specifically the Lutheran Church Orders, in the creation of the *Prayer Book of 1549*. In the 1540s, Cranmer also coauthored with Henry VIII a text entitled *The King's Prymer*. This strongly Protestant text was given to all schoolmasters, who in turn were commanded to teach it after the ABCs.[13] The extent of Cranmer's influence and his freedom to promote Lutheran doctrine can be attributed largely to the great personal bond he had with Henry VIII.

After Cranmer's marriage to the daughter of a Lutheran pastor from Nuremberg, Henry appointed him Archbishop of Canterbury, "thinking him the fittest man of all English clergy to be promoted to this high office."[14] Despite his Lutheran alliances, Cranmer found himself in the king's favor. Additionally, it was Cranmer whom Henry asked to see in the last moments of his life. The king's dying gesture, according to Reformation scholar David Starkey, was "a laying on of hands [through which the king] conferred his blessing on the new Protestant English Church and that Cranmer, more than anyone else, was to create under Edward VI."[15] It was this friendship, one that Diarmaid MacCulloch describes as one of Henry's most personal, that allowed Cranmer to exercise such great liberty as archbishop.[16] Cranmer had such a strong voice that many claim that he would have been removed from office long before had he not had such a personal bond with Henry VIII.[17] It was this friendship that allowed Cranmer, and in turn Martin Luther, to have such a significant influence on English spirituality. Although Henry VIII was not an outspoken supporter of the Protestant agenda, he allowed Cranmer much liberty. The result was the widespread influence of Lutheran doctrine through the English Bible, a text that Luther's pupil William Tyndale translated in the early sixteenth century.

Martin Luther's Protestant doctrine was spread additionally through the teachings of John Calvin. During the Marian exile, England's strongest Protestant theologians sought refuge in Geneva, Switzerland, where they worked with a community largely influenced by John Calvin's biblical scholarship. Often considered one of the greatest minds of the Protestant religion, Calvin built his ideologies on the Reformation principles established by Luther. Calvin's *Institutes of the Christian Religion* wielded a strong influence in Britain, allowing Calvin's work to influence some of the most prominent figures of British Protestantism. Some of these figures included a great host of Marian exiles, most notably the editors of the Geneva Bible and then later John Foxe and Richard Hooker.

It was Calvin's Reformation community that embraced a great majority of the English exiles. Under Calvin's tutelage, the Marian exiles were strengthened; their desire to reform the church in England was sharpened until the end of Mary's reign. It is argued by A. G. Dickens and others that this group is largely responsible for the radical shift back toward Protestantism that took place immediately after the queen's death. Dickens writes, "While the martyrs helped to ensure a reversal of Mary's policy, the eventual dynamic of that reversal may largely be ascribed to that other group of the Queen's opponents, the so-called Marian exiles. In these people abroad we see a microcosm of mid-century English Protestant opinion, free for once from the inhibiting influences of an English government."[18] On their return to England in November of 1558, the exiles were met by a government largely favorable toward Protestant theology. As Alison Shell, Christopher Haigh, Eamon Duffy, and others have pointed out, however, English culture was deeply Roman Catholic, and national conversion would not happen quickly or easily.[19]

Among the exiles were the authors of the Geneva Bible—Whittingham, Gilby, and Coverdale. As a student of Robert Barnes, the foremost Lutheran proponent in England during that generation, Coverdale undoubtedly offered a strong Lutheran bias to his work in Geneva.[20] The Geneva Bible was one that, according to Shakespearean scholar Richmond Noble, King James himself confessed to owning, that Richard Hooker and Archbishop Whitgift quoted regularly, and that preachers throughout London—Puritan or not—employed in the pulpit. Noble further claims that the Geneva Bible was "the Bible for family and personal use and its possession was no badge of party."[21] Although Noble's claim may be true, it is important to note that this translation included a foreword by John Calvin and its margins were covered with notes written by Martin Luther and other prominent Reformation theologians. A. G. Dickens writes this about the translation: "The text was more revolutionary than any since Tyndale and many of its innovations were to be followed by the Authorized Version of 1611. The critical notes, though embodying the best Reformed scholarship of the day, bore in some cases a bitter partisan flavour. Under Elizabeth this Geneva Bible was to find no close rival."[22] The notes in the margins of the Geneva Bible, written by Reformed theologians, would have an influence on how the biblical text was understood, thereby leading its readers to a strongly Lutheran interpretation of the Bible. Shakespearean critics Thomas Carter and Steven Marx support the notion that Shakespeare would have been familiar with this translation.[23]

Shakespeare would also likely have been familiar with the work of Richard Hooker. Hooker's was a Reformation voice that Shakespeare could have heard in any number of churches throughout London in the sixteenth century. Although a figure of less historical renown than either Luther or Calvin, Hooker is esteemed as a cofounder of the Anglican religious tradition. Philip Secor writes that Hooker is considered "the closest counterpart in the Anglican-Episcopal denomination to Luther for Lutherans or Calvin for Presbyterians or Wesley for Methodists."[24] As an ordained minister, Hooker held positions as rector at four very important churches from 1584 to 1600: St. Mary's Drayton Beauchamp, the Temple Church in London, Salisbury Cathedral, and St. Mary's Bishopsbourne.[25] In addition to being a well-known preacher, Hooker published a highly praised work in 1594, *Laws of Ecclesiastical Polity*.[26]

Although Hooker and the other Protestant Reformers did not find agreement in every theological doctrine, their works display a clear sense of continuity in regard to the depravity of man. Roland Frye states that Martin Luther, John Calvin, and Richard Hooker "represent and summarize the major forces which converged in the theological climate of Shakespeare's time."[27] It is the major themes of the Reformation that make their way into Shakespeare's plays.

One of the distinctive marks of Reformation theology is a humble view of humanity. The Reformers held fast to a belief in the depravity and the absolute sinfulness of mankind. It was this understanding that compelled the Reformers to speak and write about the doctrine of justification by faith. The doctrine of justification supported by Luther, Calvin, Hooker, and the great majority of Reformers in the sixteenth and seventeenth centuries came in direct opposition to the Roman Catholic vision of a man or woman who could work toward righteousness. Part of the Reformation view of justification involved the notion that men and women were spiritually depraved. According to Luther, anyone hoping to be redeemed must first recognize his or her spiritual sickness and need of a "spiritual" Physician. Only a person humbled in this way could find their place in God's grace. Only a person aware of their great spiritual sickness, their pitiable damnation, and their overwhelming depravity could truly follow Jesus Christ. The Reformers wrote many harsh words about Roman Catholic priests who refused to see humanity in this humbled state. The greatest error of the Roman Catholic Church, according to the early Reformers, was that it proposed numerous ways for men and women to reach God on their own merit by performing works of righteousness that would allow them to earn salvation. Reformation theologians condemned the practice of selling indulgences through which men and women could attain the forgiveness of sins. The Reformers' objection to the sale of indulgences and to other works of this kind focused on the fact that these acts distracted a man or woman from humble repentance. Instead of dropping to one's knees in recognition of his or her need for forgiveness, the sinner was apparently being encouraged by the Roman Catholic Church to work toward redemption through the purchase of indulgences or through the repetition of penitential prayers.

Luther's message of humiliation provided the initial attack on these practices, these religious acts based on what he claimed to be heretical doctrine. He wrote that a man was like a patient released from the hospital, grieving and wounded. This metaphor is one of Luther's most famous, and one that I contend found its way into many of Shakespeare's plays. Luther writes:

> This is like the case of a doctor who wishes to heal his patient, but finds that he is a man who denies that he is sick, calling the doctor a fool and an even sicker person than himself for presuming to cure a healthy man. And because of the man's resistance the doctor cannot get around to recommending his skill and his medicine. For he could do so only if the sick man would admit his illness and permit him to cure him by saying, "I certainly am sick in order that you may be praised, that is, be a man of health and be spoken of as such, that is, when you have healed me." Thus these ungodly and arrogant men, although they are sick before God, seem most healthy to themselves.[28]

Luther's sick man is one who is able to receive grace and healing. His sick man is cognizant of his humble position before God and man, and his humiliation serves as a catalyst for his salvation. Luther further elucidates this concept:

> Therefore we need humility and faith. What these words seek to establish and maintain is solely this, that inwardly we become nothing, that we empty ourselves of everything, humble ourselves and say with the prophet, "Against Thee, and Thee only, have I sinned, so that Thou art justified in Thy words. . . . In Thy sight I am foolish and weak, so that Thou mayest be wise and powerful in Thy words. . . . For all creation teaches. . . . that no one is exalted except the man who has been humbled, nothing is filled except that which is empty, that nothing is built except that which has been torn down."[29]

Shakespeare employs the use of Luther's "sick man" in all of his major tragedies as well as in many of the late plays. The sick man lacks proper self-knowledge, and his pride makes him unwilling to admit any deficiency in his character. The central Reformation themes that Shakespeare seemed to draw on in his creation of these plays are the need for proper self-knowledge and admission of one's spiritual sickness. These themes are worked out in Shakespeare's tragedies and late plays when the central characters have an experience with redemptive humiliation. The Roman Catholic concept of humiliation differs from the Protestant concept, the former emphasizing humiliation as a state one can think about and cultivate. Thomas Aquinas describes the Roman Catholic concept of humiliation in the following way:

> The spontaneous embracing of humiliations is a practice of humility not in any and every case but when it is done for a needful purpose: for humility being a virtue, does nothing indiscreetly. It is then not humility but folly to embrace any and every humiliation: but when virtue calls for a thing to be done it belongs to humility not to shrink from doing it, for instance not to refuse some mean service where charity calls upon you to help your neighbours. . . . Sometimes too, even where our own duty does not require us to embrace humiliations, it is an act of virtue to take them up in order to encourage others by our example more easily to bear what is incumbent on them: for a general will sometimes do the office of a common soldier to encourage the rest. Sometimes again we may make a virtuous use of humiliations as a medicine. Thus if anyone's mind is prone to undue self-exaltation, he may with advantage make a moderate use of humiliations, either self-imposed, or imposed by others, so as to check the elation of his spirit by putting himself on a level with the lowest class of the community in the doing of mean offices.[30]

In contrast, the concept of humiliation as described by Reformation theologians is one that bears a transformational power. This kind of humiliation overwhelms the sinner, causing him or her to see their "vile and damnable" souls.[31] Where we see a measure of reserve in the Roman Catholic view of humiliation—"for a needful purpose"—the Protestant view is rather violent, involving what Luther describes as "the scourging and crucifixion of the flesh."[32]

Although I will be examining the major tragedies and late plays in this study, I have chosen not to include *Macbeth* or *Pericles*. *Macbeth*, though a play that delves deeply into the notion of evil and depravity, does not invoke the theme of redemptive humiliation. The absence of humiliation in *Macbeth* creates a void that is indeed worthy of study. Why does Shakespeare arrest the progress of Leontes and yet leave Macbeth unchecked, allowing him to run headlong into disaster? Why are King Lear, Gertrude, and Alonso met by faithful ministers of redemption that lead them toward proper humiliation, while Macbeth is left alone with Lady Macbeth, her evil ambition only serving to load the fires of his own arrogance? I have chosen not to include *Macbeth* in this study because the play takes a much different shape than the other major tragedies. In *Macbeth*, redemptive humiliation, though much needed, is powerfully absent.

Unlike *Macbeth*, in *Pericles* we witness no apparent need of redemptive humiliation. In this play the great prince Pericles is a man of great wisdom, known far and wide for his discernment. In the opening scene of the play, the course of Pericles's life is altered due to his amazing ability to solve riddles and to discern the truth about the king of Antioch. When Antiochus pursues Pericles in the hope of keeping his evil secrets hidden, the humble prince takes to the seas, where his great honor is revealed in each and every encounter. Part of Pericles's character, and the key to his great vision perhaps, is an understanding of his own weakness: "My frail mortality."[33] Pericles betrays a Reformation understanding of human frailty, comparing death to a mirror "who tells us life's but breath, to trust it error."[34] This metaphor is used in *Hamlet* and, as I will argue in this book, is likely to have been drawn from Luther's Reformation writings.[35] In like fashion, Pericles affirms those who view life "as sick men do,"[36] always with a clear view of their own frailty and of the temporal nature of life. Once again lining up with one of Luther's most pervasive metaphors, Pericles seems in many ways a Reformation saint. The reason that *Pericles* does not fit into my study here, however, is the absence of redemptive humiliation in the action of the play. The primary villains in the play, the incestuous Antiochus and his daughter, are swiftly and decisively "shrivell'd up" by "a fire from heaven."[37] The secondary villains, Cleon and Dionyza, for their cruelty toward Pericles's daughter Marina, are burned by the people of their city.[38] Shakespeare stages a decisive punishment of evil in this play, choosing to employ not redemptive humiliation but what appears to be a swift and more merciless damnation.

In chapter 1 of this study, I focus on *Hamlet*. In this play, the young prince is humbled before the action of the play. Having just returned from school at Luther's highly reformed University of Wittenberg, Hamlet is well aware of his depraved condition. The focus of the play rests on prince Hamlet, a passionate young man caught in the middle of a love triangle between the living and the dead. The love triangle involves the ghost of his murdered father; his mother, Gertrude; and his uncle, Claudius. Hamlet struggles most profoundly with issues of conscience because the ghost has commissioned him to seek revenge against Claudius, who has murdered Hamlet's father and married Hamlet's mother in an effort to steal the throne and therefore the kingdom. The ghost stirs up a prophetic anger in Hamlet, urging him to take on the roles of "scourge and minister."[39] These are roles that will involve Hamlet setting the kingdom aright. Having been trained in Reformation theology at Wittenberg, Hamlet approaches his task with what appears a strong understanding of sin and redemption. He expresses a desire to see his mother "shent" or properly humiliated in order to lead her to salvation.[40] Hamlet approaches his mother with Reformation theology and with a particular set of Lutheran metaphors, a strategy by which he hopes to convince her to change her ways and seek divine forgiveness. With Claudius, however, Hamlet is far less gracious. Employing what appears to be a Roman Catholic understanding of grace and salvation, Hamlet abandons his role as minister in the hopes of seeing Claudius damned. Shakespeare portrays Hamlet as one who is thoughtful and as one who is properly fearful of the divine. In spite of this thoughtfulness, Hamlet loses control of his commission as minister and scourge. However, his desires are thwarted by the very principles of redemption he sought to employ. For in his efforts to condemn Claudius, Hamlet drives his uncle to a place of redemptive humiliation.

Chapter 2 moves on to consider *The Tempest*. Like Prince Hamlet, Shakespeare stages Prospero in *The Tempest* as a humbled minister, commissioned to take part in the workings of Providence. In *The Tempest*, Prospero is humbled to a place where he recognizes that he is a sinful man, dependent on the mercy of Providence. While serving as the Duke of Milan, Prospero develops a desperate lust for the magical arts. As a result of this lust, Prospero neglects his role as duke, allowing his disreputable brother Antonio to serve in his place. Not satisfied with sharing the dukedom with his brother, Antonio devises a scheme to banish Prospero. Prospero and his daughter Miranda are kidnapped and set on the open ocean to die a miserable death in a boat, "the rotten carcass of a butt,"[41] that has been stripped of any proper means of sailing. Through this experience, Prospero is humbled and thereby redeemed, and he is commissioned to take part in the redemptive work of Providence. By a miraculous act of God, as it is described by Prospero,[42] the broken vessel lands safely on an island. It is on this island that Prospero's magic is restored to its proper place under providential control. In this posture, humbled and broken, Prospero takes on the role of a minister, seeking the reformation of the shipwrecked sailors and of the native, Caliban. Like Hamlet, Prospero is forced to deal with ruthless men who seek to take his life. Unlike the young prince, however, Prospero does not abandon his role as minister to seek violent revenge. Instead, the former magician proves faithful as he deals humbly with the sailors and with Caliban.

In chapter 3 of this study, I examine *King Lear*, where the action revolves around the tragic consequences of the king's depraved vision. King Lear's lack of understanding is revealed in his decisions to divide his kingdom, reward his daughters according to the merit of their love speeches, and banish the people around him who refuse to tell him what he wants to hear. Lear is not left alone in his depravity; rather, he is met by faithful resistance, is broken by isolation, and is pursued by sacrificial love. The resistance Lear meets comes from his servant Kent, whose confrontation of the king bears a striking resemblance to the theological writings of Martin Luther. Lear is isolated in the wild plains, and it is here that he begins to see himself as a small part of a vast creation. This humiliation is necessary for him to accept the sacrificial love of his banished daughter Cordelia. As a truly faithful daughter, Cordelia pursues Lear with a sacrificial love that results in her untimely death. The redemptive humiliation of Lear allows him to finally see clearly. Lear becomes someone that Luther describes as capable of recognizing his sickness and who finally enjoys a redeemed understanding of himself, others, and the divine.

Chapter 4 involves an analysis of *Henry VIII*. In this chapter, I look closely at Cardinal Wolsey and his desperate need for recognition. The great cardinal is described as a fiercely ambitious man, one who was better known as "vile and importunate" than holy and devout.[43] Following what the cardinal explains as a desperate desire to please the king and to earn his praise,[44] Wolsey manipulates the king's subjects, brutally undermining any threat to his position as the king's chief advisor. The influence of Reformation theology in this play is witnessed in the nature of Wolsey's humiliating fall from power. An immediate sense of clarity overtakes Wolsey when he is finally dismissed by the king. It is important to note that Shakespeare departs from Holinshed's account of Wolsey's fall to include a more dramatic humiliation. It is here that we witness Shakespeare's employment of Reformation doctrine to create what becomes a more dramatic and perhaps more controversial redemption of Wolsey. The Roman Catholic priest is redeemed after he is humiliated; it is only here that he is able to recognize the greed and the desperate desire for recognition that had caused him to ruin the lives of so many men and women.

The final three chapters of this book focus on men who are not only greedy and desperate for recognition but also bound up by jealousy. Because of the similar natures of these protagonists, I will be treating the final three chapters cumulatively. In chapter 5, I look at *Othello*. As the story of a man who claims to have "lov'd not wisely, but too well,"[45] Othello's lack of discernment has tragic consequences, for his vulnerable mind is urged by a desperate passion. It may be argued that Othello is Shakespeare's most diseased protagonist. I contend in this chapter that although Othello would have fallen into the same violent jealousy without Iago, he might not have acted in such an extreme fashion without the aid of his lieutenant. Othello's mental and emotional sickness, though not unrecognized, goes unchecked throughout the course of the play. It is in the opening scene of act 4 that we see Othello fall into a trance. While it may be argued that Iago poisons Othello, thereby causing him to fall into such a sickness, we are persuaded to believe otherwise by Iago's own admission. While Othello's head spins, Iago confesses that only "credulous fools" are caught;[46] only men with diseased emotions and depraved hearts are vulnerable to this kind of medicine. Othello's sickened mind is also recognized by Lodovico when he witnesses Othello strike Desdemona on the face. Lodovico speaks in disbelief at the infection that has certainly taken over Othello's mind: "Is this is the noble Moor . . . Are his wits safe? Is he not light of brain?"[47]

In chapter 6, I focus on *The Winter's Tale*, where we see Leontes's fear of rejection and failure compel him to banish his wife and newborn daughter. It is this fear that serves to disrupt Leontes's vision, making him see things that do not truly exist. When the king's best friend Polixenes is convinced to prolong his visit by Hermione's persuasive gestures, Leontes creates a fictional scenario in his mind. This scenario is an elaborate creation involving a sexual affair between Hermione and Polixenes. So elaborate and farfetched are Leontes's accusations, his longtime advisor Camillo calls the king "diseas'd"[48] and begs him to be "cur'd"[49] of such dangerous imaginings.

Chapter 7 considers *Cymbeline*, where Posthumus's jealous rage leads him to demand the life of his wife, Innogen. Like Othello and Leontes, Posthumus has a violent fear of rejection and failure. This combination of character traits results in his being made vulnerable to the schemes of Iachimo. Convinced of Innogen's infidelity by what appears weak and farfetched evidence, Posthumus hastily rejects the love of one who is a picture of fidelity and grace. Just as Camillo recognizes an emotional and mental sickness in Leontes, so Posthumus's good friend Pisanio declares that a "strange infection" has overtaken Posthumus.[50]

Just as the surprise and condemnation expressed by Lodovico are unable to clear Othello's mind of an infectious fog and the censure of Camillo cannot cure Leontes, the warnings of Pisanio cannot shake Posthumus from his suspicions. Not one of these men rises from his sickbed until he is violently shaken by an experience with redemptive humiliation. This experience, drawn from the pages and sermons Reformation theology, becomes the means by which Shakespeare's most prominent characters rise from a tragic abyss into a place of brilliant clarity and divine reconciliation.

CHAPTER 1
Hamlet

A prophetic anger burns within Hamlet's soul. Hatred for Claudius and desperation to see his mother reformed stir up great emotion in him. He identifies the rank stench of injustice in Denmark, and he is mortified by the lack of understanding all around him. His sharp moral sensibilities seem to be founded on a humble knowledge of self, which the early Protestant Reformers affirmed as the basis of human wisdom.[1] John Calvin makes much of the idea of self-knowledge; he writes, "Thus from the feeling of our own ignorance, vanity, poverty, infirmity, and—what is more—depravity and corruption, we recognize that the true light of wisdom, sound virtue, full abundance of every good, and purity of righteousness rest in the Lord alone . . . Accordingly, the knowledge of ourselves not only arouses us to seek God, but also, as it were, leads us by the hand to find him."[2] The mind of the young prince bears no rival in Shakespearean literature. It is an intellect that Harold Bloom claims would drive the most devilish of Shakespeare's villains off the stage.[3] The nature of Hamlet's character, however—something that Bloom believes Shakespeare created in his "invention of the human"[4]—comes instead out of the Reformation theology of the era.[5] Hamlet is aware of the nature of his soul, and it is this knowledge that causes him to pause before the news of his ghostly father:

Hamlet: . . . and we fools of nature
So horridly to shake our disposition

With thoughts beyond the reaches of our souls?
Say why is this? Wherefore? What should we do?
(*Hamlet* 1.4.54–57)

Hamlet, so recently returned from the University of Wittenberg and sharpened by Reformation theology, is skeptical of his own disposition as a fool of nature.

Also trained in Reformation theology at Wittenberg is Christopher Marlowe's Faustus. Marlowe's *Doctor Faustus* and Shakespeare's *Hamlet* have some very significant similarities in regard to the notion of humility and Christian redemption. Clifford Davidson writes:

> Marlowe's *Dr. Faustus* seems to bear out at every point the Wittenberg theological position on the nature of the fallen man. Melanchthon in the *Loci Communes* (1521) says that, since Adam's fall, the unregenerate man's soul, "being without celestial light and life[,] is in darkness. As a result, it [the soul] most ardently loves itself, seeks its own desires and wishes nothing but carnal things and despises God."[6] Contrasted with the Christian who lives "not in himself, but in Christ and in his neighbor," Faustus' world revolves around himself from the beginning where he is discovered sitting in his study alone.[7]

It seems that in Hamlet's first encounter with the ghost, the prince expresses a measure of embarrassment at the appearance of the ghost, even before he becomes aware of the ghost's bidding of him:

Hamlet: Why, what should be the fear [of following the ghost]?
I do not set my life at a pin's fee;
And for my soul, what can it do to that,
Being a thing immortal as itself?
(*Hamlet* 1.4.64–67)

Hamlet recognizes the futility of a man's life, showing a humble opinion of himself. He does not fear that the ghost can take his soul, for his schooling at Wittenberg would have armed him against such fears. Hamlet admits some confidence in his salvation, knowing that his own soul is safely guarded by Christ:

Hamlet: My fate cries out,
And makes each petty artery in this body
As hardy as the Nemean lion's nerve.
Still am I call'd: unhand me, gentlemen;
By heaven, I'll make a ghost of him that lets me:
I say, away!

(*Hamlet* 1.4.82–86)

Hamlet's warning to Horatio and Marcellus[8] is reminiscent of Jesus's warning to Peter when the disciple objects to Christ's announcement of his impending death: "Get thee behind me Satan."[9] Peter (and in this case, Horatio) has the immediate and the temporal in mind, yet Christ—and Hamlet—is operating in the realm of the eternal. Hamlet understands the request of the ghost. The ghost bids him onward for some eternal purpose, some greater good beyond the mere physical safety of the prince.

Hamlet dares not trust his sinful soul, and he welcomes the possibility of supernatural censure, giving evidence of a spirituality that is often misunderstood by those around him:

Hamlet: But I have that within which passes show,
These but the trappings and the suits of woe.

(*Hamlet* 1.2.85)

In this scene, Hamlet stares in disbelief at the jollity present in the dead king's court. Mentioned later in his conversation with Horatio, it is here that Hamlet imagines the meats from his father's funeral reception being reused for the dinner that follows his mother's wedding. It is in this scene that Hamlet imagines the wedding guests tramping over his father's grave to stand in line at the refreshment table spread for the celebration of his mother's remarriage.

Harold Bloom and others have made assertions that in this exchange between Hamlet and his mother before the court, Hamlet reveals his self-alienated subjectivity.[10] This assertion, though nearly correct, is incomplete. Hamlet's alienation, his ability to draw conclusions in regard to the state of his own mind and soul, does not originate in himself. Hamlet's ability to draw conclusions in regard to the state of his own mind and to see himself as a depraved man incapable of making sound judgments is a result of external spiritual forces. This notion of the corrupting nature of human sin is also evidenced in Marlowe's *Doctor Faustus.*

In *Doctor Faustus*, written most likely between 1588 and 1590, Marlowe's protagonist, Faustus, speaks of having a mortal illness. The truth, however, is that Faustus's "ailment" is spiritual; he is ill of a "surfeit of deadly sin."[11] Defined by Reformer Philip Melanchthon, sin is "a depraved affection, a depraved motion of the heart against the law of God."[12] In his examination of Marlowe's text, Clifford Davidson draws on the Lutheran theology written by Melanchthon: "Sin for Faustus is an active force which corrupts his whole being; his body and soul are both committed to the power of Satan by his bond."[13] Luther would describe the saving force in Hamlet—that which is not present in Faustus—as the Holy Spirit of God. By an act of grace, the Holy Spirit enters the mind of man, allowing him to experience a more perfect self-knowledge. In Hamlet, therefore, we see a *divinely inspired* subjective alienation that can be traced back to Reformation doctrine.

On returning from Wittenberg, Hamlet does not immediately confront his mother but instead chooses to internalize his confusion and frustration. Her decision to marry Claudius is an act considered incestuous according to the ruling moral law of the day. In her analysis of this law and its impact on the play, Lisa Jardine cites the Levitical tables of consanguinity that prohibit marriage between those with close blood ties. According to Jardine, the workings of Hamlet's grief are complex: "For Gertrude has, by her remarriage, effectively cut off Hamlet from his hereditary entitlement . . . If Hamlet remains unmarried and childless, then Claudius and *his* offspring are next in line of succession to the throne of Denmark. Even if this is only a subsidiary theme of the play, it must, I think, add substance to Hamlet's obsessive preoccupation with Gertrude's *sexual* relations with Claudius, on which so many critics have commented."[14] Jardine continues by asserting that Hamlet is caught between the knowledge of an unlawful marriage, a crime committed (and perhaps two) to which the community has turned a blind eye, and a sense of personal outrage at a wrong perpetrated against himself by his close kin.[15]

Hamlet is confronted by his own mother's sin and the sin that is in his own heart. The events that transpired in his absence serve to prove the Reformation theology that he learned at Wittenberg on the frailty of man. Hamlet recognizes his own frailty as a "fool of nature" and the frailty of his mother (*Hamlet* 1.4.54). John Curran's work on *Hamlet* focuses on the Calvinistic nature of the play. While my work here focuses on the broader strokes of Reformation theology in *Hamlet*, Curran's work is important for my study in that it identifies the prince's understanding of humility and human frailty. Curran describes Hamlet as a character who, through the course of the play, develops an understanding of the power and control of God in human affairs. As a result of this understanding, Hamlet concludes that "the readiness is all" (*Hamlet* 5.2.213). This statement, according to Curran, means than man need only to prepare to "accept the way things must be."[16] This conclusion, however, isolates one of the minor points of Calvin's doctrine, failing to consider it in the context of Calvin's teaching on the responsibility of mankind. Although God has "foreseen and ordained" all things and nothing is out of His control,[17] God has, according to Calvin, chosen to enlist men and women in His redemptive and reformative work. As a redeemed man, Hamlet is not, according to Calvin's theology, limited to merely accepting the way things are; rather, he must actively participate in the work God has called him to do. Calvin writes:

> We are not at all hindered by God's eternal decrees either from looking ahead for ourselves of from putting all our affairs in order . . . For he who has set the limits to our life has at the same time entrusted to us its care; he has provided means and helps to preserve it . . . Now it is very clear what our duty is: thus, if the Lord has committed to us the protection of our life, our duty is to protect it; if he offers helps, to use them; if he forewarns of dangers, not to plunge headlong . . . These fools do not consider what is under their very eyes, that the Lord has inspired in men the arts of taking counsel and caution, by which to comply with his providence in the preservation of life itself.[18]

Calvin explains further that God often chooses to "clothe" His Providence in human form, calling men and women to take part in his plan of redemption.[19] In this way, as Curran fails to recognize, Hamlet's greater purpose is revealed through Reformation theology.

Shakespeare stages Hamlet's emotional reaction to his mother's remarriage in order to reveal sensitivity in the prince's character. T. S. Eliot's concept of the "objective correlative" in *Hamlet* deserves attention here,[20] especially as we are examining Hamlet's reaction to his mother's behavior. Eliot's concept is described in this way: "A set of objects, a situation, a chain of events which shall be the formula of that particular emotion; such that when the external facts . . . are given, the emotion is immediately evoked."[21] In other words, a character's emotional response to an event must be within means; it must not appear exaggerated or out of proportion in its relation to the behavior that elicited it. Eliot claims that Hamlet violates the objective correlative by overreacting to the actions of his mother.[22] He contends that Hamlet has no reason to act as wildly as he does. However, Eliot does not consider the fact that Hamlet is a religious man, his convictions sharpened while studying at Wittenberg, a Protestant university. Read through the lens of Reformation theology, Hamlet's grief appears realistic. The religious conviction that Shakespeare folds into Hamlet's character causes him to react passionately about his mother's incestuous act. He is angered, yet he understands that no good can come of venting his frustrations:

Hamlet: It is not, nor it cannot come to good,
But break, my heart, for I must hold my tongue.
(*Hamlet* 1.2.158)

Based on his discussion with Horatio, it is clear that Hamlet is horrified by his mother's immoral union with Claudius: "Would I had met my dearest foe in heaven / Or ever I had seen that day, Horatio" (*Hamlet* 1.2.182–83). Harold Bloom asserts that Gertrude's intense sexual appetite is to blame for her rash decisions. I find, however, the arguments of Rebecca Smith and A. C. Bradley far more convincing. Smith's contention that Gertrude is guilty of unreflective passivity seems more realistic.[23] She describes Hamlet's mother as "a compliant, loving, unimaginative woman [with an] extremely dependent personality."[24] Though Bradley is often criticized for treating characters as though they were real people,[25] his comparison of Gertrude to a "sheep in the sun" is insightful:

> But she had a soft animal nature, and was very dull and very shallow. She loved to be happy, like a sheep in the sun; and, to do her justice, it pleased her to see others happy, like more sheep in the sun. She never saw that drunkenness is disgusting till Hamlet told her so; and, though she knew that he considered her marriage "o'er-hasty" (II. ii. 57), she was untroubled by any shame at the feelings which had led to it. It was pleasant to sit upon her throne and see smiling faces round her, and foolish and unkind in Hamlet to persist in grieving for his father instead of marrying Ophelia and making everything comfortable. She was fond of Ophelia and genuinely attached to her son (though willing to see her lover exclude him from the throne); and, no doubt, she considered equality of rank a mere trifle compared with the claims of love. The belief at the bottom of her heart was that the world is a place constructed simply that people may be happy in it in a good-humoured sensual fashion.[26]

Hamlet is concerned about his mother's salvation. He treats her,  in New Testament terms, as a sheep without a shepherd,[27] lost and most certainly damned. His concern for her is shown in his confrontation of her in the bedchamber. This kind of passion may have been inspired by what Shakespeare saw in Martin Luther, a man determined to open the eyes of the common man. Hamlet's experience at Wittenberg and his internalization of Lutheran doctrine have turned him into a reflective man. Despite his concern for his mother, Hamlet's first reaction to the news of the remarriage, based on Lutheran doctrine, is to turn inward.

Part of my aim in this chapter is to put to rest the notion that Hamlet's inaction is a part of an Aristotelian tragic flaw. Indeed, it is precisely the opposite. Hamlet, refusing to be a slave to his emotions, desires to give his thoughts time to unravel and cool. Hamlet's slow progress is commendable and in every respect affirmed by the morality expressed in the play. Hamlet's comprehension of his own depravity and inability to think clearly and rationally keeps him from acting without thought. His knowledge of himself is resonant of King David's confession in the Psalms: "For I know mine iniquities, and my sin is ever before me."[28] If Hamlet is what Luther calls a man aware of his sickness and frailty, the prince is an ideal Reformation saint. Hamlet moves forward thoughtfully, revealing that which he believes is the right course of action:

Hamlet: . . . and blest are those
Whose blood and judgment are so well commeddled
That they are not a pipe for Fortune's finger
To sound what stop she please. Give me that man
That is not passion's slave, and I will wear him
In my heart's core, ay, in my heart of heart,
As I do thee.

(*Hamlet* 3.2.69–74)

In this statement Hamlet highlights the character of his best friend Horatio—an emotionally stable man with a disciplined mind. By pointing to these qualities, Hamlet reveals the battle in his mind—a conflict between passion and reason. It is clear that Hamlet wants to "wear" Horatio in his heart. By doing so, he can guard against the temptation to be passion's slave. In contrast to Hamlet's thoughtfulness is Claudius's rashness: "That we would do, / We should do when we would" (*Hamlet* 4.7.118–19). Claudius, the object of Hamlet's disdain throughout the play, lives by this notion of action—taking action immediately, seizing the moment, rushing forward without the involvement of one's conscience. This same rash behavior is also evidenced in Claudius's marriage to the queen and in the couple's desire for Hamlet to give up mourning for his father. Additionally, Claudius's manipulation of Laertes is dependent on rash action—action empowered by the heat of strong emotion.

After the dumb show, Hamlet is called forth by his mother. Before he makes his way to her chamber, he reveals his conflicted heart:

Hamlet: 'Tis now the very witching time of night,
When churchyards yawn and hell itself breathes out
Contagion to this world. Now could I drink hot blood,
And do such bitter business as the day

> Would quake to look on. Soft, now to my mother.
> O heart, lose not thy nature. Let not ever
> The soul of Nero enter this firm bosom;
> Let me be cruel, not unnatural.
> I will speak daggers to her, but use none.
> My tongue and soul in this be hypocrites:
> How in my words somever she be shent,
> To give them seals never my soul consent
>
> (*Hamlet* 3.2.379–90)

In the light of his conversation with Horatio, Hamlet is aware of the temptation to act in accordance with his passions. I do not intend to present Hamlet as a blameless figure, but rather, as a man with realistic weaknesses, at times motivated by hatred or rash and ignorant. Hamlet's awareness of his weaknesses and sin makes him akin to a Reformation saint.

Hamlet recognizes that his soul, much like the kingdom in which he resides, is an "unweeded garden" possessed only by things "rank and gross in nature" (*Hamlet* 1.2.135–36). David Kastan writes well when he claims, "If Hamlet in his efforts to restore [Denmark] to wholesome growth fails and even becomes 'a little soil'd i'th' working' (2.1.41) we cannot be surprised. Indeed we may admire him for his willingness to attempt a translation of the Ghost's intention into moral action."[29] On his way to see his mother, awareness of his weakness causes Hamlet to utter a prayer, "O heart, lose not thy nature. Let not ever / The soul of Nero enter this firm bosom" (*Hamlet* 3.2.384–85). In this prayer, Hamlet refers to a nature he aspires to, which demands that he be a minister and scourge and that he spare his mother. This is not to be confused with the nature of man, which conversely runs to that which is evil and base.

The Geneva Bible version of Romans 2:27 reads as follows: "How shall we, that are dead to sin, live yet therein?"[30] The accompanying note, printed in the margin of Shakespeare's Bible, seems pertinent to the struggle in which Hamlet is engaged: "He dieth to sin in whome the strength of sin is broken by the virtue of Christ, and so now liveth to God . . . Which is, that growing together with him, we might receive virtue to kill sin, and raise up our new man."[31] Hamlet's struggle is against his natural inclination to sin, thus the need to “kill sin.” In the book of Romans, Paul addresses this struggle and stresses man’s dependence on the “Spirit of God.”[32] Paul continues, “For I know, that in me, that is, in my flesh, dwelleth no good thing: for to will is present with me: but I find no means to perform that which is good.”[33] Again Paul admits to his struggle against sin, an admission much like Hamlet’s. The marginal note following this verse in the Geneva translation reads as follows: “He is not able to do that which he desireth to do, and therefore is far from the true perfection.”[34] Further down, the marginal note adds a stronger definition of the sinful man’s body: “This fleshly lump of sin and death.”[35]

While the depth of Shakespeare’s biblical knowledge is unknown, it is probable that he would have been aware of Martin Luther’s commentary on Romans. Luther published many sermons on this text, and the heart of his controversial Reformation doctrine focused on the idea that men and women could receive salvation by faith alone (*sola fide*) and not by works.[36]

Shakespeare has cast Hamlet in the mold of the Apostle Paul in many ways, at least in regard to Paul’s struggle to do the things he knew were right and to shun the things he knew were evil. Hamlet, consistent with the apostle’s teaching, calls on the grace of God, for this is the only way he can overcome the evil that so often hinders the regenerate man. His goal is to help his mother recognize her error and to lead her to the place of humble realization described by Luther’s redemptive humiliation. Hamlet’s words are prayerlike, bidding God not to let him act with the hatred of Nero, who killed his mother, Agrippina. Hamlet’s desire is to speak daggers—to penetrate Gertrude’s heart with the truth—and to urge her toward penitence. His hope is that she will come to a place of proper humiliation, that her heart will be “shent” (*Hamlet* 3.2.389) and that she will be saved from moral blindness. A. C. Bradley writes:

> And while the rough work of vengeance is repugnant to him, he is at home in this higher work. Here that fatal feeling, “it is no matter,” never shows itself. No father-confessor could be more selflessly set upon his end of redeeming a fellow-creature from degradation, more stern or pitiless in denouncing the sin, or more eager to welcome the first token of repentance . . . The truth is that although Hamlet hates his uncle, his

> whole heart is never in the task [of revenge]. . . . but his whole heart is in his horror at his mother's fall and in his longing to raise her.[37]

The verb "shent/to shend" is a very old word, forms of which date back to the thirteenth century, according to the Oxford English Dictionary. The word means to put to shame, to rebuke, to disgrace, and to humiliate. Hamlet has been shent by the comprehension of his place in the universe; this concept was most likely sharpened in Hamlet's mind while at Wittenberg. The circumstances of Hamlet's life have led him to further recognition of the futility of man's works and the limits of man's understanding. Stepping out in emotional fervor is something Hamlet sees neither honor nor wisdom in. This is evidenced by Hamlet's own words following his rash murder of Polonius only moments after the prince's arrival in his mother's chamber, "For this same lord, / I do repent. But heaven hath pleased it so / To punish me with this and this with me, / That I must be their scourge and minister" (*Hamlet* 3.4.172–75). In regard to this passage, R. A. Foakes writes, "Here Hamlet abandons all of his earlier wrestlings with conscience and with the biblical injunction against killing. He casually pushes responsibility away from himself with no remorse."[38] I would argue that Foakes errs here. While Hamlet does a rash and terrible thing in his murder of Polonius, he appears contrite and considerably determined to take responsibility for his crime in the lines following, "I will bestow him, and will answer well / The death I gave him" (*Hamlet* 3.4.178–79). This gesture, although given quickly, is evidence of Hamlet's contrition. He admits to his crime and vows to bestow on Polonius the respect he deserves. In promising to "answer well the death I gave him," Hamlet takes ownership of his crime, confesses to it, and acknowledges that his act of murder was wrong and cruel. Hamlet's use of a mirrored phrase, "to punish me with this and this with me," is also a reference to his murder of Polonius (*Hamlet* 3.4.176). Once again, Hamlet proves that he is aware of his sinful nature and the punishment he deserves for this murder. It is this sinful nature, one of rashness and corruption, that has led to Polonius's murder, and now Hamlet must deal with the repercussions of his act. Concerning Hamlet's conversation with Claudius in regard to the murder of Polonius, Foakes further errs when he claims that Hamlet expresses disrespect for Polonius when he "puts on [an] antic disposition in mockingly talking to Rosencrantz and Guildenstern and then to the King about what he has done with the body of Polonius."[39] Hamlet's seeming callousness is the bluff he plays in this chess match with Claudius. Hamlet must wear this  guise of madness, the guise of a wildly disrespectful knave, to keep Claudius from seeing the true color and texture of Hamlet's mind. It would be a swift execution for Hamlet if he were to show his heart to the King.

The murder of Polonius is a rash act, the likes of which Hamlet hopes to avoid with his mother. This is the nature of Hamlet's prayer before going to his mother's chamber. He hopes to keep his focus, which is the shending of his mother's heart. Hamlet strives to break  Gertrude's heart and see her properly humiliated, as is witnessed in his conversation with her in the bedchamber:

Hamlet: Come, come, and sit you down, you shall not budge.
You go not till I set you up a glass
Where you may see the inmost part of you.
(*Hamlet* 3.4.17)

Hamlet's setting "up a glass," or mirror, in which Gertrude will see the "inmost" part of her soul bears a direct relation to Luther's teachings on biblical Law. Luther compares the Law to a mirror, going so far as to say that the foremost purpose of the Law is to act as a mirror "in which we can see wherein we are lacking."[40] Hamlet hopes to use the truth  as a mirror for his mother, and to thereby save her. It is interesting to note that Luther writes with the same confidence about the saving nature of the Law: "Thus man recognizes himself in the mirror and in face of the letter of the Law—how dead he is and in what disgrace he is with God. This knowledge makes him afraid and drives him to seek the Spirit, who makes him good, godly, holy, spiritual, brings all things into accord with the Law, and leads him to God's grace."[41] In his sermons on the Gospel of John, Luther claims that the Law is given to men for the revelation of sin: "It holds a mirror before us; we peer into it and perceive that we are devoid of righteousness and life. And this image impels us to cry: 'Oh, come, Lord Jesus Christ, help us and give us grace to enable us to fulfill the Law's demands!'"[42]

In "Surpassing Glass: Shakespeare's Mirrors," Philippa Kelly offers a look at the history of the mirror and its use in literary works as it came into popular possession in the middle of the sixteenth century. Kelly draws attention to the way in which Shakespeare's poet of sonnet 62 comes to see not only his physical reflection but also the "upsetting disparity between the face he imagines he has and the face he owns. But it isn't just a physical reflection that he sees—it is also the 'sin' of his own 'self-love' that 'possesseth all mine eye, / And all my soul, and all my every part.'"[43] Hamlet wishes for his mother to experience the same awakening as did the poet of sonnet 62, an awakening that would shend her heart to a place of redemptive humiliation.

Hamlet: Leave wringing of your hands. Peace, sit you down,
And let me wring your heart; for so I shall
If it be made of penetrable stuff,
If damned custom have not braz'd it so,
That it be proof and bulwark against sense.

(*Hamlet* 3.4.34)

Hamlet is aware of how the world has dealt with the humbling nature of men. "Damned custom" is that which encourages a man to explain away or harden himself to the frailties he may recognize in himself.  In Gertrude's case, she has not been hardened by the customs and excuses that emanate from a self-centered world. Her heart is shent by Hamlet's revelation of the truth.

Gertrude: O Hamlet, speak no more.
Thou turn'st my eyes into my very soul,
And there I see such black and grained spots
As will not leave their tinct . . .
O speak to me no more.
These words like daggers enter my ears.
No more, sweet Hamlet.

(*Hamlet* 3.4.88–91, 94–96)

Gertrude's acknowledgement of her sin and shame bears a likeness to Claudius's repentance.

There is something fascinating about the nature of Claudius's prayer. Difficult to condemn and at times impossible to hate, Claudius bears the markings of a Reformation saint. The nature of his prayer in act 3 is revealing, as Claudius takes on a complexity that Shakespeare employs to wrong-foot his audience and Hamlet. In Claudius's pleading is a likeness to Reformation humility and clarity. Whereas Roman Catholic doctrine is strict concerning the nature of proper repentance, involving sacramental absolution and accompanying acts of penance,[44] Reformation doctrine emphasizes the removal of human payment and duty. This removal of the human element is reflected in Luther's statements about prayer, confession, and the sinful nature. The following passage offers insight into the mind of the Reformation Christian, insight that Shakespeare may have been working with in his construction of Claudius's character. Luther writes, "Through the Law there is knowledge of the sin which is in us, that is, of our evil will which inclines toward the evil and abhors the good. How useful this knowledge is! For he who recognizes it, cries to God and in humility begs that this will may be lifted up and healed. But he who does not recognize it does not ask, and he who does not ask does not receive, and thus he is not justified because he is ignorant of his own sin."[45] It may in fact be that Claudius is redeemed by virtue of the fact that he recognizes his sinful condition and calls on God for help. Claudius is a man who recognizes his sinful state, recognizes his inability to stop sinning, and confesses his dependence on Providence to escape what he identifies as a cursed state:

> **Claudius:** O, my offence is rank, it smells to heaven;
> It hath the primal eldest curse upon't—
> A brother's murder.
>
> (*Hamlet* 3.3.36–38)

As he struggles to understand the nature of prayer and confession, Claudius confesses that his bosom is as "black as death" and describes his soul as "limed" and "struggling to be free" (*Hamlet* 3.3.67–68). This is a man who is troubled by the sin he has committed, and yet he is unable to free himself from the web of sin his hands have spun:

Claudius: "Forgive me my foul murder?"
That cannot be, since I am still possess'd
Of those effects for which I did the murder—
My crown, mine own ambition, and my queen.
(*Hamlet* 3.3.51–55)

Claudius's question, perhaps drawn from the Reformation debate, is answered by Luther in this way: "Therefore we think: 'What shall we wretched people do, we who have been living in all the sins against the First and the Second Table? Shall we short-lived sinners (Ps. 103:15) really approach the infinite and eternal God and ask Him to alleviate these evils?' . . . Such are truly the sentiments of all human beings. Yet we must learn that we should pray even in the most desperate  evils and hope for the unexpected and the impossible."[46] Claudius wrestles with the same difficulties that Luther describes in this passage. In Claudius, we witness the struggle of a Reformation saint, a man aware of his sinful state and equally aware of his inability to save himself. An audience such as Shakespeare's would have been familiar with this difficult Reformation doctrine. Such familiarity would have stirred up debate among the Reformation and Roman Catholic sympathizers in the audience. Claudius's prayer would put such an audience into a conundrum: "Could the devilish Claudius continue in his sin and yet still retain his Christian salvation?" It  is not difficult to picture Claudius in the following description of Luther's "spiritual man." This is a man that Luther identifies as struggling in much the same way that Claudius struggles, questioning his salvation and questioning God. Luther writes, "*Wretched man that I am! Who will deliver me from the body of this death?* (v. 24). This even more clearly than the preceding statements shows that a spiritual man is speaking these words, for he laments and mourns and desires to be delivered. But surely no man except a spiritual man would say that he is wretched . . . Therefore only the perfectly spiritual man says: 'Wretched man that I am!' But the carnal man does not desire to be liberated and set free but shudders terribly at the freedom which death brings, and he cannot recognize his own wretchedness."[47] According to Reformation doctrine, the guilt that torments Claudius is evidence that the king is redeemed. The Reformation understanding of justification—that salvation is granted by grace through faith—establishes the fact that men and women do not lose their salvation by committing mortal or venial sins. By contrast, the Roman Catholic meeting at the Council of Trent of 1546 came to the opposite conclusion, emphasizing that mortal sins would indeed exclude men and women from the "kingdom of God." Chapter XV of the Council of Trent reads as follows:

> Against the subtle wits of some also, who by pleasing speeches and good words seduce the hearts of the innocent, it must be maintained that the grace of justification once received is lost not only by infidelity, whereby also faith itself is lost, but also by every other mortal sin, though in this case faith is not lost; thus defending the teaching of the divine law which excludes from the kingdom of God not only unbelievers, but also the faithful [who are] fornicators, adulterers, effeminate, liars with mankind, thieves, covetous, drunkards, railers, extortioners, and all others who commit deadly sins . . . and on account of which they are cut off from the grace of Christ.[48]

Claudius ends his prayer with pleas to the heavenly hosts and his own flesh. It is in these statements that Shakespeare may be seeking to create a sense of wonder in his audience. Claudius pleads for a humble posture and for a soft heart:

Claudius: Help, angels! Make assay.
Bow, stubborn knees; and heart with strings of steel
Be soft as sinews of the new born babe.
All may be well.

(*Hamlet* 3.3.69–72)

In this passage, Shakespeare displays a religious sensitivity in Claudius. Though Claudius in this scene appears to be struggling with Reformation doctrine, he is aware of his depravity and his need for grace. Looking at this passage through the lens of Reformation theology, especially the following commentary by Luther, it is clear that Shakespeare has staged Claudius as one who will indeed be "pardon'd and retain th' offence" (*Hamlet* 3.3.56): "As long as we are here in this world we have to sin. This life is not the dwelling place of righteousness, but, as Peter says, we look for new heavens and a new earth in which righteousness dwells . . . No sin will separate us from the Lamb, even though we commit fornication and murder a thousand times a day. Do you think that the purchase price that was paid for the redemption of our sins by so great a Lamb is too small? Pray boldly—you too are a mighty sinner."[49] As Claudius labors in prayer, vexed by the nature of grace and yet hopeful in what he understands of faith and grace, we see Hamlet prepared to kill his penitent uncle.

Standing in the doorway, Hamlet pauses behind the praying king. Hamlet engages some of the same questions of faith that Claudius has been wrestling with in prayer. Whereas Claudius in this scene appears to be struggling with Reformation doctrine, Hamlet's purpose for not killing his uncle is based largely on a Roman Catholic understanding of mortal sin. It may be that Hamlet's hatred for Claudius causes him to revert back to a Roman Catholic understanding of sin and redemption as it is this view of sin that will allow Hamlet to exert a greater measure of revenge on Claudius. The Council of Trent determined that a man lost his redemption by committing any of the mortal sins that Hamlet mentions in this scene. Hamlet hopes to catch Claudius while drunk, in a fit of rage, enjoying incestuous pleasures, or even swearing (*Hamlet* 3.3.89–91). While Reformation doctrine would not damn Claudius for engaging in any of these sins, the Roman Catholic doctrine of salvation would allow Hamlet to take part in the damnation of his uncle.

Hamlet: Then trip him, that his heels may kick at heaven
And that his soul may be as damn'd and black
As hell, whereto it goes.

(*Hamlet* 3.3.93–95)

Moving back and forth from Reformation to Roman Catholic doctrine, Hamlet betrays a confounded soul, one torn between two faiths. With his mother, Hamlet employs Lutheran sentiments, while with his uncle he employs more of a Roman Catholic posture. Part of Hamlet's delay in seeking revenge on Claudius is connected to his uncertainty regarding the nature of heaven and hell, salvation and damnation. This same uncertainty, according to Christopher

Haigh, Eamon Duffy, and others, may have also plagued the men and women that filled the seats of Shakespeare's theater.[50]

Turning back to Hamlet's rebuke of his mother, it is here that we see him switch from Roman Catholic to Reformation doctrine. Hamlet's love for his mother compels him to take a more redemptive course of action. He must, according to Reformation doctrine, help his mother recognize the sin and shame that lie on her soul. Despite his intentions, however, Hamlet's approach is flawed. The ghost presents a more accurate response to Reformation doctrine, rebuking Hamlet's harshness. For in his desire to see his mother redeemed, Hamlet would have continued in his rebuke, perhaps driving Gertrude beyond salvation and into despair. The ghost enters to soften Hamlet's charge.

> **Ghost:** O step between her and her fighting soul.
> Conceit in weakest bodies strongest works.
> Speak to her, Hamlet.
>
> (*Hamlet* 3.4.113–15)

The ghost reminds Hamlet that his mother is weak—that she is now broken and in need of comfort. Gertrude's soul has been shent; now she must be instructed in how to deal with her weakness and find a cure for her soul. The danger, according to the ghost, is in leaving the weak to their own devices. Once shown their weakness, the depraved must be instructed else they give in to conceits of dangerous proportions. If Hamlet berates his mother too violently, she may seek refuge in self-pity and despair. The ghost, whose very existence is founded on a Roman Catholic understanding of purgatory, turns Lutheran in his rebuke of Hamlet. The nature of the ghost's rebuke draws very near Luther's teaching in his sermon on the Gospel of Luke. Luther writes the following: "But the soul which is smitten by a rebuke or the preaching of the Law. . . . needs a proclamation of grace and forgiveness, or it must be overcome with despondency and despair. . . . Reprove the sin of the presumptuous and comfortable people who are not aware of their sin. . . . As for the others who know their sins and fear death, comfort them and say, 'Dear brother, you have had enough terrors, I may not frighten you any more. Before you had no God because of your presumption, but now the devil wants to lure you away from God on the other side by despair.'"[51] In the same way that Luther warns against despair, John Calvin claims that despair is employed by demonic forces to control the saints: "Satan's aim is to drive the saint to madness by despair."[52]

Hamlet's office as minister to his mother must be compared to the minister who visits Faustus in Marlowe's play. Both *Hamlet* and *Doctor Faustus* employ Reformation doctrine as they stress the importance of humiliation in a man's journey toward salvation. In *Doctor Faustus*, it is the Old Man who comes as minister to Faustus in his final hours. The Old Man's approach, though gentler than Hamlet's, bears a resemblance to the words employed by the prince in his mother's bedchamber:

Old Man: Ah, Doctor Faustus, that I might prevail,
To guide thy steps unto the way of life,
By which sweet path thou mayst attain the goal
That shall conduct thee to celestial rest!
Break heart, drop blood, and mingle it with tears—
Tears falling from repentant heaviness
Of thy most vile and loathsome filthiness,
The stench whereof corrupts the inward soul
With such flagitious crimes of heinous sins
As no commiseration may expel
But mercy, Faustus, of thy Savior sweet,
Whose blood alone must wash away thy guilt.[53]

Faustus's response does not resemble Gertrude's, for Faustus, although certain of his sin and depravity, is overcome with despondency and despair. After asking the Old Man to leave him while he thinks over his situation, Faustus falls into despair:

Faustus: Accursed Faustus, where is mercy now?
I do repent, and yet I do despair.
Hell strives with grace for conquest in my breast.
What shall I do to shun the snares of death?[54]

The ghost's warning saves Hamlet from driving Gertrude into a like despair. Hamlet seems to understand the ghost's meaning yet

complains because it has taken everything in him to remain stern in the face of such emotional matters:

Hamlet: —Do not look upon me,
Lest with this piteous action you convert
My stern effects. Then what I have to do
Will want true colour—tears perchance for blood.
(*Hamlet* 3.4.127–30)

Hamlet complains that his ability to act appropriately with controlled emotions is not natural. In this confession is another reference to the Pauline struggle against the sinful nature, as seen in Romans: "For that which I am doing, I do not understand; for I am not practicing what I would like to do, but I am doing the very thing I hate."[55]

It may be that Hamlet's most natural reaction, his sinful desire, is to tear his mother to pieces and continue berating her into unreachable despair. His divine calling prevails, however, and Hamlet follows the ghost's instruction, continuing to work on his mother and the raising of her soul. After the ghost's warning, Hamlet turns a warmer eye on his mother and gives her the comfort and instruction she needs:

Hamlet: Mother, for love of grace,
Lay not that flattering unction to your soul,
That not your trespass but my madness speaks.
It will but skin and film the ulcerous place,
Whiles rank corruption, mining all within,
Infects unseen. Confess yourself to heaven,
Repent what's past, avoid what is to come;
And do not spread the compost on the weeds
To make them ranker. Forgive me this my virtue;
For in the fatness of these pursy times
Virtue itself of vice must pardon beg.
(*Hamlet* 3.4.146)

Hamlet begs his mother not to reject the grace that has led her to see her pitiable condition. It is by grace alone, confirms Luther, that a man may realize his spiritual depravity and turn to God.[56] Luther's doctrine of grace becomes clear in this interchange between mother and son; Hamlet urges his mother to understand that her recognition of her own depravity is a gracious gift of God. Perhaps in act 5, when Hamlet claims that "there is a divinity that shapes our ends. . . . our deepest plots and their success or failure are not in our own hands" (*Hamlet* 5.2.10–11), we are to hearken back to Hamlet's plea to Gertrude that she love the grace of God and not despise the "shaping" he desires to perform in her "black and grained" soul (*Hamlet* 3.4.90). Hamlet's warning to his mother, in paraphrase, is, "Don't let your sinful mind make you think I am crazy, but understand that I speak to you in truth. Don't cover over the sin you see inside yourself, but admit your need and deal with your sickened condition. Don't let pride or conceit cause you to cover over the rank sin you see in your black heart. For in this way you become calloused to the truth about yourself and invite even more dangerous infection." Hamlet also bids Gertrude not to sleep with Claudius anymore, thereby urging her to build up a resistance against him.

Shakespeare's *Hamlet* is a complex play, speaking of themes that are rooted in a divided religious culture. Though often understood as timid and cautious, Hamlet appears more like an Old Testament prophet when viewed through the lens of Reformation theology. Hamlet is called to take part in the reformation of his mother, a calling that according to Reformation theology is contingent not on the perfection of his soul but on the power and grace of God. Seeking to turn his mother's eyes on the sin in her soul, Hamlet carefully employs Reformation doctrine to free his mother from damnation. Employing the biblical law as a mirror, Hamlet allows Gertrude to see the sin in her heart. Gertrude's recognition of the "black and grained spots" in her soul makes her a perfect candidate for redemption (*Hamlet* 3.4.90). Like Gertrude, Claudius is humiliated by recognition of his sin. Though villainous in his ambition for power, by Reformation standards Claudius bears the marks of a redeemed saint. Though it would not be accurate to classify *Hamlet* as a Reformation play, Shakespeare endows the play with some of the very difficult issues raised by the intrusion of Protestantism into English culture.

Chapter 2
The Tempest

In the opening scene of Shakespeare's *The Tempest*, the ship's master, boatswain, and mariners do not question the reality of the storm that threatens their lives. These seamen are full of terror and foreboding as the sea dismantles their ship:

> **Master:** Boatswain!
> **Boatswain:** Here, Master. What cheer?
> **Master:** Good, speak to the mariners. Fall to 't yarely, or we run ourselves aground. Bestir, bestir! *Exit.*
>
> Enter Mariners.
>
> **Boatswain:** Heigh, my hearts! Cheerily, cheerily, my hearts! Yare, yare! Take in the topsail. Tend to the Master's whistle.—Blow till thou burst thy wind, if room enough!
> (*The Tempest* 1.1.1–6)

When a sailor is left with only one option—to blow into his own sails—a terrifying storm is certainly at hand. As Gonzalo bears witness, the vessel is not only being pummeled by great waves and violent surf, but its very structure is giving way, taking on water like "an unstaunched wench" (*The Tempest* 1.1.44). The storm that opens Shakespeare's *The Tempest* is natural by all accounts until the start of the second scene. The master, the boatswain, and all the cast and crew aboard King Alonso's ship battle against what appear to be natural forces, real movements of the sky and the sea. As is revealed in the second scene, however, reality is not always what it seems. Shakespeare's turn of natural to supernatural sets the stage for a play that will dive deep into the waves of England's seventeenth-century religious debate.

In chapter 1, we saw Hamlet acting as a Reformation minister. This chapter builds on that foundation by looking at *The Tempest* and the ministerial role that Shakespeare gives to Prospero. Prospero's character is complex; the nature of his power, his humiliation, and his ultimate redemption are the subjects of this chapter. The theme of redemption runs throughout the play into the lives of characters like Alonso and even Caliban. The nature of redemption in the play has been drawn from Reformation theology, and while I draw from John Calvin and William Perkins at times, I take an especially close look at the writings of Martin Luther. A careful study of *The Tempest* will reveal that Luther's gospel for the masses, and particularly Luther's understanding of Christian redemption, are worked out within the conflict of the play.[1]

It is through an analysis of Prospero's magic that we see his need for redemption and the way in which this redemption is achieved. Though he appears damnable on many accounts, the unraveling of the Reformation theology at work in the play will reveal Prospero as among the redeemed. His redemption is, in the end, made even more certain by acts that John Calvin and Martin Luther would consider a "putting off of the old man" and a renewing of "the spirit of [Prospero's] mind."[2] Miranda's first words set the stage for our analysis of Prospero and his magic:

> **Miranda:** If by your art, my dearest father, you have
> Put the wild waters in this roar, allay them.
> The sky, it seems, would pour down stinking pitch,
> But that the sea, mounting to th' welkin's cheek,
> Dashes the fire out.
>
> (*The Tempest* 1.2.1–5)

In this opening scene, it is important to note that Miranda, moved with pity for the sailors, is quick to blame Prospero, recognizing the form of his handiwork and knowing this to be his kind of conjuration.[3] This is not the first time Prospero has stirred the seas with violence, nor is it the first time he has allowed his daughter, or others perhaps, to witness the workings of his power. It was while he was Duke of Milan that Prospero opened graves, "waked their sleepers," and "let 'em forth" (*The Tempest* 5.1.49).[4]

By acts of this kind, Prospero is able to fill his "creatures" with such awe that they would have fought for his release, "So dear the love my people bore me" (*The Tempest* 1.2.82, 141), if they had known of his arrest and banishment by King Alonso and Antonio. Prospero explains that it is more than the money and status of a dukedom that corrupts Antonio; it is in fact Prospero's dukedom, so infused with the art of magic, that provides more power and authority than Antonio's moral strength can handle:

> **Prospero:** He being thus lorded,
> Not only with what my revenue yielded,
> But what my power might else exact . . .
> (*The Tempest* 1.2.97–99)

It may be that the legend of Prospero's dukedom, expanded by the workings of the miraculous, lives on in the legends of Milan long after Prospero's banishment. It is this legend, we may conclude, to which Ferdinand refers when he is reintroduced to his father at the end of the play: "She / Is the daughter to this famous Duke of Milan, / Of whom so often I have heard renown, / But never saw before" (*The Tempest* 5.1.191–94).

Prospero has great powers while governing Milan, and it is in Milan that he is corrupted by a lust for said powers and supernatural authority. In Milan, Prospero is lost in selfish ambition, which draws him from his post as public servant to secret chambers, from leadership and authority over the people of Milan to a dark corner of the kingdom where he seeks to better his mind and strengthen his powers. As H. R. Coursen suggests, Prospero's turning over his dukedom to Antonio must force a comparison to King Lear, another erring ruler who gives up his kingdom and his duties, shirks his responsibilities, and thereby chooses a life of selfishness over a life of self-sacrifice.[5] Just like Lear, Prospero neglects civil duty and pursues his own self-serving course. Prospero justifies neglecting his official duties because he is dedicated "to closeness, and the bettering of my mind" (*The Tempest* 1.2.89). As S. C. V. Stetner and O. B. Goodman claim in their work on Lear and the nature of his abdication, Shakespeare might have us view Prospero's abdication in the same way. They argue that Shakespeare's audience "could only view an act of abdication as foolish, irresponsible, and damnable, since it invited civil war and disasters sufficient to rock the macrocosm."[6] Stetner and Goodman refer to Celestine V, the pope who offered to abdicate his throne and to leave three cardinals in charge, as a historical parallel to Lear. Like Lear, the abdicating pope was also viewed as a foolish man, full of self-interest. Prospero, like Lear, is not only a wounded soul as he is driven from Milan but also a wounding soul. He is responsible in many ways for the deterioration of his own family: his wife's disappearance, his brother's corruption, and his daughter's banishment. Prospero, like Lear, sins more than he is sinned against.

H. R. Coursen cites a number of examples of neglected rule in English history that ended badly for all involved. He also references neglected duty in Norton and Sackville's *Gorboduc* published in 1561, in *Mirrour for Magistrates*, and in Shakespeare's *Richard II*, whose protagonist Coursen claims "used his kingdom like a credit card."[7] Prospero too, it may be argued, uses his dukedom as a source of money. His dukedom pays for his books, and instead of working for his salary, he draws additional money from his subjects and hires his brother Antonio to do the work of the kingdom for him. Charles V, Holy Roman Emperor and infamous abdicator, also requires our attention as a possible source for *The Tempest*.[8] Charles's connection to Spain and Italy and his involvement in the controversial restructuring of kingdom of Naples make him an interesting historical parallel to Prospero.[9] The abdication of Charles V was viewed as unwise by his contemporaries, many of whom were "aghast . . . thinking it the strangest thing ever to happen,"[10] but it is the emperor's desire to retain the advantages of rule that aligns him most with Prospero. As M. J. Rodriguez-Salgado explains, "The problem was that Charles realized a man without money and patronage was nothing in this world."[11] When planning his retirement to a monastic retreat,

Charles was adamant about retaining significant financial power; as he famously explained to one of his servants, "I will be quite capable of granting favours there."[12] This is the hope that Prospero entertains when he turns the governance of Milan over to Antonio. Prospero's desire to live a life of contemplation and study, to neglect "worldly ends," and to concentrate on the "bettering" of his mind are selfish desires that parallel the kind of lifestyle that Charles V also desired (*The Tempest* 1.2.89, 90). As described by William Maltby, "No ascetic, Charles nevertheless attended Mass regularly in the chapel of the Jeronimite monks, which was connected to his villa by a covered walkway, and pursued a daily routine based in large part on prayer and contemplation. Much of the time he spent in the sun on his terrace overlooking the beautiful valley of the Vera. His wish to put the great world behind him was nothing if not genuine."[13]

While there is much debate over the nature of Prospero's magic, the mage's damnable state in Milan has little to do with the magic itself but rather with Prospero's obsession with magic and the study thereof. After a close examination of what appears to be the dominant theological opinion of magic and the miraculous, I find myself at odds with Jerry Brotton, who argues that Shakespeare meant to make his audience feel suspicion and anxiety about Prospero's magic. Brotton writes, "Magic and the secretive, closeted scholarship which it entailed were deeply suspect activities, precisely because of the difficulty of establishing just what the scholar was doing behind closed doors . . . Like the traveler, the magus or 'intelligencer' inspired unease precisely because of the difficulty of situating his activities within a comprehensible frame of cultural reference, where his activities could be seen and understood."[14] When understood in the context of Reformation theology, however—particularly the writings of Martin Luther—a more optimistic view of magic and those who command the miraculous takes shape. Luther writes the following about miraculous signs and wonders and those who possess this kind of "knowledge":

> This knowledge is a good and most natural one. It is the source of everything that physicians, and those like them, know and describe about the powers and uses of herbs, fruits, iron, minerals, and so on. It is often referred to in Scripture when in similes it mentions animals,

> minerals, trees and herbs, etc. This knowledge was highly developed in Persia and Arabia, and these countries of the East studied it and looked upon it as honest knowledge which produced wise people . . . These are the arts which the magi studied, and great wisdom lies hidden in them concerning Christ and how man should conduct himself in his life.[15]

Much of the criticism surrounding Prospero's magic points to a well-known magician and astrologer of Shakespeare's day named John Dee.[16]

Known to have had a large library of "about 4000 bookes: whereof, 700 were ancientlie written by hand," Dee bears a strong resemblance to Prospero. As a controversial figure, Dee is often demonized by critics, but much like Prospero, Dee appears strangely Christian in his personal expression. When his library was attacked by some of his opponents, Dee credited God's Providence for saving a majority of the most important books.[17] In a letter dated 1604, Dee wrote to the Archbishop of Canterbury defending his magic as an art that "proceed[es] and ascend[es] . . . from things visible, to consider of things invisible; from things transitory, and momentary, to meditate of things permanent; by things mortall . . . to have some perceiverance of immortality."[18] Because of the controversial nature of his art, Dee was reduced to a poor and humiliating station, yet up to his death, he continued to write letters to the king and Parliament in defense of what he called Hermetic beliefs and practices.[19]

I dare not build a case for John Dee's Christian orthodoxy, but I find him an interesting character for his blend of the occult and Christianity. Dee's confession of faith, found in a letter he wrote to the Prague court of Rudolf II in 1585, is of a form that would most certainly have made orthodox sixteenth-century Christians very suspicious: "It pleased God to send me his Light; and his holy Angels, for these two years and a half, have used to inform me . . . Moreover, the Lord hath made his covenant with me: [. . .] If you will forsake your wickednesse, and turn unto him, your Seat shall be the greatest that ever was: and the Devil shall become your prisoner: Which Devil, I did conjecture, to be the Great Turk. This my Commission, is from God."[20] The nature of Dee's ideology is not easily understood; scholars of the present and past are undecided whether Dee operated in white or black magic and whether he was a Christian or a pagan.[21] In Dee, Shakespeare finds a complex individual who sacrifices everything in his search for God and the powers of heaven. Dee, like Prospero, would have been in agreement with Pico della Mirandola's sixteenth-century confession: "Who would not long to be initiated into such sacred rites? Who would not desire, by neglecting all human concerns, by despising the goods of fortune, and by disregarding those of the body, to become the guest of the gods while yet living on earth, and, made drunk by the nectar of eternity, to be endowed with the gifts of immortality though still a mortal being?"[22] In Dee, we have an ideology and a passion that we cannot easily unravel. It is this complexity that we see in Shakespeare's construction of Prospero, a complexity that forces his audience to pause as one before a great mystery.

Emperor Rudolf II of Bohemia, a controversial European ruler deposed of his throne in 1606, is another important historical connection to Shakespeare's Prospero. Like Prospero, Rudolf lost his kingdom by neglecting his duties for the preferred study of magic. He was one of the European emperors visited by John Dee in 1584 on his "European Mission." Though the emperor did not grant the magician more than one meeting, it is possible that the emperor was influenced by the nature of Dee's work.[23] Sir Henry Wotton (1568–1639), English author and diplomat, wrote that as early as 1591, "[Rudolf seems] now rather to bear the title of Emperor for fashion sake, than authority to command by virtue of it."[24] Rudolf's throne was taken from him by the Habsburg archdukes and conferred on his brother Matthias, who later commented that "his majesty is interested only in wizards, alkymists, Kabbalists, and the like, sparing no expense to find all kinds of treasure, learn secrets, and use scandalous ways of harming his enemies."[25] David Scott Kastan suggests that the resemblance between Rudolf and Prospero is not accidental. He claims that by renouncing his magic, Prospero is allowed to "escape the damning parallel with Rudolf."[26] Prospero is not, however, allowed to escape the humiliation that Rudolf suffered. This Shakespearean twist is in fact another important historical element that Shakespeare inserts alongside the life of Rudolf. Shakespeare borrows from Reformation theology by redeeming his protagonist through humiliation. While Rudolf's humiliation is followed by a hopeless banishment, Prospero's is followed by a redeeming self-knowledge that allows him to be reconciled with Providence.

Although Barbara Mowat's essay "Prospero, Agrippa, and Hocus Pocus" is important for the connections it makes to the body of magic influencing Shakespeare's England, the essay fails due to its ambiguous conclusion: "The 'reality' or fakery of the magician's power and our inability to fix this power as supernatural or as sleight-of-hand are central to the play and our vision of life, just as they point to the central ambiguities in our own vision of man in the natural and supernatural worlds."[27] Though Shakespeare maintains the mystery of the natural and supernatural worlds in this play, this is not done by his creation of a loosely developed character. If we follow Mowat's conclusion, we must accept the fact that Shakespeare overlooked some of the inconsistencies in Prospero's character. We must accept the fact that Shakespeare fails to make sense of a Prospero who works with demons and angels. William Empson suggests that while we do not know whether or not Christopher Marlowe sends Dr. Faustus off of the stage in the final scene of his play screaming in terror or delight,[28] we are certain that he is drawn off by the forces of hell. In contrast, a clear understanding of the theology of Shakespeare's England reveals a Prospero who deals in white magic and surrenders himself to the will of an omniscient God. Shakespeare gives his playgoer evidence to support an understanding of Prospero and the nature of his magic. In an age that David Hirst describes as reactionary toward "learning, rediscovery of the art[s], [and] scientific exploration," Shakespeare had no room to be inconclusive or ambiguous about the nature of Prospero's magic.[29] If like John Dee, Prospero seeks God in and through his supernatural dealings, if he seeks to better understand Christ through a Luther-like understanding of magic, then Prospero's character takes on a new clarity. His cries to Providence and his humility before his enemies are neither inexplicable nor inconsistent, but they are most certainly important within a historically based and theologically rich play.

When Prospero is accosted by Alonso, Antonio, and a "treacherous army," the arresting party is aware, as Caliban becomes aware during the course of his exile, that Prospero is powerless without his books, his cloak, and his staff.

Caliban: . . . without them
He's but a sot, as I am, nor hath not
One spirit to command

(*The Tempest* 3.2.89–93).

Abandoned on the open ocean in a stripped vessel without "tackle, sail, or mast" (*The Tempest* 1.2.147), the helpless father and daughter are destined for certain death but for the grace of "Providence divine" and the kindness of Gonzalo. It is the "noble Neapolitan" who knew which of Prospero's books and cloaks to put aboard the ship, and it may in fact be, as Stephen Orgel suggests, that Providence governs "not only their coming ashore but Gonzalo's charitable intervention as well."[30] In any case, the intertwining of Providence and Prospero's magic makes a strong case for a positive, rather than suspicious, understanding of Prospero's art.

Prospero's banishment, his helplessness at sea, and his exile on the island serve important purposes in his life. Miranda's question in regard to being exiled elicits a confession from Prospero:

Miranda: O the heavens!
What foul play had we, that we came from thence?
Or blessed was 't we did?
Prospero: Both, both, my girl.
By foul play, as thou sayst, were we heaved thence,
But blessedly holp hither.

(*The Tempest* 1.2.59–63)

Prospero's banishment as well as his deliverance are of divine making. The humiliation he suffers as a result of his subjection to the sea serves to save him from damnation for a life lived in selfishness and conceit. In Milan, Prospero is blind to the schemes of his brother and the state of his own soul. It is not magic that is the cause of his damnation but his dedication to selfish ambition and greed. Prospero does not understand his place before Providence until he is thrust out on the open ocean, humiliated and subjected to the mercy of the gods. Through this humiliation, Prospero begins to understand the true nature of his magic, most importantly that it is not worthy of worship.

Prospero confesses to Miranda that it is "By Providence divine" that they make it to shore and again that it is by "bountiful Fortune" that the King of Naples and his retinue are brought to the island (*The Tempest* 1.2.159, 178). Yet as we witness, Prospero's magic has much to do with the process as well. Stephen Greenblatt, contradicting a tide of criticism that seeks to demonize Prospero's magic, describes Prospero as an artist who is "at once the bestower of life and [at the same time] the master of deception."[31] While I appreciate the fact that Greenblatt recognizes the complexity of Prospero's art, he fails to make sense of Prospero's relationship with Providence, an important "character," if you will, in *The Tempest*. Prospero's understanding of his magic, himself, and—most importantly—Providence allows him to move into a place of clarity, a byproduct of his redemption. Barbara Mowat affirms a more complex view of Prospero's character, describing the play as "the story of a man's personal growth from vengeance to mercy, and from rough magic to deep spirituality."[32] Mowat is correct in her assessment of Prospero, but she stops short of shedding light on how Prospero arrives at this place. Prospero's move toward spirituality is modeled after the Reformation process of redemption, a process by which the magician is humiliated in order to be redeemed. This is a process in which, like many biblical characters,[33] the prideful, self-centered Duke is humbled and brought into a right relationship with self, others, and God.

Unlike Lear, whose humiliation is accompanied by a shedding of royal robes, and Leontes, who loses his kingly authority and is reduced to taking orders from his subjects, Prospero's humiliation is more subtle but equally significant. As previously argued, Prospero's recognition of providential authority is the first part of his humiliation, for this act signals a humbling of self and a recognition of weakness before God. Second, Prospero's experience of grief aboard the abandoned ship, "the rotten carcass of a butt" (*The Tempest* 1.2.146), serves as a moment of change:

Prospero: Thou didst smile,
Infused with a fortitude from heaven,
When I have decked the sea with drops full salt,
Under my burden groaned, which raised in me

> An undergoing stomach, to bear up
> Against what should ensue.
>
> (*The Tempest* 1.2.153–58)

Prospero's grief, covered by a "fortitude" that he understands to be divinely inspired through the child, Miranda, results in a baptism of tears. Lois Feuer claims that what we find in this passage is a "birth metaphor,"[34] a birth that is meant to signal Prospero's Christian "rebirth" by humble contrition. This concept of rebirth plays largely into the theology of Martin Luther, who describes the goal of redemption as such: "All is lost without a rebirth through the water and the Spirit. Don't imagine that you will enter the kingdom of God unless you have been reborn through water and the Spirit. These are clear and powerful words; they demand that we be born anew, that is, that we pass from the birth of sin to the birth of righteousness. Otherwise we will never come into the kingdom of heaven. And then good works must follow this birth of righteousness."[35] The notion of rebirth by "water and the Spirit" describes the action of *The Tempest*, relating both the physical and the spiritual components of the play. This powerful rebirth is signaled, according to Luther, by an experience of redemptive humiliation: "A man with a true [or redeemed] heart [must] detest himself and confess his sin and, at all events, punish himself inwardly . . . Therefore judgment is nothing else than disparagement or humiliation of self from the heart and knowledge of self, that one is indeed a sinner and altogether unworthy."[36] In William Perkins's writings, we find another description of the redemptive process, which involves the acknowledgment of one's sin and an experience in which one is "pricked with the feeling of God's wrath, for sinne."[37] A theologian of the Reformation tradition in Shakespeare's England, Perkins describes the redeemed sinner as expressing his worship to God in faith by yielding "subiection to him in all his commandments"[38] and by making God "to be our Refuge, our castle, our rocke, and tower of defence."[39] Perkins lists three actions of faith that take place in the life of the redeemed: "The first of faith's 'actions in the heart' in times of affliction 'makes us to depend on gods promises . . . to trust without limitation of time . . . and to behold him with the eyes of faith."[40] In Prospero's tears, we see the action of faith described by Perkins. The magician's faith allows him to draw near to God and to recognize the presence of divine grace in Miranda's smile.

Prospero's baptism of tears aboard the skeleton vessel results in the birth of that which allows him "to bear up / Against what should ensue" (*The Tempest* 1.2.158). Prospero's tears flow as a result of his recognition of sin, the selfish ambition that has destroyed his life and threatens to destroy the life of his daughter. By acknowledging his sin and subjecting himself to Providence, Prospero is redeemed and begins to see the hand of Providence as that which sustains him. His own magic takes a subservient role to providential design.

Prospero's confrontation with his own sin and shame leads him to a redeemed state in which true moral action is possible. John D. Cox affirms the kind of change Prospero experiences: "The fact that Prospero possesses such incredible powers and still recognizes the need for self restraint and forgiveness of his enemies is perhaps the single most remarkable feature of *The Tempest* . . . this is what is most profoundly miraculous about the play . . . Prospero's growing moral insight and capacity for moral action."[41] *The Tempest* reveals Prospero's transformation from damned to deliverer, for over the course of the play Prospero becomes a man who will help lead others, even his enemies, to a state of redemption. In his work on *Henry IV*, Michael Davies addresses a concern that many will have with my claims about Prospero. Davies writes this about Hal: "However uncomfortable we may feel about a Shakespeare who seems willing to dramatize matters of repentance and reformation, and who presents Falstaff [in my case Prospero] within the frame of Calvinist reprobation, nevertheless a Reformed reading of these plays, along these lines, can help us make more sense of them in some important historical and dramatic ways."[42] In much the same way that Davies argues for a redeemed and even pastor-like Hal, I contend that Prospero moves into a position of care and concern for the souls of those who hurt him. The mercy that Prospero deals to Alonso and Antonio, the two men who planned his banishment to the seas, becomes more realistic if we see the magician as one who has been "reborn" by Reformation standards.[43]

Prospero's handling of his enemies becomes an important factor as I seek to prove his regenerated state and his accompanying desire to show mercy. We first witness Prospero's mercy when he chooses not only to save his enemies from death in the opening storm but also to restore them to a condition better than before the storm. This physical restoration is significant as we analyze the spiritual restoration that Providence, with Prospero's assistance, aims to enact:

Prospero: But are they, Ariel, safe?
Ariel: Not a hair perished.
On their sustaining garments not a blemish,
But fresher than before; and as thou bad'st me,
In troops I have dispersed them 'bout the isle.
(*The Tempest* 1.2.216–20)

Prospero's extension of kindness and mercy to those who have sought to end his life is preposterous without an understanding of the theological workings within this play. He is a "new creation" by Reformation standards, and this fact explains his desire to serve those who hurt him. Luther writes much about men like Prospero:

> Such a man begins to fear God with all his heart, he trusts Him under all conditions of his life, he calls upon Him in all his needs, he is steadfast in the confession of His Word, by his life he praises God before all the world, and for His sake he suffers and bears whatever God is pleased to send him. Such are genuine and true forms of service, and they please God very well because they are done with faith in Christ. They proceed from within the heart, which has now become "a new creation" in Christ, as St. Paul calls it in Galatians 6:15.[44]

Examples of men and women being given grace to act mercifully in spite of their anger or desire for revenge abound in the scriptures, but as it is with the scriptural characters, for Prospero the merciful acts are not easily carried out. In many ways, the Old Testament account of Joseph resembles Prospero's experience with the men who banished him.

Like Prospero, Joseph is the victim of a surprise assault, resulting in his banishment to a distant land. The abuse Joseph suffers comes as a result of the attention he receives from his father, whose gift of a "coat of many colors" stirs up jealousy in his brothers.[45] Although the coat is not described as having any magical power, it is interesting to note that immediately after receiving this gift, Joseph has a series of prophetic dreams.[46] After Joseph is exalted by his father and granted this gift, his brothers are clearly threatened by him.[47] It is in this climate, much like the climate in which Prospero is abused, that the brothers dispose of him. Though Joseph suffers violent abuse and many years in prison, he eventually emerges from his captivity by several acts of Providence, one of which involves his miraculous interpretation of the pharaoh's dream. This magical work earns Joseph the most exalted position in the Egyptian government, a position which involves his control over a massive food distribution campaign bringing relief to famine victims throughout the land. The famine reaches Joseph's family and draws them to Egypt to purchase food. As Providence would have it, Joseph meets up with his brothers when they come to make their request. Joseph is at first unrecognizable to his brothers, and instead of revealing himself to them right away, he remains in disguise, perhaps as a means of bringing his brothers to a place of redemptive humiliation. In disguise, Joseph accuses his brothers of being spies from Canaan, sent to size up the land. Although they deny his charges, the brothers are imprisoned and further questioned. Unprompted by Joseph, his brothers confess that their bad luck comes as a result of the terrible treatment they had imposed on Joseph so many years before:

> We *are* verily guilty concerning our brother, in that we saw the anguish of his soul, when he besought us, and we would not hear; therefore is this distress come upon us. And Reuben answered them, saying, Spake I not unto you, saying, Do not sin against the child; and ye would not hear? therefore, behold, also his blood is required. And they knew not that Joseph understood *them*; for he spake unto them by an interpreter. And he turned himself about from them, and wept; and returned to them again, and communed with them, and took from them Simeon, and bound him before their eyes.[48]

Much like Prospero's dealings with his captives, Joseph leads his sinning brothers toward recognition of their sin, which results in their redemption. As a powerful Egyptian authority, Joseph could have ordered the torture and imprisonment of his brothers. They, like Antonio and Alonso, have never paid for their crimes against him, and Joseph could have chosen to exact a severe penalty from them.

Instead, Joseph acts with grace and mercy toward his brothers. In spite of his resolve to act mercifully, Joseph's emotions are deeply troubled as he listens to his brothers argue about the crime they committed against him so many years before. The task of forgiveness required of Joseph is a difficult one, demanding something from him that runs contrary to his flesh and his fierce desire for revenge. Joseph turns from his brothers to disguise his tears, which are drawn from a broken heart that would act more naturally in vengeance than in mercy. In her comparison of *The Tempest* and the Joseph narrative, Lois Feuer claims that the tears Joseph sheds in the passage cited above signify his "moving from pity for his younger self, to love for his full brother Benjamin, to forgiveness and love for all his brothers."[49]

Like Joseph, Prospero is troubled by the task of forgiveness that he is required to perform. His emotional strife is visible at one point in the play, Miranda and Ferdinand commenting:

Ferdinand [*to Miranda*]**:** This is strange. Your father's in some passion
That works him strongly.
Miranda: Never till this day
Saw I him touched with anger so distempered.
(*The Tempest* 4.1.143–45)

Ferdinand and Miranda recognize Prospero's "vexed" state, but before they can inquire about his "distempered" condition, he begins his speech about the empty nature of life. It is only in sacrifice and submission, he might have added, that one finds redemption and that which is of true and eternal weight. Prospero explains to Miranda and Ferdinand that human beings and all their pomp and circumstance are nothing more than a "baseless fabric . . . [an] insubstantial pageant" (*The Tempest* 4.1.151, 155). Prospero continues with what appears to be very Luther-like sentiments regarding human life:

Prospero: We are such stuff
As dreams are made on, and our little life
Is rounded with a sleep.
(*The Tempest* 4.1.156–58)

Luther employs the same metaphor as he attempts to explain a Reformation view of human life and the humble nature of human wisdom and power:

> However, this whole life which we live is sheer dreaming and dark night. For no light shines in the world except this earthly and bodily light. The light of the sun is a cause of error for us so that we believe that we are in the light. But we are really wandering as though we were in a black night. Therefore our life is truly sleep and night spiritually . . . Moses attests the same thing in Ps. 90:5, saying: "Thou dost sweep men away; they are like a dream," that is our life is fleeting, flying, and transient, just as the Elbe is always flowing or any river is borne along by its swift current; "as water rushes past, so Thou hast made men a raging stream and a passing torrent." Job also says (14:1–2): "Man that is born of a woman is of few days and full of trouble. He comes forth like a flower and withers; he flees like a shadow and continues not." What is more, Moses adds: "[Men] are a dream" (Ps. 90:5), that is, our life is a dream by comparison with eternal life.[50]

Prospero explains to Miranda and Ferdinand the lesson he has learned through the course of his banishment—that a life of selfish ambition is insubstantial and fleeting, lived for no purpose, only a chasing after the wind.

Prospero is prompted to think these heavy thoughts by news of Caliban's treachery. Caliban, in addition to Alonso and Antonio, will require Prospero's forgiveness. Prospero reveals more emotional struggle over the task of forgiveness when Ariel brings word to him that the hour of confrontation is at hand:

> **Ariel:** Your charm so strongly works 'em
> That if you now beheld them, your affections
> Would become tender.
>
> (*The Tempest* 5.1.16–18)

Unlike Jonathan Bate, who argues that Prospero is moved to pity for his enemies in this exchange with Ariel, I suggest that Prospero's tone here is parental.[51] Bate fails to identify the conflicting emotions evident in Prospero's dialogue with the spirit. Though he agrees in part with Ariel's conclusion, Prospero proceeds to communicate some of the complexity of human forgiveness, a complexity that Ariel will never understand:

> **Prospero:** Dost thou think so, spirit?
> **Ariel:** Mine would, sir, were I human.
> **Prospero:** And mine shall . . .
> Though with their high wrongs I am struck to the quick,
> Yet with my nobler reason 'gainst my fury
> Do I take part. The rarer action is
> In virtue than in vengeance. They being penitent,
> The sole drift of my purpose doth extend
> Not a frown further.
>
> (*The Tempest* 5.1.25–30)

Prospero agrees that he will indeed be moved to pity his enemies. His pity, however, like the pity that is drawn from any wounded human soul, must first travel through the difficult web of anger and frustration. A key part of Prospero's redemptive humiliation leads him to this act of forgiveness, an act that is born out of personal sacrifice. Like the biblical story of Joseph, a man betrayed by his brothers, Prospero's expressions of forgiveness and mercy come through a brokenness that he suffers at the hand of Providence. The tears that Prospero shed while stranded aboard the skeleton vessel so many years before, revealing his brokenness before God and his recognition of his own depravity, are a close parallel to the tears shed by Joseph in the company of his brothers.[52] Though Prospero does not become a perfected saint, a state that Reformation theologians claim is only reached when redeemed men and women are taken to heaven,[53] the redeemed magician is aware of his own dependence on Providence. This awareness is the key to his acts of mercy and forgiveness toward those who hurt him. Joseph betrays this same knowledge when he tells his brothers that it is God who has guided the course of his life: "I am Joseph your brother, whom ye sold into Egypt. Now therefore be not grieved, nor angry with yourselves, that ye sold me hither: for God did send me before you to preserve life . . . God sent me before you to preserve you a posterity in the earth, and to save your lives by a great deliverance. So now it was not you that sent me hither, but God."[54] It must not be misunderstood that in either Joseph's case or in Prospero's forgiveness comes easy. It is clear that in each story the men struggle with anger and a desire for revenge. Feuer writes, "Despite these transformations, neither text presents forgiveness as easily arrived at; Joseph's motives are at least momentarily ambiguous as, with his brothers at last in his power, he remembers his dreams of them (and presumably their mocking of these dreams, though the minimalist style leaves that unsaid)."[55] Prospero's forgiveness of Antonio bears a similar struggle; it may be that the magician mutters his forgiveness of Antonio with teeth clenched, disgusted by the traitorous man before him, yet compelled by a greater calling that challenges him to take the more virtuous course.

As Prospero imposes on Alonso a desperation that may seem cruel, keeping him in the belief that his son is dead, in truth Prospero and Ariel work as ministers of Providence, revealing to Alonso his great sin and need for redemption. Alonso is made to feel responsible for the death of his son and for the certain deaths of all those stranded on the island:

Ariel: You are three men of sin, whom Destiny,
That hath to instrument this lower world
And what's in't, the never-surfeited sea
Hath caused to belch up you, and on this island,
Where man doth not inhabit—you 'mongst men
Being most unfit to live.

(*The Tempest* 3.3.53–58)

Ariel betrays more evidence of Reformation theology in this passage and more evidence in support of my claim that Shakespeare represents Providence as at work in the lives of men and women.

Ariel's claim that a personified Destiny uses the lower world, and in fact has used the sea and a chosen magician in this case, to carry out things that are spiritual resonates with Luther's debate against those of his day who did not believe that God uses imperfect and even sinful men and women to carry out His divine plan. Luther writes, "Our fanatics, however, are full of fraud and humbug. They think nothing spiritual can be present where there is anything material and physical, and assert that flesh is of no avail. Actually the opposite is true. The Spirit cannot be with us except in material and physical things such as the Word, water, and Christ's body and in his saints on earth."[56]

Understood in its Reformation context, the play supports the idea that Arial is here employed as a type of minister. He speaks to Prospero's enemies about things they do not yet understand—their chance for redemption:

Ariel: Ling'ring perdition, worse than any death
Can be at once, shall step by step attend
You and your ways; whose wraths to guard you from,
Which here, in this most desolate isle, else falls
Upon your heads, is nothing by heart's sorrow,
And a clear life ensuing.

(*The Tempest* 3.3.77–82)

That their life hangs in the balance is clear enough, but Ariel's reference to "heart's sorrow" and "a clear life ensuing" are most clearly explained within the context of Reformed theology. Sorrow of the heart is a condition described by Luther as essential for a sinner to enter into a redeemed state.[57] The sorrow Alonso feels leads to an experience of redemptive humiliation, which works "like poison" in his mind, killing the old man and preparing for the birth of one who is redeemed (*The Tempest* 3.3.105). Alonso's redemption is made certain in the final act when he is humbled by Prospero and restores to him his dukedom. It is in the final scene that Alonso acknowledges the hand of Providence, following Gonzalo's pronouncement of the marriage blessing with a bold "Amen!" and confessing that there is "in this business more than nature / Was ever conduct of" (*The Tempest* 5.243–244).

Although Providence confers every opportunity for redemption on Antonio, he refuses to repent. Prospero's response to his brother's arrogance serves as additional proof that Prospero is indeed redeemed:

Antonio: Flesh and blood,
You, brother mine, that entertained ambition,

> Expelled remorse and nature, whom, with Sebastian,
> Whose inward pinches therefore are most strong,
> Would have killed your king, I do forgive thee,
> Unnatural though thou art . . .
> . . . For you, most wicked sir, whom to call brother
> Would even infect my mouth, I do forgive
> Thy rankest fault—all of them . . .
> (*The Tempest* 5.1.74–79, 129–34)

Prospero's final rebuke of his brother Antonio is full of pain and sorrow. An awkward silence follows Prospero's rebuke. This is a silence not unlike that of Iago, who in the closing act of *Othello* stares silently into the face of the general.[58] Like Iago, Antonio does not give his accuser the satisfaction of a response, thereby making Prospero's act of forgiveness the more painfully dealt but the more nobly served.

After his painful forgiveness of Antonio, Prospero must face Caliban. Shakespeare's presentation of Caliban, even his naming of the brute, is bestial and savage.[59] Caliban has attempted to rape Miranda, and he is guilty of many other criminal acts on the island. In light of these facts, it is significant that Caliban is permitted to live and even more compelling that he is given the opportunity to be redeemed in the closing moments of the play. Prospero's dealings with Caliban are important on many levels. Lisa Hopkins claims that "one of the most interesting things about Shakespeare's representation of Caliban is how little we are actually told about him."[60] It is possible, as Hopkins and others have suggested, to read Caliban's name as a reference to the cannibals of the New World, about which stories were sent back to England in the early 1600s.[61] What must not be done, however, is to compare the abuse dealt to New World natives with Prospero's treatment of Caliban.

There is much debate over the nature of Caliban's position and place on the island. In her essay on Caliban, Julia Reinhard Lupton claims that Prospero's treatment of Caliban is criminal and abusive.[62] She rightly claims that Caliban must be rescued from colonialist readings, for his character is complex, and he must not be classified as a simpleminded beast.[63] Lupton's handling of Caliban's attempted rape and murder, though gracious and thoughtful, would benefit from a more realistic approach to these crimes. Caliban actions in the play establish him as a violent criminal, a sexual aggressor, and a rather dangerous conspirator.[64] I am convinced by Lupton's work that it is reasonable and very important to view Caliban as a "minor," not by virtue of his age but in moral and emotional matters.[65] In spite of this, however, we are left with a man that Shakespeare portrays as strong and determined, a certain threat to island peace and security.

Prospero is not left with many options for the reformation of a young and dangerous Caliban. I agree with Lupton's charge that Prospero failed as a duke,[66] but I do not agree that he is a complete failure as a father figure to Caliban, deserving as Lupton claims, to be "chastened by his imperfect exercise of paternal duty."[67] While Caliban claims to be imprisoned in a "hard rock" (*The Tempest* 1.2.342), we witness his free movement about the island, even his freedom to choose a new master (*The Tempest* 2.2.167). Caliban is supposedly pinched by spirits and at times watched by Ariel, but in act 2, Shakespeare establishes Caliban as an unreliable source as he casts off Ariel and takes Stephano on a tour of the island. Caliban's complaints regarding the severely limited freedom offered to him by Prospero are invalidated in this scene:

Caliban: I'll show thee the best springs; I'll pluck thee berries;
I'll fish for thee, and get thee wood enough . . .
I'll bear [Prospero] no more sticks, but follow thee,
Thou wondrous man.

(*The Tempest* 2.2.149–52)

By revealing Caliban as prone to extreme exaggeration, Shakespeare allows very little room for his audience to sympathize with Caliban as a brutalized native. Caliban clearly lacks what Lupton describes as "moral maturity," but the aggressive sexual advances of a twenty-four-year-old man[68] must not be mildly dismissed as the innocent sexual explorations of a small child.[69] Caliban betrays certain knowledge that his continued rape of Miranda would result in his populating "this isle with Calibans" (*The Tempest* 1.2.351). As Lupton suggests, Shakespeare reveals that Caliban is not a creature of "unregenerate incorrigibility."[70] Caliban is indeed reformed through the course of the play by fair and reasonable limitations; these limitations are designed and enforced by Prospero. Though at times he is supposedly limited to a section of rocks, the greater action of the play reveals that Caliban's sentence involves minor limitations to his freedom and a rather short list of chores that fall well-within his physical capabilities.[71]

As it does for Prospero, the play incriminates Caliban as a man that is in need of redemption. It seems unfair and, more important, inaccurate to compare Prospero's treatment of Caliban to the New World colonists' treatment of natives. Meredith Skura treads this unfair territory in this passage: When Prospero has Caliban pinched by the spirits, he shows a "similar sadism" to that of the Haitian masters who "roasted slaves or buried them alive," or when Prospero and Ariel hunt Caliban with spirit dogs, they are equated to the Spaniards who hunted Native Americans with dogs.[72] While the colonialist argument is compelling for its revelation of power relations within the text, there is far too much compassion and reconciliation in Prospero's character to accurately cast him in a colonialist mold. Skura's comparison is unfair, since pinching is far different than the roastings and live burials of the colonial period.[73] In regard to Ariel's "hunting" of Caliban, the text does not support the same kind of brutal capture of natives as related by colonial writers. Ariel's pursuit of Caliban is more adequately compared to the contemporary process of searching for criminals with dogs, a process that was considered acceptable practice in Shakespeare's England just as it continues to be in the United States, Great Britain, and nearly every country of Western Europe in the twenty-first century. Though Caliban is fishlike and grotesque in appearance, Caliban is not described as a soulless creature. He is, in fact, a creature who is redeemable as well as damnable. Taking note of Caliban's "exquisite dreams and visions," Ewan Fernie claims that like the other men and women in the play, Caliban is endowed with a humanlike spirituality.[74]

Prospero describes Caliban as being difficult to teach and motivate, but it is significant for our understanding of Prospero's character that the magician seeks such activities. Speaking of his efforts to teach Caliban, frustrated by the native's inclination toward evil, Prospero compares him to a devil. Taken in context, Prospero's description of Caliban is properly understood as hyperbole:

> **Prospero:** A devil, a born devil, on whose nature
> Nurture can never stick; on whom my pains,
> Humanly taken, all, all lost, quite lost;
> And as with age his body uglier grows,
> So his mind cankers.
>
> (*The Tempest* 4.1.189–93)

Prospero's desire is to protect Caliban and to find a place for him on the island. Shakespeare forces his audience to take sides for or against Caliban in the first act of the play. It is here that Caliban claims he has been mistreated by Prospero, that the magician has unjustly taken the island from him. Throughout the conversation, Caliban utters rude curses at Prospero, asking for "All the charms / Of Sycorax . . . light on [Prospero]" (*The Tempest* 1.2.340). Meredith Skura's colonialist reading of this scene seems unbalanced, for in her haste to condemn Prospero, she fails to consider Shakespeare's balancing of the characterization. While Skura's work is important for the way in which it gives value to Caliban as a human, the play does not offer sufficient grounds for the condemnation of Prospero as a heartless slave master. We learn in act 1 that Prospero allowed Caliban to live in his home and that Miranda taught Caliban to speak English (*The Tempest* 1.2.353). It is in this setting, before he has been reduced to the status of slave, that Caliban attempts to rape Miranda. Prospero refuses to kill him, however, perhaps evidencing that Prospero has compassion and that he values Caliban as a human being. Prospero's acknowledgment of Caliban at the close of the play, "this thing of darkness . . . mine" (*The Tempest* 5.1.276), must not be understood as Skura explains: "Prospero's acknowledgement of Caliban is considered a mistake, a moment of inadvertent sympathy or truth, too brief to counter Prospero's underlying colonialism . . . in calling Caliban 'mine,' [Prospero] is simply claiming possession of him: It is as though, after a public disturbance, a slave owner said, 'Those two men are yours; this darkie's mine.'"[75] I disagree with Skura and propose that Prospero's claiming of Caliban is gracious.

By claiming him and pardoning him, it appears that Prospero is finally able to convince Caliban of his desire to see the savage redeemed. It may be that in the closing lines of the play Caliban recognizes what Robert Hunter refers to as the "good governance" of Prospero.[76] It is through this recognition that Caliban is able to understand the futility of his ways and the need to repent before a sovereign God. This notion fits within a pattern that is established in the play by the similar recognition and more prominent humbling of Prospero. It is this theme of redemptive humiliation that allows the reader to more fully appreciate Caliban's very humble statements at the close of the play:

> **Caliban:** Ay, that I will; and I'll be wise hereafter,
> And seek for grace. What a thrice-double ass
> Was I to take this drunkard for a god
> And worship this dumb fool!
>
> (*The Tempest* 5.1.295–98)

Caliban's suit for grace betrays a connection to Reformation doctrine. Luther's teaching on this matter points out that anyone who hopes to be redeemed must "yearn and seek for grace," as we see Caliban do in this final scene. Luther writes:

> For in its true and proper work and purpose [the Law] humbles a man and prepares him—if he uses the Law correctly—to yearn and seek for grace. For only when a man's sin is disclosed and increased through the Law does he begin to see the wickedness of the human heart and its hostility toward the Law and toward God, the Author of the Law . . . Now he is forced to confess that there is nothing good in him at all. When he has been crushed and humbled this way, he acknowledges that he is truly miserable and damned. Therefore when the Law forces a man to acknowledge his evil this way and to confess his sin sincerely, it has performed its function; its time has come to an end, and the time of grace has come, when the Blessed Offspring is to arrive, who will raise up and comfort the man who has been frightened and wounded by the Law.[77]

As Stephen Greenblatt claims, "Caliban is not a Noble Savage; [he is] lecherous, evil-smelling, idle, treacherous, naïve, drunken, rebellious, violent, and devilworshipping."[78] Caliban is fully human, his shortcomings only lining him up more fully with the Reformation understanding of mankind. Greenblatt's description of Caliban bears a resemblance to the portrait of humanity painted by Paul in the New Testament book of Romans: "Being filled with all unrighteousness, fornication, wickedness, covetousness, maliciousness; full of envy, murder, debate, deceit, malignity; whisperers, Backbiters, haters of God, despiteful, proud, boasters, inventors of evil things, disobedient to parents, Without understanding, covenantbreakers, without natural affection, implacable, unmerciful: Who knowing the judgment of God, that they which commit such things are worthy of death, not only do the same, but have pleasure in them that do them."[79] Luther writes dozens of pages about this idea, for the depraved state of humanity is central to his theology of grace. According to Luther, one must recognize and repent of depravity before he or she can be redeemed.[80] It may in fact be that Caliban is to be considered a Pauline symbol of depraved humanity. The comparison between Caliban and sinful humanity allows us to see Caliban as a redeemed soul. As John Cox writes, "Caliban's determination to be wise hereafter and seek for grace would in fact seem to be the ultimate expression of anyone's humanity in *The Tempest*."[81] Though bestial in appearance, Caliban is not unredeemable, and his final confession evidences the humanity in his soul. The nature of Caliban's redemption betrays one more intersection between Reformation theology and Shakespeare's *Tempest*.

In conclusion, it is my contention that Prospero is in sin while serving as Duke of Milan for his worship of magic and his neglect of duty. He is deposed by Providential design, humbled on an island with one subject and a simple "cell," and finally comes to realize that even though he is armed with powerful magic, he must submit to Providence and live a life of humble service. As a redeemed man, Prospero is given the opportunity to take part in the ministry of Providence. Newly armed with a proper understanding of his own magic, Prospero becomes a Luther-like minister of Providence and takes part in the humiliation of Alonso and Caliban, a process through which both men are redeemed. The concept of redemptive humiliation at work in *The Tempest* is drawn from Reformation theology and particularly the writings of Reformation theologians Martin Luther and John Calvin.

Chapter 3
King Lear

In chapters 1 and 2, we have seen humiliated protagonists take part in the redemptive humiliation of others. Both Hamlet and Prospero are cast in the role of Reformation minister. In this chapter, we examine *King Lear*, wherein the humiliation of the protagonist dominates the action of the play. In an essay describing Christian pessimism in *King Lear*, Kenneth Myrick argues that the Elizabethan audience, trained in Reformation theology, would not have been surprised by what unfolds in *King Lear*. Myrick writes, "One by one, the five villainous characters in *Lear* are destroyed in the exact circumstances in which the Elizabethan had been trained to see and dread the judgment of an angry God."[1] According to Myrick, Elizabethans would have been familiar with the preaching and the printed sermons of Richard Hooker (1554–1600) and Henry Smith (1550–1591). Smith preached about the "false security" and "downfall of evildoers."[2] In one sermon, he describes the process in this way: "First, God takes him in his fault, that he might see his fault . . . Then he takes him suddenly, because he contemneth his warning . . . Thirdly God takes him where he is pleasantest and lustiest, and safest . . . Vengeance doth stay until sin be ripe, and watch the time when they are most occupied, then judgment steps forth, like the Angell to stop Balaam in his way, because the punishment is more grievous and terrible when they look not for it."[3] It is in this way, modeled after what Myrick calls the "tragic sense" or the "tragic note" of Elizabethan Christianity that five of the villains in *King Lear* meet their ruin. Myrick is here referring to Goneril, Regan, Cornwall, Edmund, and Oswald. The first of these to die in the play is Cornwall, stabbed by the servant who seeks to protect Gloucester. Cornwall's death is not anticipated, thus allowing it to take on the "more grievous and terrible" characteristic as described by Smith. The servant's rise against Cornwall is unexpected:

1 Servant: Hold your hand, my lord.
I have served you ever since I was a child,
But better service have I never done you
Than now to bid you hold.
Regan: How now, you dog?
1 Servant: If you did wear a beard upon your chin,
I'd shake it on this quarrel. What do you mean?
Cornwall: My villein?

(*King Lear* 3.7.70–77)[4]

Both Regan and Cornwall are surprised at the servant's audacity, Cornwall confessing that this injury comes on him too early: "Regan, I bleed apace; / Untimely comes this hurt" (*King Lear* 3.7.97–98).

Oswald is the next to die in this list of villains. His death is also unexpected, as his earlier conflict with Kent confirms that Oswald would not be one to draw on someone he thought might prove a good fighter. We witness Oswald run in fear from Kent in act 2, Kent calling him a coward, a "lily-livered, action-taking knave [and a] glass gazing . . . finical rogue" (*King Lear* 2.2.16–19). As an "action-taking knave," Oswald is claimed to be one who takes legal action rather than fighting; as a "finical rogue," he would be one who is affected or fussy.[5] In his exchange with Edgar, it may be that Oswald is fooled by the dialect Edgar feigns, one of a country peasant, thereby leading Oswald to believe that he would not be a well-trained fighter.[6] Like Cornwall, Oswald also claims that his death is untimely, further betraying his surprise.

In act 5, both Regan and Goneril die. Regan is secretly poisoned by her sister, clearly an unexpected death, and Goneril, though she kills herself, does so as a desperate act of frustration. Goneril kills Regan so that she may have Edmund for herself, yet in the process discovers that Edmund will not have her. The frustration that overtakes Goneril is unexpected, and her suicide is carried out in a passionate rage.

Edmund's ruin is of a different nature than the previous four. He is faced with his own ruin; he is taken, as stated by Henry Smith, "in his fault, that he might see his fault."[7] After being brought to his knees by Edgar, Edmund is charged for his crimes by Albany, to which he confesses:

> **Edmund:** What you have charged me with, that have I done,
> And more, much more; the time will bring it out.
> 'Tis past and so am I . . .
>
> (*King Lear* 5.3.160–62)

He also confesses to Edgar, after Edgar confronts him about the treatment Gloucester is forced to endure:

> **Edgar:** The gods are just and of our pleasant vices
> Make instruments to plague us:
> The dark and vicious place where thee he got
> Cost him his eyes.
> **Edmund:** Thou'st spoken right, 'tis true;
> The wheel is come full circle, I am here.
>
> (*King Lear* 5.3.168–73)

Though it appears that Shakespeare was familiar with Smith's ideas regarding the punishment and judgment of evil men and women, Myrick—like Roland Frye—does not claim that Shakespeare was a religious man or that Shakespeare even read the works of Reformation preachers. Myrick writes, "Whether Shakespeare ever . . . heard a sermon by Henry Smith is of no particular relevance. What is important is that Smith and [Bartholomew] Parsons [we can reasonably include Hooker here as well] are representative. It would be absurd, of course, to say that every religious writer of the age was gifted with the tragic sense . . . But the frequency of the tragic note in Elizabethan Christianity is undeniable."[8] In Shakespeare's *King Lear*, we see more support for what Myrick describes as the "tragic note in Elizabethan Christianity"[9] in the fall of the play's antagonists, but I will here extend his analysis, and demonstrate that the impact of Reformation theology on Shakespeare's *King Lear* can be witnessed in the plain dealing of Kent, the humiliation of the king, and the compassion of Cordelia.

As I propose to focus on what may seem minor elements of Reformation theology, it is important to note that the new doctrines of Protestantism would not have been considered minor to an Elizabethan. As acknowledged by Alison Shell, "There was considerable personal and literary interaction between individuals of opposing religious views. Catholics and Protestants lived side by side, sometimes spoke to each other without quarrelling, and read each other's books."[10] Kent's plain dealing and Lear's humiliation provide evidence of Shakespeare's ability to glean from his culture, a characteristic of the playwright praised by Harold Bloom.[11] From the religious storms that rage around him, Shakespeare employs what appears to be the essence of Reformation doctrine. In Shakespeare's *King Lear*, we see these passionate teachings played out in the lives of Kent and Lear.

In the first act of the play when Kent confronts Lear in regard to the banishment of Cordelia, Kent understands that the king is exercising poor moral vision:

Lear: Out of my sight!
Kent: See better, Lear, and let me still remain
The true blank of thine eye.

(*King Lear* 1.1.147–67)

The Arden Shakespeare edition notes that Kent here invites Lear to look to his servant for good advice.[12] "See *me* better," is perhaps what Kent implies, as he responds to Lear's command. Kent understands, perhaps, that he alone is able to see the danger that Lear has fallen in to. In "let me still remain," Kent is trying to get Lear to recognize that he is the only one who sees Lear's madness clearly. Offering himself as a potential focal point of sorts, Kent understands that Lear, like a blind man, needs a guide. Ben Schneider Jr. argues in his essay "King Lear and the Culture of Justice" that Kent is of the classic plain dealer mold, praised in the Renaissance as one who is unafraid to speak the truth.[13] The spirit of the Reformation is one steeped in the tradition of plain dealing. Luther's very act of nailing his Ninety-five Theses to the church door in Wittenberg and proclaiming the truth as he saw it was, in these terms, an exemplary act of plain dealing. In Luther's "Warning to His Dear German People," the German Reformer supports those who would stand up against a corrupt government:

> One might tolerate an evil life; but one can and must not tolerate, much less help to defend, a person who condemns doctrine and God's word and who elevates himself over God. They have disseminated so many doctrinal abominations within Christendom that these cannot be numbered. They repent of none of them, nor do they want to change them, but they openly defend them all and rigorously insist on being in the right. All of that would rest on your neck and conscience. You would make yourself a partner of all such abominations and you would be guilty if you helped to defend them.[14]

Calvin concludes his *Institutes of the Christian Religion* with a warning to those who lack the courage to stand up to a corrupt ruler or king:

> So far is the praise of modesty from being due to that pretence by which flattering courtiers cloak themselves, and deceive the simple, when they deny the lawfulness of declining anything imposed by their kings . . . I know the imminent peril to which subjects expose themselves by this firmness, kings being most indignant when they are contemned. As Solomon says, "The wrath of a king is as messengers of death" (Prov. 16:14). But since Peter, one of heaven's heralds, has published the edict, "We ought to obey God rather than men" (Acts 5:29), let us console ourselves with the thought, that we are rendering the obedience which the Lord requires, when we endure anything rather than turn aside from piety. And that our courage may not fail, Paul stimulates us by the additional consideration (1 Cor. 7:23), that we were redeemed by Christ at the great price which our redemption cost him, in order that we might not yield a slavish obedience to the depraved wishes of men, far less do homage to their impiety.[15]

Hooker is no less plain in his writings, arguing that men must know the truth and be willing to stand up for it, be it against priest, king, or other guide: "If the guides of the people be blind, the common sort of men must not close up their own eyes and be led by the conduct of such; if the priest be partial in the law, the flock must not therefore depart from the ways of sincere truth, and in simplicity yield to be followers of him for his place' sake and office over them."[16] We can find models for Kent in all three of these prominent, very plain-dealing writers. While plain dealing was praised long before the Reformation, the religious movement and especially the works of Luther, Calvin, and Hooker put a new emphasis on the power and honor of speaking the truth plainly and boldly. Just as Huston Diehl claims that the Reformers reinvigorated the notion of original sin, "adamantly insisting that everyone is depraved by nature and sharply critiquing the Catholic ideals of celibacy, monasticism, and good works that imply otherwise,"[17] so too did the Reformers reinvigorate the importance of the plain dealer. It is Martin Luther whose statements about the pope make him the clearest model among Reformation theologians of plain dealing. Luther challenged the Roman powers of his day, wrote profusely about the damage he believed the pope was doing to the church, and made controversial claims about the pope, calling him the "Antichrist," the "devil incarnate," and one who "signifies the terrible wrath of God."[18] With a Luther-like plain dealing, Shakespeare's Kent is not afraid to step "between the dragon and his wrath" (*King Lear* 1.1.122) or even to appear rude and unmannerly:

Lear: The bow is bent and drawn; make from the shaft.
Kent: Let it fall rather; though the fork invade
The region of my heart: be Kent unmannerly
When Lear is mad. What wouldst thou do, old man?
Think'st thou that duty shall have dread to speak,
When power to flattery bows? To plainness honour's bound
When majesty falls to folly.

(*King Lear* 1.1.146–52)

Kent alludes to himself as one who sees honor in "plainness," contesting that plain speaking must come before mannerly behavior. The question Kent poses to Lear is an interesting one, "What wouldst thou do, old man?" (*King Lear* 1.1.149). Kent identifies that the kingdom has fallen into a state of emergency; it is he alone who sees the danger of Lear's request for flattery. Kent claims that this is madness, and his addressing of Lear as "old man," though an outrageous breach of decorum, is part of what Kent claims to be his duty. Lear's calling on Apollo, the archer god known for clear-sightedness, gives Kent an additional opportunity to press Lear about his poor moral vision:

Lear: Now by Apollo—
Kent: Now by Apollo, King,
Thou swear'st thy gods in vain.
Lear: O vassal! Miscreant!

(*King Lear* 1.1.161–64)

Kent recognizes that Lear is unable to see, that his eyes are clouded over with madness. Kent also recognizes that Lear's shout to Apollo is more an expression of exasperation, a taking of the god's name in vain, than a serious plea to the most clear-sighted of the gods. Kent believes that Lear truly needs to cry out to Apollo for guidance and vision.

In this opening act, Kent is cast in the role of a spiritual physician; he has the proper prescription for Lear, yet tragically, Lear is unable to hear his servant's wise counsel:

Kent: Do, kill thy physician, and thy fee bestow
Upon the foul disease. Revoke thy gift,
Or whilst I can vent clamour from my throat
I'll tell thee thou dost evil.

(*King Lear* 1.1.164–67)

Kent does not seek to win an argument or to be vindicated through his passionate conflict with Lear. As he claims, Kent is trying to save his beloved king. The language he employs, referring to himself as Lear's physician, is the very language employed by Martin Luther in his *Lectures on Romans*. Luther writes, "This is like the case of a physician who wishes to heal his patient, but finds that he is a man who denies that he is sick, calling the physician a fool and an even sicker person than himself for presuming to cure a healthy man. And because of the man's resistance the physician cannot get around to recommending his skill and his medicine. For he could do so only if the sick man would admit his illness and permit him to cure him."[19] Lear is too arrogant to see that he is sick. Just like Lear, the sick man in Luther's example proclaims that the person who tries to help him is a miscreant—a word that the Oxford English Dictionary defines more similarly to heretic and misbeliever than to "wretch" or "villain."[20] Though Kent seeks to protect the well-being of his king, Lear proclaims that his physician is not a proper spiritual guide but rather a damnable heretic. Kent does not seek honor or power by claiming to be Lear's physician; rather, Kent risks his life by stepping into Lear's rage. Luther's illustration is meant to point out man's need to humbly confess his illness, trust the scriptures, and seek God's grace. Luther further elucidates this concept:

> Therefore we need humility and faith. What these words seek to establish and maintain is solely this, that inwardly we become nothing, that we empty ourselves of everything, humble ourselves and say with the prophet, "Against Thee, Thee only, have I sinned, so that Thou art justified in Thy words. . . . In Thy sight I am foolish and weak, so that Thou mayest be wise and powerful in Thy words. . . . For all creation teaches. . . . that no one is exalted except the man who has been humbled, nothing is filled except that which is empty, that nothing is built except that which has been torn down."[21]

Kent's plain dealing and the language he employs to confront Lear bear a close resemblance to the plain-dealing Reformation theologians and especially the writing of Martin Luther. The "tearing down" of prideful Lear, still claiming to be "more sinned against than sinning" (*King Lear* 3.2.59) long after he has isolated himself from his family, is the second place we find major strands of Reformation influence.

The humiliation of Lear comes as a result of his poor moral vision. There is a desperation that dominates this play, which made Samuel Johnson and many others of the eighteenth century glad of Nahum Tate's revised version of the play. It was Dr. Johnson's prediction that playgoers would "rise better pleased from the final triumph of persecuted virtue."[22] Civilized society, in the opinion of Geoffrey Bickersteth, "had grown too much sophisticated, too consciously aware of its own exquisite refinement, to be capable of responding with any real sympathy 'to the primitive scene, the moral and physical humiliations and the desperate challenge of such a play as *King Lear*.'"[23] It may be, as Stephen Greenblatt writes, that in *King Lear* the Catholic Church is "revealed to be the persecuted elder brother forced to defend himself by means of theatrical illusions against the cold persecution of his skeptical bastard brother Protestantism."[24] But Greenblatt's premise misses the more consuming issue at hand in *King Lear*, the fact that the humiliation of man, central to the play, was of paramount concern to Protestant writers during the Reformation. That men and women would recognize their sinful state and understand that they were unable to save themselves were two of the chief goals of Luther, Calvin, and Hooker. Luther writes, "Nobody doubts that man with all his faculties was created by the eternal Word of God, as were all other things, and that he is God's creature. Nevertheless there is nothing good in him; this means (as Moses says in Genesis 6[:5]), that all his thoughts and senses with all faculties are continually inclined to evil. Thus although the flesh is truly God's creation it is not inclined to chastity but to unchastity; although the heart is truly God's creation, it is not inclined to humility, to love of neighbor, but to pride and to self-love."[25] In the opening lines of *Institutes of the Christian Religion*, Calvin writes, "We are accordingly urged by our own evil things to consider the good things of God; and, indeed, we cannot aspire to Him in earnest until we have begun to be displeased with ourselves. For what man is not disposed to rest in himself . . . so long as he is contented with his own endowments, and unconscious or unmindful of his misery?"[26]

Hooker follows in the same way, writing thus: "We are not dust and ashes, but worse; our minds from the highest to the lowest are not right; if not right, then undoubtedly not capable of that blessedness which we naturally seek, but subject unto that which we most abhor, anguish, tribulation, death, woe, endless misery."[27] In her work on the tradition of common prayer in Elizabethan Christianity, Ramie Targoff cites a passage from Hooker, revealing the Elizabethan preacher's mistrust of the nature of man: "[Common prayer is] a mechanism that successfully molds the naturally flawed impulses of the worshipper, whose faith can only be stimulated through regulated external forms."[28] The notion of human depravity stands at the forefront of Reformation theology, and it was this issue that we find played out in Shakespeare's humiliation of Lear.

Martin Luther employs the use of marred human vision to describe the futility of human reason and the truth of human weakness. Luther claims that humans are "blind" to the truths of God and that the result is that religious institutions oppress their members as Lear oppressed his daughters. As Lear orders each daughter into a posture of confession, he requires of them an offering of praise:

> **Lear:** Which of you shall we say doth love us most,
> That we our largest bounty may extend
> Where nature doth with merit challenge.
>
> (*King Lear* 1.1.51–53)

The sisters are here ordered to perform an act of religious dedication, to publicly proclaim their love for Lear. Lear's demand parallels what Luther described as the demands of the Roman Catholic Church of the sixteenth century. Luther writes this about the priesthood of his day: "[Any priest that demands such outward signs of devotion] is as blind as a bat and says that we must fast, pray, sing, and do the works of the law. It continues to fool around in this manner with works, until it has gone so far astray and thinks we serve God by building churches, ringing bells, burning incense, reciting by rote, singing, wearing hoods, having tonsures, burning candles, and by other countless foolish acts of which the world is full, indeed more than full."[29] Lear's blindness, in many ways symbolic of the blindness of all mankind, is foundational to the human struggle found in the text. Bickersteth refers to Lear's blindness as "a hideous rashness against the moral order of Nature."[30] He fails to consider the emotional and spiritual implications of Lear's blindness. Lear does indeed lash out at the moral order, but more importantly, he lashes out at the emotional and spiritual order around him. Lear knows himself only "slenderly," and his understanding of his daughters and other loved ones around him is equally shallow. Lear rushes forward in haste by what Luther would call the natural light of his own depraved logic. This natural light, or human reason, is marred by sin. Luther writes: "But the natural light cannot reach so far that it could determine which things are good and which are bad."[31] Although the thrust of my work here is focused on the character of Lear, it is worth mentioning that Gloucester's physical blindness is included in the play to drive home the point that Lear's tragedy "is no isolated instance of a single life gone wrong."[32] Buechner here moves us toward my central thesis. Lear's story is not an isolated incident but in some ways a playing out of one of the major theological views of Shakespeare's day: that prideful men are brought into a right relationship with themselves, others, and ultimately God only after being brought to their knees through a humiliating experience. Gloucester's physical blindness, acquired at the hand or perhaps the spur of Cornwall, and his literal fall, staged for him by his son Edgar at the imaginary cliffs of Dover, act as a frame for Lear's emotional-spiritual blindness and his ultimate fall.[33] In his essay "Grief, Authority and the Resistance to Consolation in Shakespeare," Frederic B. Tromly writes the following about Gloucester's fall: "[Edgar's purpose] was to convince [Gloucester] that there is a divine providence in which his life matters . . . Edgar stages a kind of miracle play to convince Gloucester that his attempt at suicide has been foiled by divine intervention . . . [the plan was constructed] to save his father from the spiritual death of despair."[34] Tromly's explanation, though partly accurate, falls short by failing to recognize the historical relevancy of Edgar's "treatment" of his father. Gloucester, suffering from a depression that an early modern audience would possibly have recognized as melancholy, begs Edgar, disguised as Poor Tom, to lead him to the Dover Cliffs (*King Lear* 4.1.73–80). Winfried Schleiner writes that Gloucester's despair bears a similarity to the symptoms of one suffering from schizophrenia, "with its attendant false images of the world . . . fear, pain, and despair."[35] The scene that follows, and more specifically the remedy that Edgar seeks to apply to his psychologically ailing father, bears a similarity to the remedies employed by Renaissance doctors as well as by Martin Luther to the melancholics who were brought to him for pastoral treatment.

In act 4, scene 6, Edgar leads Gloucester up an imaginary hill. This scene, involving the deception of Gloucester, is not cruel as Richard Wilson claims but, by Reformation standards, full of grace and mercy.[36] Recognizing the merciful nature of Edgar's staging of Gloucester's fall, Robert Miola describes this "theatrical fiction" as "a salvific action performed with costume."[37] Edgar's ploy to heal Gloucester's imagination through the imagination was consistent with Renaissance psychiatric theory.[38] Edgar must work to entangle Gloucester in an imaginary world:

Gloucester: When shall I come to th' top of that same hill?
Edgar: You do climb up it now; look how we labour.
Gloucester: Methinks the ground is even.
Edgar: Horrible steep. Hark do you hear the sea?
Gloucester: No, truly.
Edgar: Why then, your other senses grow imperfect
By your eyes' anguish.
Gloucester: So may it be indeed.
Methinks thy voice is alter'd, and thou speak'st
In better phrase and matter than thou didst.
Edgar: Y'are much deceiv'd: in nothing am I chang'd
But in my garments.
Gloucester: Methinks y'are better spoken.
Edgar: Come on, sir; here's the place. Stand still.
How fearful
And dizzy 'tis to cast one's eyes so low!
The crows and choughs that wing the mid-way air
Show scarce so gross as beetles. Half-way down
Hangs one that gathers samphire—dreadful trade!
Methinks he seems no bigger than his head.
The fishermen that walk upon the beach
Appear like mice; and yond tall anchoring bark
Diminish'd to her cock; her cock, a bouy
Almost too small for sight. The murmuring surge
That on th' unnumb'red idle pebble chafes
Cannot be heard so high. I'll look no more;
Lest my brain turn, and the deficient sight
Topple down headlong.
Gloucester: Set me where you stand.

(*King Lear* 4.6.1–19)

Gloucester's challenge of Edgar, claiming not to notice any incline and claiming to hear not the sea but rather a slight change in Edgar's feigned accent forces Edgar to work even harder at the creation of an imaginary world. The detail he employs, from birds to bugs, fishermen and samphire, creates in Gloucester a confidence in a world that does not exist. Edgar must draw his father from a world of despair into his own world of hope and promise. It is in Edgar's world of hope that Gloucester is redeemed. The old man's fall and, more importantly, his redemption serve as key parallels to King Lear's fall and his ultimate redemption.

Edgar: Thy life's a miracle. Speak yet again.
Gloucester: But have I fall'n, or no?
Edgar: From the dreadful summit of this chalky bourn . . .
. . . therefore, thou happy father,
Think that the clearest gods, who make them honours
Of men's impossibilities, have preserved thee.
Gloucester: I do remember now. Henceforth I'll bear
Affliction till it do cry out itself
"Enough, enough" and die . . .
Edgar: Bear free and patient thoughts.

(*King Lear* 4.6.55–57, 72–79)

Sixteenth-century records of psychiatric cases and their respective treatments describe patients with maladies of a very similar nature to that of Gloucester. Some patients held strange notions that they had an alternative identity; others believed that they had a unique physical make-up or a dangerous internal problem; still others believed that God had called them to perform different acts of purgation. One patient of Martin Luther's, a case recorded in Luther's *Tischreden*, is described as one who was certain that God had called him to abstain from urinating. The case was handled in much the same way that Edgar handles Gloucester's melancholy. Luther's experience is related thus:

> Then someone came to him saying that he was doing right in castigating his body and that he should certainly stay with his resolve (to serve God and to make himself suffer), for one entered into heaven

> through many crosses and tribulations. The same person also pretended that he too had taken a vow not to urinate, but that since he had prided himself on this pledge and had thought to gain heaven by it, he had sinned more than if he had urinated; indeed, he had almost become a murderer of his own body. "Thus all the world will say similarly of you, that you do so out of pride. Therefore give up your resolve and let nature have its course." In this way he persuaded the melancholic to urinate.[39]

This course of therapy, orchestrated by Martin Luther, involved creating an imaginary world. Like Edgar, Luther sought to save the delusional man by bringing him into another world in which God does not demand men and women to castigate themselves but where men and women are forgiven and blessed with grace. This was in fact what Luther sought to do to the church at large through the Reformation.

Luther sought to offer men and women a paradigm shift in the way they thought about God, verified by a close reading of scripture. Just as Luther freed his patient, so Edgar freed Gloucester. Although Gloucester claims to "shake patiently my great affliction off" (*King Lear* 4.6.36), in truth his attempted suicide betrays his great impatience with affliction. Gloucester's greatest affliction is his knowledge of his own sin and shame. Just as Luther's patient was afflicted by a false theology—that God wanted him to pay for his sins and earn his forgiveness—so too is Gloucester afflicted. Certain that he must pay for his bad behavior and cognizant of his helpless situation—his inability to fix what he has destroyed—Gloucester seeks to end his own life. Edgar's assurance that the gods have saved Gloucester and spared him, allowed him to float down from the great cliffs like "gossamer, feathers, air" (*King Lear* 4.6.49), is all the assurance Gloucester needs in order to live on and accept his fate. Edgar's final command to "Bear free and patient thoughts" (*King Lear* 4.6.79) is of special significance in light of Luther's connection to this episode. Luther's theology was one that put a particular emphasis on the freedom of the Christian. Free from blame, free from sin, free from damnation, Luther emphasized that the Christian did not need to perform acts of purgation. Luther affirmed that God's grace was free and that men and women did not need to earn their salvation. Acts of penance and other forms of castigation, even the purchasing of indulgences, according to Luther, were not necessary. Luther criticized the Roman Catholic

Church for burdening men and women with harmful theology and for failing to teach of God's free grace and forgiveness.

Gloucester's melancholy, much like the melancholy described in Luther's *Tischreden*, is brought on by a theological misunderstanding. Much like Lear, Gloucester and Luther's patient must be humbled before they can enter into a healthy relationship with God and with others. In the psychiatric terms of the early modern period, Gloucester's broken imagination is healed by a work of the imagination. In the religious terms of the Reformation and the Renaissance, Gloucester and Luther's patient are healed by recognizing what Martin Luther called a man's proper place before God.[40] These men, according to the writings of Martin Luther, were bound by a false understanding of God and of themselves. Through a humiliating revelation, both men are able to recover their emotional and spiritual vision and to move forward, bearing "free and patient thoughts" (*King Lear* 4.6.79).

Lear's fall can be described in terms of a downward spiral, a movement that begins at the banishment of Cordelia. Lear's moral blindness secures him a tenuous position between two competitive daughters. Goneril and Regan have no patience with their father and are grateful to see him choose to leave their homes than to stay with a smaller following. While it seems strange to argue in support of Goneril and Regan, Shakespeare does not give us much reason to hate the two sisters in the early stages of the play. When called on to flatter their father, Goneril and Regan's acquiescence does not seem villainous next to Cordelia's seemingly harsh refusal. Later, when Lear's soldiers are wreaking havoc on Goneril's home, the logic Goneril employs for not allowing her father so many knights is reasonable:

Goneril: This man hath had good counsel—a hundred knights!
'Tis politic, and safe, to let him keep
At point a hundred knights! Yes, that on every dream,
Each buzz, each fancy, each complaint, dislike,
He may enguard his dotage with their powers
And hold our lives in mercy.

(*King Lear* 1.4.315–20)

At the outset of the play, we see Lear engage his fancy and demand an offering of praise from his daughters. The text gives us every reason to trust Goneril's concern in this passage, for how can we be sure that more "dark purposes" do not still lurk in the aging mind of Lear? If we take Regan at her word, her home is too small to house all one hundred of Lear's attendants.

> **Regan:** This house is little; the old man and's people
> Cannot be well bestowed.
> **Goneril:** 'Tis his own blame; hath put himself from rest
> And must needs taste his folly.
> **Regan:** For his particular, I'll receive him gladly,
> But not one follower.
> (*King Lear* 2.2.479–82)

Regan is not moved by Goneril's statement of frustration, that Lear deserves to learn his lesson, but insists that she would gladly take him into her home. Even Regan's locking of the doors against Lear, shortly after his departure, seems excusable. She justifies her action by explaining once again that she fears Lear's potential for rage:

> **Regan:** Shut up your doors.
> He is attended with a desperate train,
> And what they may incense him to, being apt
> To have his ear abused, wisdom bids fear.
> (*King Lear* 2.2.494–97)

In this same passage, Regan echoes Goneril's prophetic word, claiming that Lear will grow in wisdom through a series of injuries, "O sir, to wilful men / The injuries that they themselves procure / Must be their schoolmasters" (*King Lear* 2.2.493–95).

Goneril and Regan do not sin against their father at the beginning of the play. Their flattery, though in many ways contemptible, is part of the courtly life they are a part of. Lear's claim to be "more sinned against than sinning" (*King Lear* 3.2.59) is not true but instead is further evidence of the king's moral blindness, his inability to see himself and the people around him clearly.[41] Like Lear, the abdicating pope Celestine V of the thirteenth century was also viewed as a foolish man, full of self-interest. Lear is not a wounded soul as he departs from Regan's house but a wounding one. He is responsible for the deteriorating family, much more sinning than sinned against.

As the storm tears the clothing from Lear's body, it also takes from him his damning pride. The king is reduced to a humble man, and by act 4, he begins to speak thoughtfully, no longer blinded by pride, and is even able to give proper instruction to Gloucester:

Lear: Thou must be patient. We came crying hither:
Thou knowst the first time that we smell the air
We wawl and cry. I will preach to thee: mark me.
Gloucester: Alack, alack the day!
Lear: When we are born we cry that we are come
To this great stage of fools.

(*King Lear* 4.6.174–79)

This is the language of humility, Lear finally seeing himself as he truly is, a fool on a stage. The violence of Lear's humiliation is evidence of its Protestant design. Different from the mild employment of humiliation, as proposed by Aquinas, Lear is not "using humiliations as a medicine."[42] The violent humiliation that Lear experiences is one that he has no control over; it is a humiliation that Reformation theologians would attribute to divine grace. Luther describes God as a father that disciplines those he loves with "scourges and blows."[43] It is this kind of discipline, according to Luther, that leads to clear self-knowledge and spiritual redemption.[44] In this manner, Lear is reduced to a humble state; his clear self-knowledge is evidenced by the fact that he does not fight to keep his dignity but confesses his human frailty:

Lear: I know not what to say.
I will not swear these are my hands: let's see—
I feel this pinprick. Would I were assured
Of my condition.

(*King Lear* 4.7.54–57)

Though he swings in and out of sanity in the final acts of the play, it is certain that Lear is conscious of his human frailty. His expression of self-doubt signals a change in Lear from proud to humbled before man and before the gods.

Lear's confession draws us back to Regan's statement regarding Lear, that he "hath ever but slenderly known himself" (*King Lear* 1.1.294–95). Lear's confession here indicates that he is not in full possession of himself and that there are things he does not understand about himself and life. As Ewan Fernie writes, through the course of the play Lear moves "through shame toward relationship."[45] Lear does not refuse to admit weakness and ignorance, and thus his confession is a model of that which John Calvin describes as the perfect posture of a man.[46]

Lear's fall is compatible with Hooker's view of man, which the preacher expresses in this way: "But for most men the doom of suffering is a necessity if they are to know the profundities of life."[47] Though the play ends tragically, Lear leaning over the dead body of his beloved daughter, it may be argued that his sufferings have led him to a place where he can at last experience the greatest profundity of life: true and sincere love for another.

Chapter 4
Henry VIII

> I come no more to make you laugh. Things now
> That bear a weighty and serious brow,
> Sad, high, and working, full of state and woe,
> Such noble scenes as draw the eye to flow,
> We now present . . .
>
> (*Henry VIII* Prologue 1–5)[1]

As we have seen in chapter 3, the humiliating fall of King Lear leads to his redemption, evidenced in the restoration of his vision and in his reconciliation with Cordelia. This chapter builds on this idea in the humiliation of Cardinal Wolsey. William Shakespeare's *Henry VIII* opens with a conversation between the Duke of Norfolk and the Duke of Buckingham. The Duke of Norfolk relates the details of his experience in Calais where Henry VIII and Francis I met for a royal event called the Field of Cloth of Gold. This event, documented in Raphael Holinshed's *Chronicles of England, Scotland, and Ireland*, took place in the Val d'Or, a shallow valley on English soil halfway between Guisnes and Ard.[2] Luxurious banquets, dances, a "feat of arms," and engagements between the two kings and their queens were orchestrated by Cardinal Wolsey. The royal accommodations were noted as being especially magnificent.[3] Historian Joycelyne G. Russell records that the French pitched more than three hundred tents, all of them covered with velvet and cloth of gold "emblazoned with the arms of their owners and surmounted by pennants or golden apples."[4] Russell also documents that King Francis's tent, taller than the others, "was supported by two ship's masts lashed together, covered with cloth of gold and topped by a life-sized statue of St. Michael."[5] The description continues, "An eye-witness described the French tents as more magnificent than 'the miracles of the Egyptian pyramids and the Roman amphitheatres'. However, many people were more impressed by the temporary palace erected by Henry VIII near Guisnes. This had walls of timber painted to look like brick and many large windows. Even Leonardo, an Italian commented, could not have done better."[6] Shakespeare opens his play with the Duke of Norfolk, exhilarated by his experience in Calais:

Norfolk: 'Twixt Guynes and Arde.
I was then present; saw them salute on horseback;
Beheld them when they lighted, how they clung
In their embracement, as they grew together;
Which had they, what four throned ones could have weighed
Such a compounded one?

(*Henry VIII* 1.1.7–12)

Though his presence at the event is documented by historians, Shakespeare's Buckingham reports to having been sick with a fever when King Henry and King Francis meet in the valley "'Twixt Guynes and Arde."[7] Whether or not Buckingham's bitterness over the event causes him to break out in fever cannot be determined, but it is clear, however, that the Duke is not happy about the role he is forced to play. In this opening exchange, Norfolk, despite his comrade's disturbance, continues with much excitement and explains that the event grew in grandeur with each passing day:

Norfolk: . . . till the last
Made former wonders its. Today the French,
All clinquant, all in gold, like heathen gods,
Shone down the English; and tomorrow they
Made Britain India: every man that stood
Showed like a mine.

(*Henry VIII* 1.1.17–22)

The Field of Cloth of Gold, though marketed by Cardinal Wolsey as an important political engagement between England and France, did not result in the establishment of any lasting treaties between the countries. According to Joycelyne Russell, the event actually became "a household word among both nations [standing] for any superlative luxury or splendour, with no need for justification or thought of cost."[8] It is further reported that the engagement actually concluded poorly between the two kings, Raphael Holinshed stating that during the event, "there was such an hideous storm of wind and weather, that many conjecture it did prognosticate trouble and hatred shortly after to follow between princes."[9] Russell further documents that "no sooner was the meeting [between Henry VIII and Francis I] over than Francis began to fortify Ardres, and with the very wood from the pavilions."[10] The Field of Cloth of Gold takes place at the height of Cardinal Wolsey's power and authority. By choosing to open his play with a discussion of the event, Shakespeare focuses the attention of his audience on Wolsey's lust for fame.

It is only after Norfolk ceases to praise the royal engagement that Shakespeare reveals the source of Buckingham's bitterness. Buckingham is aware of the superfluous nature of the Field of Cloth of Gold. He and many of the other English nobles are enraged when Wolsey usurps their authority as a royal council and demands that they pay for the elaborate festival. Buckingham exclaims, "No man's pie is freed / From his ambitious finger" (*Henry VIII* 1.1.52–53). Holinshed records that it was the Duke of Buckingham who raised the loudest complaint. It is on this report that Shakespeare builds his character: "But namely the Duke of Buckingham, being a man of lofty courage but not most liberal, sore repined that he should be at so great charges for his furniture forth at this time, saying that he knew not for what cause so much money should be spent about the sight of a vain talk to be had, and communication to be ministered of things of no importance; wherefore he sticked not to say that it was an intolerable matter to obey such a vile and importunate person [as the cardinal]."[11]

Buckingham's bitterness at the beginning of Shakespeare's *Henry VIII* finds its focus in Cardinal Wolsey. Instead of calling to remembrance a meeting of nobles, richly clad and engaged in friendly games, the Field of Cloth of Gold could only have reminded Shakespeare's audience of the pride and vanity that characterized the work of Cardinal Wolsey. Though the play bears the name of the king, the focus of the play never travels far from the pride of Wolsey.

Shakespeare's *Henry VIII* is more a story about the king's chief advisors than a story about the king himself. Cardinal Wolsey, in particular, is a character that Shakespeare displays as arrogant and dangerously manipulative. It is the Cardinal's story that dominates more than two thirds of the play's action. As E. Pearlman writes, "Unlike the greater history plays, in each of which the monarch is the principal figure, *King Henry VIII* does not center on the king himself . . . The character of King Henry is less well defined and less interesting than either Buckingham, Katherine, or Wolsey."[12] In *Henry VIII*, Shakespeare seems not so interested in the reign of a king as in the fall of a priest. It does not seem farfetched that John Fletcher, the playwright many believe Shakespeare collaborated with in writing this play, could have had some influence over the way in which the cardinal is portrayed within the play. Fletcher's father, the onetime Bishop of London, infamously lost his post for marrying a widow supposedly known for her ill repute.[13]

In *Henry VIII*, Shakespeare moves beyond the medieval *de casibus* tradition to present a desperate and controversial view of humanity. While true to the medieval form in its description of a sudden fall from power and in its presentation of worldly power as fleeting and vain,[14] *Henry VIII* finds Shakespeare experimenting with a religious concept newly reintroduced to the Church by Protestant Reformers. It is the concept of the total depravity of man that shook the foundations of European spirituality, forcing men and women to adopt a new understanding of themselves and the God they served.[15] In *Henry VIII*, Shakespeare wrestles with the concept of humiliation as an agent of change in the life of Cardinal Wolsey. This concept, I argue, is drawn from the religious debates of the sixteenth and seventeenth centuries between Protestants and Roman Catholics. Of these debates and the religious culture in which Shakespeare lived, Debora Shuger writes, "If it is not plausible to read Shakespeare's plays as Christian allegories, neither is it likely that the popular drama of a religiously saturated culture could, by a secular miracle, have extricated itself from the theocentric orientation informing the discourses of politics, gender, social order, and history."[16] Stephen Greenblatt weighs in on the debate surrounding Shakespeare's theological interest by claiming that the Protestant Reformation offered Shakespeare an "extraordinary gift"[17]: "the broken fragments of what had been a rich, complex edifice—and he knew exactly how to accept and use this gift. He was hardly indifferent to the success he could achieve, but it was not a matter of profit alone. Shakespeare drew upon the pity, confusion, and dread of death in a world of damaged rituals."[18] In *Henry VIII*, we witness Shakespeare using and experimenting with unsettling Reformation "gifts": the doctrine of human depravity and the nature of the human conscience. In this play, Shakespeare borrows heavily from Reformation theology as he displays the concept of humiliation at work in the life of Cardinal Wolsey.

In his work *Shame in Shakespeare*, Ewan Fernie examines the multidimensional nature of shame in several of Shakespeare's works. In his chapter on *King Lear*, Fernie writes the following: "By the end of Act 1 Scene 1, we have learned that shame, as exemplified by Cordelia and thrust off by her father, is a painful good and that shamelessness, as exemplified by Lear and his elder daughters, is aligned with wickedness. It is the most emblematic revelation of Shakespeare's ethical vision of shame in the canon; it exposes this ethical vision in its most radical aspect."[19] Fernie continues in this manner: "France has been invaded by an inspiring vision of Lear's youngest daughter and, even as he moves to take her hand, he wonders if she is not set apart from marriage and life in the world. His curious speech as a whole plunges us deep into the enigmatic spiritual territory of ecstatic mortification and shame."[20] Fernie describes an otherworldly view of shame that we must employ in our understanding of Wolsey's humiliation in Shakespeare's *Henry VIII*. We cannot properly understand the powerful nature of shame and humiliation in Shakespeare's works, however, without examining the way in which this concept was embedded within the Reformation agenda. Portrayed in the writings of Martin Luther and John Calvin, the otherworldly shame, which Fernie describes as a path to the world outside the self, is the principal way in which men and women are required to come to God by newly established Reformation standards. Reformation doctrine demands that men and women "despair of self,"[21] for it is only by recognizing one's moral sickness and humbling depravity that one may find true enlightenment.[22] In Wolsey's case, as in Lear's, an enlightened moral vision comes only after the subject has been humbled; it is then that they are brought into a correct understanding of themselves and their relationship with the God of the universe. What is even more humbling about the Reformation view of salvation and divine enlightenment is that this process takes place within in spite of the individual. Much like his presentation of Lear, Shakespeare's portrayal of Wolsey is one of pride and selfish ambition, not as one looking for spiritual enlightenment. According to the Reformers, it is by an act of God's grace that a man or woman's soul is invaded by the divine, broken by a clear view of their sinful souls, and then escorted by the Spirit of God into a right relationship with self, with the universe, and—most importantly—with God.[23]

The Reformation understanding of God's invasive work in the hearts of depraved men and women came in direct conflict with the reigning Roman Catholic understanding of the innate goodness of mankind. The doctrine of the depravity of mankind—famously debated by two theologians, Pelagius and Augustine, in the fifth century AD—is ripe with doctrinal and philosophical consequences that continue to divide Christian denominations in the twenty-first century. A purely Pelagian philosophy denies the existence of original sin and Christian grace, maintaining that "the moral strength of the human will unaided by grace was sufficient to attain perfection."[24] Though not purely Pelagian in its view of mankind, the early modern Roman Catholic Church was highly influenced by this doctrine.[25] A man or woman who was not fully depraved but still retained some moral goodness could participate in the working out of his or her salvation. In contrast, the Reformers stood behind a view of human sin and depravity as proposed by Augustine of Hippo. Allegiance to an Augustinian understanding of the total depravity of mankind required that one accept that a man or woman was entirely unable to please God by any religious act or sacrifice. The Augustinian approach to salvation is considered passive in nature, due to the fact that men and women are dependent on the movement and work of God in their minds for salvation. Any movement toward God and that which is godly is initiated by God, and therefore any religious activity performed by a man or woman is described in Reformation terms as fruitless. Christopher Marlowe's infamous protagonist, Doctor Faustus, struggles against the passive understanding of Christianity proposed in Reformation theology. It is the passive nature of theology that Faustus expresses disdain for, choosing instead to pursue a more active course in "cursed Necromancie":[26]

> **Chorus:** That shortly [Faustus] was grac'd with Doctors name,
> Excelling all, and sweetly can dispute
> In th'heavenly matters of Theologie,
> Till swolne with cunning, of a selfe conceit,
> His waxen wings did mount above his reach,
> And melting, heavens conspir'd his over-throw[27]

Faustus expresses frustration in the passive nature of a Christianity that requires only that one confess one's sins and passively acknowledge the divinity of Christ. Faustus dismisses Christianity, for in his understanding, it only offers "everlasting death."[28] Faustus claims to desire a life of action, one in which he can exert power and control and an active rather than a passive pursuit is rewarded with the fruits of knowledge and pleasure:

> **Faustus:** O what a world of profit and delight,
> Of power, of honour, and omnipotence,
> Is promised to the Studious Artizan?
> All things that move betweene the Poles
> Shall be at my command[29]

Faustus condemns the fact that Christianity demands passive acceptance, while he is burning with a desire to do more. Faustus struggles with what appears to be the Reformation view of works, a view that states that only after God has saved a man or woman can he or she perform works of righteousness. Even in this redeemed state, however, a man or woman is still at the mercy of the will of God and not given authority to perform the miraculous for selfish gain. The theology of Luther and Calvin emphasized the servant role of the redeemed, and it is this role that Faustus rejects. In his text *Augustinianism and Modern Theology*, Henri de Lubac writes that an Augustinian view of humanity believes that "we [humanity] need grace in the sense that to begin with we are deprived of it, we have need of it . . . We are by nature in want."[30] Reformation theology emphasizes the idea that there are no free-agent Christians, somehow empowered to free themselves from sin and shame. Marlowe endows Faustus with a fierce desire to be a so-called free agent.

As described by Luther, the theology of Pelagianism offered men and women the power and importance they naturally desired.[31] Acts of penance and good works therefore became of central importance as men and women were allowed to participate in the process of salvation.[32] As confirmed by the Council of Trent (1545–1563), it was through works of penance that sinners avoided purgatory.[33] The passive role of the Reformation convert runs in direct contrast to the active role of the Roman Catholic convert. Though often characterized as a movement of the mind, books, and intellectual activity on the part of converts, the Reformation movement affirmed the discipline of study and Bible reading not as a means of earning divine favor but only as a free response of one who desires to experience a greater sense of freedom, joy, and enlightenment.[34] Maurice Hunt describes the Reformation view of works or good deeds "with good deeds being viewed as an *expression* of faith rather than as a passport to salvation."[35] Study of the scriptures and other works of intellectual discipline, though highly encouraged, did not lead an unconverted person to conversion. Luther writes the following regarding salvation by works and faith: "He must needs be a Christian and righteous before . . . he doeth good works in deede, but they do not make him a Christian. The tree bringeth forth and giveth fruit, and not the fruit the tree. So none is made a Christian by workes but by Christ."[36] It was only by divine intervention that a man or woman could be delivered from their depraved state. For even faith, according to the Reformers, was a gift that had to be given to the unredeemed before they were capable of expressing belief in the saving power of God. Luther writes the following:

> So far as we are concerned, therefore, this is a very elusive matter, because we are so unstable. In addition, we are opposed by half of our very selves, namely, by reason and all its powers. Moreover, because the flesh cannot believe for sure that the promises of God are true, it resists the spirit. Therefore it contends against the spirit and, as Paul says, holds the spirit captive (Rom. 7:23), to keep it from believing as firmly as it wants to (Gal. 5:17). This is why we continually teach that

> the knowledge of Christ and of faith is not a human work but utterly a divine gift; as God creates faith, so He preserves us in it. And just as He initially gives us faith through the Word, so later on He exercises, increases, strengthens, and perfects it in us by that Word.[37]

Luther continues with what appears to be strong Reformation support for what Fernie correctly refers to as "spiritual territory,"[38] and that which is opposed to the worldly and unspiritual: "Thus by Scripture we are led to believe things that are absurd, impossible, and contrary to our reason. For this is the work of God to humble the proud and exalt the humbled, to make something great of the least and vice versa. Just so he does here with the wealthy city of Tyre. Let this be an example to our arrogant tyrants!"[39] Although my attention in this work focuses on the influence of Protestantism in Shakespeare's work, given what we have in terms of historical data, we cannot prove that Shakespeare was a Protestant. David Daniell writes about the literary contributions of the Protestant translators, who brought Christian doctrine into much closer proximity to Shakespeare and those he walked among: "The stories in the Gospels are not, or not only, about moral outcasts: [they are] more fully about losing and finding again, an existential experience that can make one weep, like finding oneself unexpectedly at home again . . . Shakespeare met suffering people, registered in the ordinary language of the people, in the texts of the Gospels in English, ultimately Tyndale's English. He interiorised their suffering, and put them on his stage. That is the great bequest of Protestantism."[40] It is my desire to take the argument regarding the spiritual nature of Shakespeare's plays a step further than Ewan Fernie's. In *Henry VIII*, Shakespeare gleans from his culture and the religious debate therein. The unsettling nature of Reformation doctrine defies a "worldly" morality, and it invites an otherworldly perspective of humiliation.

The otherworldly humiliation of Wolsey that Shakespeare describes in *Henry VIII* does not occur in the account of the fall as documented in Raphael Holinshed's *Chronicles of England, Scotland, and Ireland*. In his departure from the historical source, we find Shakespeare fleshing out what was certainly a difficult and devastating shift in thought regarding the natures of God and man. Though we find the report of Wolsey's fall in the Holinshed, the account does not portray Wolsey in the same depth of humiliation as the cardinal experiences in Shakespeare's play. In fact, in the Holinshed account, Wolsey's famous reflections on his fall are more accusatory than repentant and humble. Although he changes the nature of Wolsey's fall, Shakespeare preserves what is believed to have been Wolsey's arrogance. In his work *Life of Wolsey*,[41] George Cavendish writes, "Here is the end and fall of pride and arrogance of such men, exalted by fortune to honour and high dignities. For I assure you, in his time of authority and glory he was the haughtiest man in all his proceedings that then lived, having more respect for the worldly honour of his person than he had for his spiritual profession."[42] In much the same manner, Shakespeare presents an ambitious and arrogant cardinal in the opening act where Abergavenny claims that he can see Wolsey's pride: "Peep through each part of him" (*Henry VIII* 1.1.69). Also in act 1, Buckingham describes Wolsey in this manner:

Buckingham: This holy fox,
Or wolf, or both (for he is equal rav'nous
As he is subtle, and as prone to mischief
As able to perform't), his mind and place
Infecting one another, yea reciprocally,
Only to show his pomp as well in France
As here at home . . .

(*Henry VIII* 1.1.158–64)

In act 3, on delivering the news of Wolsey's final undoing, Surrey identifies the cardinal's ambition as his most potent sin, which leads him to rob the kingdom of good and noble men (*Henry VIII* 3.2.254–55). It is Wolsey's ambition and his thirst for status that motivate him to remove capable men, who by their very goodness, could threaten his position and thereby keep him from acquiring more power.

Though his portrait of the arrogant Wolsey is consistent with the historical account, Shakespeare alters the proceedings of Wolsey's fall. The Holinshed account reports that the cardinal spoke the following words as he was dying: "I see the matter how it is framed; but if I had served God as diligently as I have done the king, he would not have given me over in my gray hairs: but it is the just reward that I must receive for the diligent pains and study that I have had to do him service; not regarding my service to God, but only to satisfy his pleasure."[43] In this account, Wolsey praises himself as a diligent servant who tried with notable unselfishness to serve the king and satisfy his pleasures. Shakespeare reshapes the Holinshed account, removing that which is more accusatory than regretful and replacing it with a powerfully repentant exchange between the cardinal and his disciple Cromwell:

> **Cromwell:** How does your grace?
> **Wolsey:** Why, well:
> Never so truly happy, my good Cromwell.
> I know myself now; and I feel within me
> A peace above all earthly dignities,
> A still and quiet conscience.
> (*Henry VIII* 3.2.378–81)

Shakespeare transforms the bleak Holinshed account by inserting a redemptive and most certainly Reformed experience with humiliation. Wolsey's claim to "know" himself bears a distinctly Calvinistic flavor. On the opening page of Calvin's *Institutes*, the Reformer claims that without knowledge of self, "there is no knowledge of God."[44] Calvin further affirms proper self-knowledge: "we are prompted by our own ills to contemplate the good things of God; and we cannot seriously aspire to him before we begin to become displeased with ourselves. For what man in all the world would not gladly remain as he is . . . so long as he does not know himself . . . ignorant or unmindful of his own misery?"[45] Howard Felperin identifies a pattern in Shakespeare's late plays, one in which the falling character "leaves his trial, mounts the scaffold, or faces ignominy and death with a new access of spiritual strength and self-knowledge."[46] Before seeing it in Shakespeare's *Henry VIII*, Renaissance playgoers witnessed this pattern in Thomas Dekker and John Webster's *The Famous History of Sir Thomas Wyatt*.[47] In this work, Lady Jane Grey and her husband Guildford Dudley are convinced to usurp the throne of England upon the death of King Edward VI. The play begins with announcement of the death of Edward VI, whereupon the Duke of Northumberland and the Duke of Suffolk begin plotting:

Suff. How fares the King, my Lord? Speakes he cheerily?
North. Even as a dying man, whose life
Like to quicke lighting, which is no sooner seene,
But is extinct . . .
Suff. . . . That will confirme my Daughter Queene.
North. Right, and my Sonne is marryed to your daughter.
. . . What though the King hath left behinde,
Two Sisters, lawfull and immediate heires,
To succeed him in his Throane.
Lyes it not in our powers to contradict it?
Have we not the King and Counsels hands unto it?
Tut, wee stand high
In mans opinion, and the worldes broad eye.[48]

Jane Grey's father, the Duke of Suffolk, is certain that his good reputation and his power over the court will be enough to convince the people to accept Lady Jane as the new queen. The Duke of Northumberland is equally excited by the opportunity, and the two men move forward in their greed without considering the implications of their actions—especially as it regards their children. The play portrays Lady Jane and Guildford as being innocent of any unlawful action in regard to the throne. These two become victims of their father's greed and that of other court members:

Guildford: Our Fathers grow ambitious,
And would force us saile in mightie tempests,
And are not Lordes of what they doe possesse.
Are not thy thoughts as great?
Jane: I have no thoughts so ranke, so growne to head,
As are our Fathers pride.
Troth I doe enjoy a Kingdome having thee.[49]

Lady Jane and Guildford are portrayed as innocent lovers caught in a tempest of family greed. In addition to the pressing of her father, Jane is further convinced to accept the crown by the Earl of Arundel, who tells her, "You are by the Kings will, and the consent / Of all the Lords, chosen for our Queene."[50] Even after this proclamation, Jane is reluctant to accept the crown, claiming that "The heated blood that covets to be royall, / Leaves off ere it be noble."[51] When the conspiring dukes fail, it is clear that they are repentant, but Felperin's pattern of humiliation and spiritual regeneration is portrayed in the innocent Lady Jane. Although she is innocent of the crimes she is on trial for, Jane leaves her trial and mounts the scaffold with spiritual strength. Though Guildford rails against the unjust system and continues to appeal the decision until he is face to face with the headsman, Jane is at peace, claiming that "to a prepared minde death is a pleasure, / I long in soule, till I have spent my breath."[52] When asked to remove her "night-Gowne" before the guillotine, Jane betrays further spiritual vision and insight:

Jane: Good Mistris Ellin lend me a helping hand,
To strip me of this worldly ornaments.
Off with these robes, O teare them from my side,
Such silken covers are the guilt of pride.
Insteede of gownes, my coverture be earth,
My worldly death for new Celestiall bearth . . .
How hardly can we shake off this worldes Pomp,
That cleaves unto us like our bodies skinne?
Yet thus O God shake of thy servants sinne.[53]

Though Lady Jane and Guildford are deceived by their father's pride and thereby convinced to seek the throne after Henry's death, their failure to reject the throne incriminates them in a traitorous act. Like Wolsey, Jane experiences a spiritual strengthening through a process of humiliation. In this way, we may understand that both Lady Jane and Wolsey experience what Felperin describes as a "fortunate fall."[54]

Shakespeare's historical revision is further witnessed in his choice of Wolsey for this Protestant fall. Although he died before the English Reformation properly began, Wolsey is an excellent choice, as Shakespeare employs the cardinal's spiritual journey as foreshowing for the Reformation. The shape of Wolsey's fall, drawn from the humbling view of mankind proposed by the Reformers, was one of the most difficult, if not the most devastating element of Reformation doctrine. The participatory nature of late medieval Roman Catholicism is witnessed in a myriad of religious traditions and activities, the most familiar perhaps being the traditions of pilgrimage, indulgence, and penance. In their purest sense, these traditions encourage the participation of the Christian in the process of salvation. In their important works on the Protestant Reformation, Eamon Duffy and Christopher Haigh describe the Reformation as a painful stripping away of traditional religious practices from the English people. The Protestant Reformation, according to Duffy, Haigh, and others, is now understood as being just as much a cultural reformation as a religious reformation. It was the traditions and practices of common men and women that were attacked by this new spirituality. Haigh writes, "The theological foundation of works-religion was challenged, and the 'ignorant multitude' mocked for its reliance on artificial aids and external acts . . . The hallowed routines of the religion of doing were forbidden . . . The ordinary way to God was declared closed."[55] The traditions of pilgrimage, indulgence, and penance offered the medieval Roman Catholic an opportunity to please God and to "work out" his or her salvation.[56] By affirming works of participation, the Roman Catholic Church placed a measure of value on the spiritual exercises of men and women. When the Reformers came along, it was this participation in the salvific process that was attacked. In the face of a more optimistic view of man's ability to do what was then considered proper penance, the Reformers stressed the depraved state of mankind and therefore man's inability to perform any works that were pleasing to God.

As Martin Luther writes, true salvation involves a violent and terrible despair, one that changes the way a man or woman understands him- or herself and the world in which he or she lives: "You see, then, what it means to be justified through faith in Christ. It means that after learning to know your iniquity and weakness through the Law you despair of yourself, of your own strength, of your knowledge, of the Law, of works, in short, of everything, and that with trembling and confidence you humbly implore the right hand of Christ alone . . . And at the same time you see that the whole human race, no matter with how much wisdom and righteousness it may shine before men, is nothing but an accursed mass of perdition."[57] Recent work on the Protestant Reformation contends that well into the Elizabethan settlement, England was still a very Roman Catholic nation.[58] While A. G. Dickens and Diarmaid MacCulloch argue that England's return to Roman Catholicism under Queen Mary was brief and insubstantial, more recently Christopher Haigh has written of an England that moved swiftly back to its religious foundations with little government compulsion:

> The rapid restoration of the mass and altars, common anticipation of orders to set up roods and images . . . voluntary giving, and a jovial round of church ales—all are a far cry from the Protestant gloom and Catholic doom prominent in most accounts of Mary's reign or the English Reformation . . . the Marian restoration was not a external act, inflicted on parishes by official decree and enforced by grinding bureaucratic procedure. Rather, it was achieved in the parishes, by the parishes, and with only intermittent (and often unnecessary) official prodding. The real hallmark of the Marian Church . . . was local enthusiasm, an enthusiasm which produced large sums of money, raised at great speeds in bucolic ways, to devote to popular projects.[59]

Although the Protestant reforms of the Elizabethan settlement finally saw the nation convert from Roman Catholicism, recent scholarship describes this national conversion in painful, wrenching terms. Of this spiritual struggle Duffy writes, "The Reformation represented a deep and traumatic cultural hiatus . . . a process and a labor, difficult, drawn out, and whose outcome had been by no means a foregone conclusion . . . The Reformation had not been achieved on a tidal wave of popular enthusiasm, but had to be worked out, by force, persuasion, and slow institutional transformation."[60] According to Eamon Duffy, Christopher Haigh, Norman Jones and others, it wasn't until the 1580s that the Protestant missionary project had really begun to bear substantial fruit. If this was truly the case, it is realistic to assume that, as a boy in Stratford, Shakespeare would have been affected by the raging religious tension of a divided England. Haigh cites the influence of the writings of English Reformers, inspired by the works of Martin Luther and John Calvin, that did much to disrupt and overturn the spiritual direction of early modern England. Haigh writes:

> The preachers and printers of Elizabethan England offered the message of Christian hope and endurance. Its content was well summarized in John More's best-selling *Brief and Necessary Catechism*, first published in 1572. More's catechism begins with a call to humility and to

> the recognition of one's depraved state: "By the Ten Commandments," writes More, "I see my miserable estate, that I deserve death, damnation, and the curse of God, which must be paid because God is just; and whereas I myself am not able to pay it, the Holy Ghost through the preaching of the Gospel worketh in me faith"[61]

The Reformers, by a flood of printed materials, sermons, and government influence, attacked the notion that a man or woman could participate in their own salvation. For the Reformers, salvation was an act of grace alone, and no pilgrimage, however long; indulgence, however costly; or penance, however painful, could earn the favor of the God of the Reformation. As is made clear in the writings of Luther, Calvin, More, and a host of others, it was no longer the works of a man or woman, but the humility of a repentant sinner that was the surest sign of salvation. A confrontation with one's own depravity, brought on by a gracious movement of God in a man or woman's life, resulted in what the Reformers called an outpouring of repentance and in a divinely inspired view of life and truth.

It is an inspired view of life and truth that is manifested in Wolsey when the prideful cardinal falls; this man who for the first half of the play sought self-promotion by any means necessary. It is well before the cardinal has any opportunity to seek formal absolution from his sin that he experiences a distinctly Reformed redemption. It is in this third act that Wolsey comes to realize that far from bearing the ability to participate in the process of his own salvation, he is as Luther writes, "nothing but an accursed mass of perdition."[62]

Wolsey: I have ventured
Like little wanton boys that swim on bladders,
This many summers in a sea of glory,
But far beyond my depth; my high-blown pride
At length broke under me . . .
O how wretched
Is that poor man that hangs on princes' favours!
(*Henry VIII* 3.2.358–64)

That Wolsey is rewarded with moral vision in his fall is evidenced in the nature of his dialogue with Cromwell and in the witness of

Katherine's servant, Griffith. Only moments after the announcement of his fate, the cardinal has the ability to see with clarity his sin and that which led to his downfall. As Luther writes,[63] Wolsey is able to see the truth about his own soul because of the law that is proclaimed about him:

> **Wolsey:** The king has cur'd me,
> I humbly thank his Grace; and from these shoulders,
> These ruin'd pillars, out of pity taken
> A load would sink a navy, too much honour . . .
> 'tis a burden
> Too heavy for a man that hopes for heaven!
> (*Henry VIII* 3.2.381–86)

Wolsey's confession is a perfect model of what Luther describes as the prayer and confession of a righteous man.[64] Wolsey's ability to give advice regarding the dangers of ambition, the futility of corrupt dealings, and the importance of honoring God above men is evidence, according to Reformation doctrine, that the cardinal has been redeemed.[65] That these lessons come so quickly to a man who has so recently fallen is evidence that Shakespeare has indeed woven Reformation theology into this violent redemption. The queen's attendant, Griffith, whose defense of the cardinal before the banished queen seems risky not to mention ill timed, states that the cardinal found blessing in his fall, for in it he "found the blessedness of being little . . . he dies fearing God" (*Henry VIII* 4.2.66–68).

In *Spiritual Shakespeares*, Ewan Fernie argues that spirituality in Shakespeare is often associated with "ideas of emancipation and an alternative world."[66] It is this kind of spirituality, one involving the emancipation of Thomas Wolsey in Shakespeare's *Henry VIII*, that may indeed be the central issue at play. Cardinal Wolsey's fall, though it is "sad, high, and working, full of state and woe" (*Henry VIII* Prologue 3), offers us a powerful picture of spiritual redemption or, as Fernie writes, emancipation. Unlike Fernie's, my work here draws on the theology of the Protestant Reformation. From Reformation doctrine, Shakespeare gleans the concept of redemptive humiliation, a concept that transcends restrictive denominational categorizing. The spirituality of *Henry VIII* is most poignantly illustrated in Wolsey's fall from power, for in this fall, Shakespeare preserves what Kiernan Ryan explains as "everything that confounds common sense."[67] In Wolsey's fall is a curious rise; in his shame is a peculiar honor; and in his banishment is a certain initiation into a life of freedom, vision, and moral clarity.

Chapter 5
Othello

In chapters 3 and 4, we have looked at the falls of King Lear and Cardinal Wolsey through the lens of Reformation theology. These men, though guilty of selfish ambition and corrupt political maneuvering, are saved through an experience of redemptive humiliation. This chapter will examine the fall of a more violent criminal, Othello, whose jealousy and fear lead him to murder his wife.

In the opening act of Shakespeare's *Othello*, Iago feigns panic when he warns Othello of an approaching mob of men: "Those are the raised father and his friends, / You were best go in" (*Othello* 1.2.29). Although he responds to Iago with confidence, "Not I, I must be found" (*Othello* 1.2.30), Othello's soul is soon to be tested, and his confidence will be broken. Othello's soul—"perfect," as he claims (*Othello* 1.2.32)—is spun by a craftsman who drew inspiration from a culture steeped in religious controversy and violence. Othello is a prideful man whose tragic fall and subsequent rise are modeled after the Reformation process of salvation. Though often pitied as an outsider and even more often condemned as a jealous monster,[1] Othello is a Reformation saint whose struggle with sin and depravity places him within the ranks of an everyman. Othello's flawed character, not an issue of his race but of his sin and depravity, is drawn from a view of man that was widely propagated in Shakespeare's England by Reformation theologians, pastors, preachers, and writers. This study of *Othello* will engage most specifically with the works of Martin Luther and John Calvin as they relate to the nature of redemptive humiliation.

Othello's damning pride and self-justifying habits are the most potent elements of his ruin. Robert Watson writes, "Pride is as fundamental to the tragedy of *Othello* as jealousy, and the psychological melodrama comports a lesson in soteriology—the theology of salvation."[2] In this chapter, I seek to move beyond what is so often the focus of *Othello* criticism—the character of Iago and his diabolical structures of jealousy—to Othello's damning pride and his habit of self-justification. I do not seek to promote a fixed view of Othello's character, one that condemns him as a brutal egoist, but to present Othello with a complexity that is very human. In this way, I hope to leave ample room, as E. A. J. Honigmann writes, for seeing Othello "as a time traveler, burdened like every human being with too much psychic luggage . . . with which we refuse to face the facts."[3] Othello's terrible journey runs a parallel course with the Reformation journey of a redeemed sinner. Othello is an everyman struggling against a storm of pride and insecurity. At a time when the meaning and substance of religious justification was being debated, when men and women were losing their lives over particular elements of faith, Shakespeare creates *Othello*. In this tragedy, we witness the playing out of the Reformation view of redemptive humiliation, a painful process that uncovers the depravity of Othello's soul, ultimately purifying his murderous hands.

In many ways, Othello's story resembles that of the New Testament author Paul the apostle. Paul's writings were a source of controversy during the Protestant Reformation. As a brilliant Jewish teacher, Paul entered the early Christian narrative as an outsider and a powerful and violent enemy. Broken and humiliated in a supernatural encounter with God, Paul becomes aware of his depravity. Though once arrogant and proud, Paul is reduced to a humble man. It is in this place of humility that God redeems Paul and commissions him to a life of service. Like Paul, Othello is also introduced into the play as an outsider.

Othello, a black man in what appears to be a predominantly white society, is brought to a place of humiliation. In this painful state, Othello is for the first time able to see clearly the truth about his life and those he loves. Through a process of humiliation, Othello experiences an enlightened state that enables him to take a penitent posture before God. Othello is described as a convert to Christianity in the text, yet like the preconverted Paul, Othello's religious belief is wrapped in a self-centered legalism. Just as Paul is freed from the hypocrisy of what he considered Pharisaical Judaism, Othello is freed from what Reformation theologians criticized as the legalistic or Pharisaic nature of Roman Catholicism. Until his humiliation, Othello is consumed by the deeds of satisfaction; he understands God to be an exacting, judging Being, one that demands satisfaction for wrongs committed. Men and women must pay for their sins, and Othello is willing to take on the role of Desdemona's judge because her supposed infidelity threatens his own reputation. Othello's use of divine judgment—his claim that if not stopped by his hand Desdemona is certain to lay waste the dignity of more men (*Othello* 5.2.6)—is evidence of a conceited delirium. Ironically, what we see in Othello is a blending of insecurity and fear and a fragile pride with the violent attributes of a judging God.

In the history of the early Christian church, Paul is known as a persecutor of Christians; he sought to condemn those who broke free from Jewish laws and practices to follow what was believed by the reigning Jewish religious authorities to be a heretical cult. Luther describes Paul, before the apostle's conversion, as a figure of repressive legalism who "was puffed up by his own righteousness,"[4] believing himself to be "an outstanding zealot for the traditions of the fathers, a devotee of the righteousness of the Law."[5] In this way, early Christian literature describes Judaism as a works religion, a belief system that reveals God to be an exacting judge. Taking up the language of the early Christian church, Reformation theologians attacked the Roman Catholic Church, claiming that it was identical to Pharisaic Judaism. The Reformers attacked the Roman Catholic doctrine of justification. Claiming that it promoted a legalism that led to damning self-worship, the Reformers sought to uproot the Roman Catholic understanding of justification. This doctrine required that men and women participate in the redemptive process by performing, as the Council of Trent of 1546 states, "satisfaction by fasts, alms, prayers, and the other pious exercises of a spiritual life."[6] Luther attacks this doctrine in this way:

> There are two kinds of righteousness: mine and Christ's. The Gospel proclaims that we must be put into the righteousness of Christ and must be translated from our righteousness into the righteousness of Christ. Thus Paul says in Rom. 3:24 that we "are justified by His grace

> as a gift"; and in 1 Cor. 1:30 he says that Christ was made by God "our Wisdom, our Righteousness and Sanctification and Redemption." But the pope has instituted new kinds of life by which righteousness should be provided before God, namely, one's own deeds of satisfaction. If the pope taught that our righteousness is nothing and that we are saved solely because of the righteousness of Christ, then he would say: "Therefore the Mass is nothing. Therefore the monastic life and one's own deeds of satisfaction profit nothing," and thus the whole kingdom of the pope would be overturned. To be sure, they say that Christ's merit saves us; but they mix in their own righteousness.[7]

In much the same way, John Calvin criticized what he believed was the Pharisaical nature of Roman Catholic doctrine. About the erring papacy and the importance of rejecting works-based theology and legalism, Calvin writes, "There these cruel butchers, to relieve the wounds that they had inflicted, applied certain remedies, asserting that each man should do what lay in his power. But again new anxieties crept in. Indeed, new tortures flayed helpless souls: 'I have not spent enough time'; 'I have not duly devoted myself to it'; 'I have overlooked many things out of negligence'"[8] Calvin continues, "Thus from the feeling of our own ignorance, vanity, poverty, infirmity, and—what is more—depravity and corruption, we recognize that the true light of wisdom, sound virtue, full abundance of every good, and purity of righteousness rest in the Lord alone . . . Accordingly, the knowledge of ourselves not only arouses us to seek God, but also, as it were, leads us by the hand to find him . . . we cannot seriously aspire to him before we begin to become displeased with ourselves."[9] The Reformers taught that at the heart of legalism was a confidence in one's ability to please God. This confidence, according to both Luther and Calvin, is rooted in a pride that results from man's faulty knowledge of himself. The theme of self-knowledge is one that is vital to our understanding of Shakespeare's *Othello*.

On the subject of self-knowledge John Calvin writes, "Without knowledge of self there is no knowledge of God."[10] Calvin begins his multivolume work with this very statement, from which he relates that men and women cannot be satisfied with themselves if they hope to have a proper understanding of God. Calvin continues, "For we always seem to ourselves righteous and upright and wise and holy—this pride is innate in all of us—unless by clear proofs we stand convinced of our own unrighteousness, foulness, folly, and impurity."[11] Though an Aristotelian reading of the play would identify Othello's hamartia as poor self-knowledge and identify his anagnorisis in the final moments of the play, if we fail to move beyond a secular analysis, we overlook the powerful way in which Renaissance Protestantism informs the play.[12] Othello's peripeteia, as examined through the lens of Reformation theology, involves more than a reversal of fortune but a gracious act of Providence that serves to lead Othello beyond anagnorisis to spiritual redemption.[13] A clear knowledge of self is what Paul claims to receive when he is confronted by the power of God. In the same way, Othello is plagued by faulty self-knowledge, compelling him to seek out the unrighteous in order to destroy them. If Paul had seen in his own life's hypocrisy and sin, he would have lost some of the vigor with which he sought to condemn wayward Jews. The same can be said of Othello, who in fact claims to have a "perfect soul" (*Othello* 1.2.31). In Othello's damnation of Desdemona, he is unaware of the rumors that drift abroad about him.

Iago makes reference to Othello's reputation when he claims, "And it is thought abroad that 'twixt my sheets / He's done my office" (*Othello* 1.3.386–87). In act 4, Emilia confirms the existence of this rumor when she chides Iago:

Emilia: I will be hanged if some eternal villain . . .
Have not devised this slander . . .
. . . some such a squire he was
That turned your wit the seamy side without
And made you to suspect me with the Moor.
(*Othello* 4.2.132, 135, 148–50)

Of this struggle and rumor, Othello seems not to know. He does not possess the proper self-knowledge that would allow him to move forward in his jealousy with more caution and self-control. Othello's elevated view of himself compels him on a course of disastrous haste.  Blindness to his own pride and insecurity keeps Othello on course to destroy whatever rises to threaten his position and his reputation. Like Paul in his persecution of the early church, Othello cannot see that his self-righteousness puts him in opposition to God. Luther describes his condition in this way: "Now the true meaning of Christianity is this: that a man first acknowledge, through the Law, that he is a sinner, for whom it is impossible to perform any good work . . . Therefore everything [the self-righteous] think, speak, or do is opposed to God. Hence [they] cannot deserve grace by [their] works . . . Trying to merit grace by preceding works, therefore, is trying to placate God with sins, which is nothing but heaping sins upon sins, making fun of God, and provoking His wrath . . . Thus the first step in Christianity is the preaching of repentance and the knowledge of oneself."[14] With this notion of pride in place, we must now turn our gaze onto the character of Othello.

Othello's disability is specifically pride, the most prominent sin according to Reformation theologians that keeps men and women from recognizing that they cannot add to the righteousness of Christ. Irving Ribner locates Othello's pride in the Moor's intense desire to justify himself and protect his reputation: "This reputation theme runs through the entire play, but Shakespeare makes a careful distinction between a just self-esteem which a man in his honour must defend and a worship of false appearance without regard to the inner reality. Such a concern for reputation is a manifestation of pride . . . this false concern for reputation Iago arouses in Othello, leading him to the murder of Desdemona in the delusion that only thus can he preserve his good name."[15] Othello is guilty of worshiping a false appearance; he worships himself and the fictional structures that have allowed him to succeed in this foreign nation. In terms of fictional structures, I am referring to Othello's fanciful descriptions of foreign travels:

Othello: Of moving accidents by flood and field,
Of hair-breadth scapes i'th' imminent deadly breach,
Of being taken by the insolent foe
And sold to slavery; of my redemption thence
And portance in my travailous history;
Wherein of antres vast and deserts idle,
Rough quarries, rocks and hills whose heads touch
heaven

> It was my hint to speak—such was my process—
> And of the cannibals that each other eat,
> The Anthropophagi, and men whose heads
> Do grow beneath their shoulders.
>
> (*Othello* 1.3.136–46)

What are we to make of these wild details? Has Shakespeare given us ample evidence of Othello's integrity and of his reliability?

For its ability to draw together some important works on this issue, Thomas Moisan's "Repetition and Interrogation in *Othello*" is an important study. By first drawing from Geoffrey Bullough's compilation of the narrative sources that surround *Othello*, Moisan establishes that Shakespeare's audience would have been familiar with the Italian *novelle* that poured into London in the late sixteenth century.[16] Moisan further asserts that many would have been equally familiar with royal tutor Roger Ascham's rebuke of the like for their obsession with "sensational love *cum* violence" and their ability to "mar men's manners in England."[17] Moisan continues his study by looking at Rosalind Johnson and Karen Newman's studies of the various travel accounts of Africa, namely, *The History and Descryption of Africa*. Here, Moisan makes some important claims about the interpretive abilities of Shakespeare's audience. This was a people, according to him, who marveled at Leo's tales of exploits and yet responded—as did John Pory, the narrator of *The History and Descryption of Africa*—with certain skepticism.[18] Merely accepting the details of Othello's story as truth does not allow for a proper concern that we are to feel in regard to Othello's character. Michael Mangan writes:

> But it is also possible that Shakespeare was more skeptical, that he found tales of Anthropophagi and their like rather far-fetched, even amusing, and that he included them here in order to give Othello's traveler's tale precisely that air of unreality, of fictionality, which I believe it has. For *Othello* is a play in which the making of fictions is a central issue . . . From the first time we see him, [Othello] is engaged in constructing plots—not malevolent plots against other people like Iago's, but literary plots. He writes himself into various kinds of

> stories: in Act I he writes himself into a traveller's tale; by Act V he has written himself into a tragedy.[19]

Othello is grand; he is indeed, as A. C. Bradley claims, "by far the most romantic figure among Shakespeare's heroes."[20] Othello is poetic and creative, a perfect storyteller. To borrow from Bradley once again, "there is no love, not that of Romeo in his youth, more steeped in imagination than Othello's."[21] And yet, how are we to follow Bradley in his belief in the nobility of this man? Can a spinner of tales and a bender of truths be respected as a man of honor?

Othello is indeed likeable, but his lack of self-knowledge and his apparent need for acceptance betray a dangerous vulnerability. He is unable to see any sin in himself; he does not recognize the frail nature of man, as Hamlet does, but sees himself as possessing a "perfect soul" (*Othello* 1.2.31). Failing to regard what Ribner calls Othello's "inner reality" is the central point of Othello's failing.[22] The general's inner reality is simply his sinful pride. A seventeenth-century audience, one tutored in and perhaps in some cases pummeled by Reformation theology, would be suspicious of a character who claims to have a perfect soul. This same audience would find it difficult to put their trust in a man who expresses a greedy thirst for gossip, is moved to jealous insanity, and slinks after his suspects.

As we witness in act 3, Othello's thirst for gossip is unnaturally strong. Coming upon Cassio and Desdemona in a private conversation, Othello is moved to jealousy without the hinting of Iago. When Iago begins to offer scandalous warnings to his general, Othello's response is all too enthusiastic. In his greed to gather the gossip, Othello betrays a sense of fear and uncertainty, perhaps even a bit of insecurity. This is no surprise to those who had earlier recognized the inherent desperation in Othello's prideful claims to Iago and in his pompous fictionalizing before the Senate. Othello does not have a perfect soul but one that is racked with fear and self-doubt.[23] In her racially sensitive work, Ania Loomba writes, "[Othello's] 'magic' consists of invoking his exotic otherness, his cultural and religious differences as well as his heroic exploits, which involve strange peoples and territories. He oscillates between asserting his non-European glamour and denying his blackness, emphasizing through speech and social position his assimilation into white culture. He thus is hopelessly split; as Homi Bhabha writes in relation to Fanon's split subject: 'black skins, white masks is not . . . a neat division; it is a doubling, dissembling image of being in at least two places at once which makes it impossible for the devalued . . . to accept the colonizer's invitation to identity.'"[24] Othello is, as Loomba asserts, living a double life, one in which he is unable to be authentic. In his conversation with Iago, Othello betrays an insecurity that may be rooted at least partly in his foreignness, but it is not an insecurity that is foreign to the human condition. Ewan Fernie accurately describes Othello as a "shameful Everyman,"[25] and in the context of Reformation theology, nothing is more common to humanity than sin and shame. In this way, Othello is more accurately described as a Reformation everyman, full of sin and shame, quick to self-justification, and full of pride. It is this focus that reveals the play's cultural sensitivity. In this way, Shakespeare proves to be, as Harold Bloom claims, "the most curious and universal of gleaners."[26] From the religious storms that rage around him, Shakespeare gleans the heart of the religious controversy, man's identity before God. Othello's racial "otherness" may in fact serve only to point to mankind's condition of separation from God, the sin and shame that has kept him from a proper knowledge of himself, others, and God.[27]

Shakespeare's audience, most certainly familiar with the Reformation debate over the total depravity of man, would have been alarmed by Othello's claim to a "perfect soul" (*Othello* 1.2.31). In her excellent study of *Othello*, Julia Lupton argues that Othello is "Islamicized [and] Judaized . . . Brought back into contact with a law [a legalistic mentality] that should have been dissolved by the rite of baptism."[28] I contend that Othello is more realistically, by virtue of the play's historical context, *Roman Catholicized*—that is, brought back into contact with the man-centered doctrine of the Roman Catholic Church.[29] Othello may not have an Islamic or Jewish nature but, more accurately, a Roman Catholic nature. Martin Luther criticizes Roman Catholic works of righteousness in this way:

> Many among us are disciplinarians of works; nor can they rise beyond the active righteousness. Thus they remain exactly what they

> were under the pope. To be sure, they invent new names and new works; but the content remains the same. So it is that the Turks perform different works from the papists, and the papists perform different works from the Jews, and so forth. But although some do works that are more splendid, great, and difficult than others, the content remains the same, and only the quality is different. That is, the works vary only in appearance and in name. For they are still works. And those who do them are not Christians; they are hirelings, whether they are called Jews, Mohammedans, papists, or sectarians.[30]

Luther draws a clear line between works-centered religious expressions and his understanding of biblical Christianity. He claims that religions that require works of this sort are pagan, no matter what their title or claim. Calvin asserts the same when he writes, "The Romanists wish [church power] to consist in the making of laws. From this source have arisen innumerable human traditions—so many nets to ensnare miserable souls. For they have no more scruples than the scribes and Pharisees about laying on other men's shoulders burdens which they would not touch with their finger."[31] He establishes a distinct relationship between the Roman Catholic Church and the Pharisaical Judaism of the Old Testament. The Catholic Church, writes Luther, twists scriptural truths so as to create a system by which to control the people.[32] Luther finds support for his rebuke of the Roman Church in the New Testament book of Matthew, wherein Jesus makes this rebuke of the Scribes and Pharisees: "Woe be unto you, Scribes and Pharisees, hypocrites: for ye compass sea and land to make one of your profession: and when he is made, ye make him two fold more the child of hell, then you your selves."[33] In *Othello*, the paganization of the Moor comes as a result of Othello's own corrupting pride. While some have found it easier to blame Othello's ruin on Iago, Othello's pride and fear are what draw him into his self-fashioned abyss. The so-called corrupted theology of the Roman Catholic Church, as described by Reformers throughout Shakespeare's England, is found in the character of Othello. It is here, on the bleak stage of Othello's soul, that Shakespeare plays out the repercussions of this belief system as it is proposed by the most dominant Reformation theologians. In the course of the play, we see the fabric of Othello's character exposed.

In hindsight, Othello's first difficult conversation with Iago in act 3 becomes of much greater importance:

Othello: And when I told thee he was of my counsel
In my whole course of wooing, thou criedst "Indeed?"
And didst contract and purse thy brow together
As if thou then hadst shut up in thy brain
Some horrible conceit. If thou dost love me
Show me thy thought . . .

And then moments later Othello pleads,

Othello: . . . and give thy worst of thoughts
The worst of words.

(*Othello* 3.3.114–19, 134–36)

Once Othello's violent pride is revealed, the "horrible conceit" he begs Iago to reveal must be seen as a conceit that Othello shares with his evil friend. Moisan writes, "It can be argued that what Othello 'drags out' of Iago, what he seeks to hear from Iago, are not 'the facts' Iago has invented, but the voiced confirmation of Othello's own 'exsufflicate and blown surmises.'"[34] Iago gives voice to the groans of Othello's "black vengeance" that he calls to when in the heat of rage (*Othello* 3.3.450). Moisan continues by claiming that Othello's demand would be better phrased, "Give *my* worst of thoughts *thy* worst of words."[35] While Iago clearly poisons Othello's soul, it is my contention that the Moor would have arrived at this place of jealous and murderous rage without the conjuring of Iago. Othello's own pride is what propels him toward his humiliating end; in many ways, the Moor uses Iago to feed this raging pride.

Many of Othello's actions in the play bear a likeness to Roman Catholic tradition: kneeling before the priestlike Iago, depending on the relic-like handkerchief, and sacrificing the seemingly sinful flesh of Desdemona and Cassio. The Reformers criticized these actions as legalistic, and it is possible that Othello's moral and emotional blindness in the play results from his dependence on these harmful traditions. When Othello's vision is restored, he finds himself in his private chamber staring at the bloody frame of his beloved. He cries out once again to the audience of authorities, but he no longer cries out in the pompous manner with which we have grown familiar. Othello's final cry is muted by a clarity that he has lacked up to this point. This new self-knowledge comes as a result of Othello's redeeming humiliation. Like the Apostle Paul, whose eyes are opened through a humiliating encounter with the Savior in the New Testament account, Othello's eyes are cleared of the once-blinding pride. Othello sees himself as he truly is:

> **Othello:** Soft you, a word or two before you go.
> I have done the state some service, and they know't:
> No more of that. I pray you, in your letters,
> When you shall these unlucky deeds relate,
> Speak of me as I am. Nothing extenuate,
> Nor set down aught in malice. Then you must speak
> Of one that loved not wisely, but too well;
> Of one not easily jealous, but being wrought,
> Perplexed in the extreme
>
> (*Othello* 5.2.336–44)

Othello no longer sees fit to describe himself in grand proportion. This is a noticeable change from his speech to the Senate in which he plays himself up as the king of seas and a conqueror. To have done the state a service was to place himself not among the ranks of the great Odysseus, as his former tale seems to do, but to place himself among the most humble of state officials. Even after this meager self-praise, Othello seems to quiver, and he rebukes himself for the mentioning of it: "No more of that" (*Othello* 5.2.338). Othello's bid to the hearers is to tell his story in all its humiliating gore, not to exaggerate as he once did, but to set the lesson down for the benefit of future egoists.

In this humiliating place, Othello sees himself as he truly is, depraved and incapable of earning his own salvation. The Moor takes on the shape of what Martin Luther would consider the ideal form of the redeemed: "Therefore those who consider themselves darkness and unworthy are already righteous, because they give to themselves what is their own and to God what is His, and for that reason the light rises to them . . . Therefore God gives His grace to the humble (1 Pet. 5.5). Hence above all things we must be humbled so that we may receive light and grace; indeed, that we also preserve them."[36] Of this humiliation, Calvin writes in much the same way: "Humility 'is an unfeigned submission of our heart, stricken down in earnest with an awareness of its own misery and want. For so it is everywhere described by the Word of God.'"[37] In this humiliating place, finally aware of his own "misery and want," Othello admits to being wrought and he admits to being perplexed. Othello sees his service as the Apostle Paul sees his righteous deeds after his enlightenment and conversion. Paul writes, "But ye things that were vantage unto me, the same I counted loss for Christ's sake. Yea, doubtless I think all things but loss for the excellent knowledge sake of Christ Jesus my Lord, for whom I have counted all things loss, and do judge them to be dung, that I might win Christ, And might be found in him, that is, not having mine own righteousness, which is of the Law, but that which is through the faith of Christ, even ye righteousness which is of God through faith."[38] It is significant that Shakespeare chooses not to have Othello blame Iago in his final moment of life. Othello does not shift the blame because, in this final moment, his sin becomes real to him; he is made aware of the fact that Iago indeed had little to do with the unwise path Othello chose to walk.

Othello recognizes the fact that he chose to walk in darkness and cries out this curse on himself:

> **Othello:** Arise, black vengeance, from the hollow hell,
> Yield up, O love, thy crown and hearted throne
> To tyrannous hate! Swell, bosom, with thy fraught,
> For 'tis of aspics' tongues!
>
> (*Othello* 3.3.450–53)

At the close of the play, Othello expresses a belief that he alone must pay the penalty for his sin. He turns his own judging eye on himself; his legalistic theology and crucifying doctrines turn inward, and he sees himself clearly for the first time. Gordon Braden describes Othello's self-curse as a foreshadowing of violent self-judgment: "Like Medea, Othello is rousing himself to an ideal of murderous

constancy by annexing his own resolve to the power of vast and distant natural forces. Such language is very much a part of the mood of Shakespeare's play—it helps set the scale for Othello's grandiose self-judgment—and can easily be paralleled elsewhere in his work."[39] Othello at last understands the law as the Reformers would have understood it; he is finally relating to the law as it was meant to be related to. Othello sees the law in the way Luther describes it, as judge and accuser and as a mirror before one's sin and shame.[40] He no longer appears to be trying to measure up to the law; no longer does he appear to be pure in his own sight, but he is now guilty and ashamed. At the close of the play, Othello is enlightened to his own sin and shame, yet he is not aware of his redemption. As G. R. Eliot writes, Othello is "too full of repentant grief to let himself live."[41] Eliot further claims that Othello recognizes Desdemona's grace in his life; he is aware of her sacrifice, and that he has discarded a "pearl of great price."[42] Eliot's reference to Desdemona as the "pearl of great price" comes from the parable Jesus tells in the New Testament book of Matthew. In this parable, Jesus describes a man who finds a pearl and sells all his belongings to purchase it: "Again the kingdom of heaven is like to a merchant man, that seeketh good pearls, Who having found a pearl of great price, went and sold all that he had, and bought it."[43] Alexander Cruden, in his commentary on the New Testament, writes, "The transcendent excellency of Christ and his grace made known and offered in the gospel, is compared to a pearl of great price."[44] In other words, Christ and the grace he offers make up the priceless nature of the pearl. Instead of preserving and protecting the pearl, Othello throws the pearl away, thereby breaking the command Christ gives to his disciples in the seventh chapter of Matthew: "Give ye not that which is holy, to dogs, nether cast ye your pearls before swine, lest they tread them under their feet, and turning again, all to rent you."[45] Although he does not appear to know he has been redeemed, Othello's reference to Desdemona as a pearl of great value and his repentance before her dead body suggest that he has accepted her grace.

As one who is now enlightened to the state of his soul, newly aware of his proper relationship to the things of heaven and of earth, Othello is not repulsed by Desdemona's cold, judging eyes,[46] nor does he think again of her gaze as one that will "hurl [his] soul from heaven" (*Othello* 5.2.272). Othello is drawn to her lips and with his final breath confesses his crime:

> **Othello:** I kissed thee ere I killed thee: no way but this,
> Killing myself, to die upon a kiss.
>
> (*Othello* 5.2.356–57)

In this final statement, we find Othello's confession of sin and his confession of faith. He confesses that he is a murderer, one who was confused and ignorant enough to throw Desdemona away, yet now with a kiss finds himself reunited with her in truth and in love. Othello's sincere confession in this final scene leads Ewan Fernie to claim that Othello is spiritually heroic. Fernie writes, "Othello is morally degraded—we must never forget that he has killed his wife—but he is also a spiritual hero, one who shows up the cosseted and frightened self-deception of those who thrust off and misplace shame . . . Othello's electric experience takes the audience in the theatre to the heart of our shameful condition."[47] Unlike the shameful kiss of Judas in the Garden of Gethsemane,[48] there is no hidden shame in Othello, no Judas individualism that would cause him to run off and murder himself in a distant field.[49] Othello's kiss is not a deceiving kiss but one that kills in ignorance and unites in repentance.[50] Fernie continues in this way:

> But in the dying moments of the tragedy, Othello, too, emerges from the darkness of the self and its selfish concerns, and recognises the blinding reality of his wife. He kills himself to die upon her kiss (5.2.359), which gives us an amazingly concentrated image of the whole hard process of embracing shame and mortality in order to achieve love. He has murdered Christian shame by killing Desdemona, but his passion of repentant shame over her dead body has restored spiritual shame to the world of the play . . . Within a drama which is substantially a nightmare of shame we therefore find a strong hint of penitence, with intimations of redemption and atonement.[51]

The image Fernie describes here, of the "whole hard process of embracing shame," is an image that sits at the heart of Reformation doctrine. To embrace shame, as Fernie describes, is to arrive at a place of redemptive humiliation. To embrace shame, according to Reformation theologians, is to come to a true understanding of oneself and thereby open the door to the grace offered by God to mankind.[52] It is to recognize one's sickness, as Luther writes, and to give one's self over to the care of "a divine Physician."[53] The "penitence . . . redemption and atonement" described in Fernie's important work find their roots in Reformation doctrine. While Fernie is reserved in his workings on Desdemona, his hinting leads us to see Desdemona as a Christ figure. She is the "love" that is "achieved" when Othello embraces shame and mortality. In Reformation terms, Othello's embrace of shame and mortality is his recognition of his depravity before God and man. Othello perceives and confesses his guilt and shame, his sin and inability to earn salvation, and thereby finds the clarity and truth he has lacked throughout the play.

Othello accepts his savior's touch—Desdemona's kiss—and more importantly her unconditional love and grace. His acceptance of her sacrifice, though it is in the shape of lifeless lips, is an acceptance of the healing power of grace. In his final confession, Othello makes this request of the men present:

Othello: When you shall these unlucky deeds relate,
Speak of me as I am. Nothing extenuate,
Nor set down aught in malice. Then must you speak
Of one that loved not wisely, but too well;
Of one not easily jealous, but, being wrought,
Perplexed in the extreme

(*Othello* 5.2.346–51)

Othello's confession requires close examination for all that it reveals about his state of mind at the close of the play.

This is not the Othello of act 1, full of pride and pomp, excited by any opportunity to relate the story of his life. This is not the Othello who exaggerated the details of his past so as to win favor among the Senators, not to mention the very hand of his bride. The fact that Othello desires to have his story told in the simplicity of truth, without exaggeration, is clear evidence of the change, the reform if you will, in the Moor's misguided soul. Othello has been humbled, and he no longer values the praise earned from the telling of false tales.

When Othello bids the men to tell of one who "loved not wisely, but too well," he speaks of Desdemona. In the same way that the Reformers describe as the incomprehensible work of Christ suffering a criminal's death, so too Desdemona suffers a criminal's death for the man she loves. Much like Dostoyevsky's Idiot, Desdemona lives by a divine set of principles, and she is unwilling to change or compromise to save her own life. Desdemona stays true to her promise in the prayer she utters at the close of act 4:

> **Desdemona:** God me such usage send
> Not to pick bad from bad, but by bad mend!
> (*Othello* 4.3.105–6)

In this prayer, Desdemona refuses the "earthy and pragmatic relativism" proposed by Emilia.[54] She does not see the world as Emilia does but contends for a higher calling. The temptation offered to Desdemona in this way resembles the temptation of Christ: "Again the devil took [Jesus] up unto an exceeding high mountain, and showed him all the kingdoms of the world, and the glory of them, And said to him, All these will I give thee, if thou wilt fall down, and worship me."[55] In this passage, the devil seeks to drive Jesus off of His chosen path by leading him to distrust God and to forsake the purpose of His incarnation. The offer to own the world for what seems a minor compromise is the same offer Desdemona and Emilia consider in act 4. Desdemona asks Emilia if she would commit marital infidelity for all the kingdoms of the world:

> **Emilia:** The world's a huge thing: it is a great price
> For a small vice.
> **Desdemona:** Good troth, I think thou wouldst not.
> **Emilia:** By my troth, I think I should, and undo't when I
> had done. Marry, I would not do such a thing for
> a joint-ring, nor for measures of lawn, nor for gowns,
> petticoats, nor caps, nor any petty exhibition. But for
> all the whole world? ud's pity, who would not make
> her husband a cuckold to make him a monarch? I
> should venture purgatory for't.
> (*Othello* 4.3.69–78)

Desdemona does not see the world as Emilia does. Emilia's earthy vision, one that allows the end to justify the means, is the same vision that Jesus sees in Peter, as written in the New Testament, when the rash young disciple tries to shift Jesus from his chosen path:

> From that time forth Jesus began to show unto his disciples, that he must go unto Jerusalem, and suffer many things of the Elders, and of the high Priests, and Scribes, and be slain, and rise again the third day. Then Peter toke him aside, and began to rebuke him, saying, Master, pity thy self: this shall not be unto thee. Then he turned back, and said unto Peter, Get thee behind me, Satan: thou art an offence unto me, because thou understandest not the things that are of God, but the things that are of men . . . For what shall it profit a man though he should win the whole world, if he lose his own soul?[56]

Jesus's rebuke of Peter came as a result of the disciple's bid for self-preservation. Peter did not have the same perspective as Jesus, one that had its eyes set on the salvation of the world by the sacrifice of an innocent Savior. Peter saw an earthly kingdom and an earthly redemption. Jesus refers to Peter as "Satan" for his desire to derail the purpose of Christ's incarnation. Christ had already been tempted by Satan to forsake the purpose, and in much the same way, Peter is here seeking to get Christ to set up an earthly kingdom and lay claim to the kingdoms of the earth. Peter encourages Jesus to pity Himself, focus on self-preservation, and value His earthly life enough to give up on God's higher calling for one that offers a more immediate result. Emilia sees no value in self-sacrifice; rather, she warns men to treat their wives with respect or to expect that their wives will seek revenge:

> **Emilia:** Then let them use us well: else let them know,
> The ills we do, their ills instruct us so.
>
> (*Othello* 4.3.103–4)

In spite of the pressure placed on her by Emilia, Desdemona expresses her commitment to a higher calling in the sacrifice she makes for Othello. She is certain of her innocence, yet she does not incriminate Othello.

Othello's humiliation results in his elevated moral vision; this is his redemption. His moral vision is elevated, and he is able to recognize Desdemona's innocence and her great love for him. Although he is redeemed, the question of Othello's suicide must be addressed, for according to Roman Catholic doctrine, suicide guarantees a person's damnation.[57] Anthony Gilbert describes Othello's suicide as something that "transfixes the audience by its horror, by its moral truth, and by its transgression of conventional categories of meaning and morality."[58] Othello's redemption is the climactic moment of the play. His suicide is, as Gilbert claims, horrific, the horror resulting from the unexpected nature of the act. Othello rises to a place of moral clarity, evidenced by his recognition of truth and purity, and yet he is unable to transcend the despair that results from his murder of Desdemona. As Gilbert claims, Othello's suicide transgresses conventional understanding and does not result in his damnation.[59] However, it must not be presumed that Othello escapes damnation because of his noble heart, as Gilbert suggests,[60] but because of divine grace. Martin Luther's writings contradicted the conventional understanding of suicide in his time, supporting the notion that suicide did not guarantee one's damnation. Luther writes, "I don't share the opinion that suicides are certainly to be damned. My reason is that they do not wish to kill themselves but are overcome by the power of the devil . . . Such persons do not die by free choice or by law . . . they are examples by which our Lord God wishes to show that the devil is powerful and also that we should be diligent in prayer."[61] Luther claims that people who commit suicide are overcome by despair and that they are not entirely responsible for the act. This view of suicide is consistent with the Reformation view of sin and human depravity. Even after one's redemption, he or she will continue to sin and continue to struggle against doubt and despair. Suicide is something that Luther wrote about in several works, always contesting that men and women—pagan or redeemed—will suffer under the oppression of their depravity.[62] Part of the oppression of one's depravity involves limited vision and a tendency to succumb to a despair that leads to suicide.[63]

It is through the lens of Reformation theology that we are able to better understand Othello's journey. Othello's pride and fear propel him toward his humiliating end. While Iago guides Othello at times, giving him further reason to distrust Desdemona and Cassio, it is clear from the text that Othello's own fear and pride are the most powerful forces behind his action. Othello's fall does not lead to his damnation, however, for Shakespeare's staging of Reformation doctrine gives the play a far more complex framework. In the Reformation process of salvation, Othello first experiences a great humiliation, second an  enlightened vision, and third a complete redemption.

Chapter 6
The Winter's Tale

In the play discussed in the previous chapter, we see Othello's jealous rage boil over, causing him to murder his innocent wife. In this chapter, we look at King Leontes, who, much like Othello, is blinded by fear and motivated by a jealous rage. The fate of Leontes, from his jealous rage to his humiliating fall to his ultimate redemption, is staged by a craftsman who was acquainted with the theology of the Protestant Reformation. In *The Winter's Tale*, we witness Shakespeare's use of the controversial religious issues of his day. The atmosphere in the kingdom of Sicilia is ripe with controversy as the play opens up on a debate over that which is owed and that which is given freely. This key tension invites the audience to consider the ideas about judgment and redemption at work in the play, as well as the nature of the hope of grace as personified by the birth of young royalty. The Protestant nature of Leontes's redemption is set in contrast to the Roman Catholic theology of works, which is personified in the priestlike characterization of Paulina. *The Winter's Tale* is often seen as a play about the nature of creative art,[1] or as a stage in the literary evolution of the pastoral.[2] It is also, as I argue in this chapter, a play about Protestantism. Various people, such as René Girard, Louis Martz, Jeffrey Knapp, and Maurice Hunt[3] have engaged with the redemption in the play in various senses, and it is to this strand of recent criticism that my reading here is a contribution.

In the opening act of *The Winter's Tale*, Camillo and Archidamus, lords in the service of their respective kings, are engaged in a discussion that revolves around the laws of hospitality:

> **Archidamus:** If you shall chance, Camillo, to visit Bohemia, on the like occasion whereon my services are now on foot, you shall see, as I have said, great difference betwixt our Bohemia and your Sicilia.
>
> **Camillo:** I think, this coming summer, the King of Sicilia means to pay Bohemia the visitation which he justly owes him.
>
> **Archidamus:** Wherein our entertainment shall shame us: we will be justified in our loves: for indeed—
>
> **Camillo:** Beseech you—
>
> (*The Winter's Tale* 1.1.1–10)

Archidamus's first statement offers an important value judgment. He has been the beneficiary of some lavish hospitality in Leontes's kingdom, and he feels compelled to prepare Camillo for the more simple arrangements available in Bohemia. In this passage, Archidamus seems to be reacting to the Stoic tradition of hospitality, an understanding that has its roots in the writings of Cicero, specifically in *De Officiis*, where Cicero reflects on various forms of hospitality. Cicero notes that although giving generously to one's peers is a noble act, the receiver of gifts will be expected to return a gift of comparable value, thereby putting a certain measure of pressure on the receiver.[4] Cicero further warns that one must give thoughtfully, as overgiving may be recognized as shameful ambition or simple foolishness.[5]

In this opening conversation, Archidamus reveals that he is aware of custom and fears that his kingdom will not measure up to the standard of excellence set by Sicilia. Bohemia will not be able to reciprocate with an equal gift of hospitality. When Archidamus speaks of being shamed in his conversation with Camillo, he invites the reader to consider the meaning of grace. It is grace that must be offered by Sicilia, according to Archidamus, who understands that any form of kindness must be repaid in like degree. Archidamus hopes his country will be able to give an offering of love, an offering that will justify them before the Sicilian king.

The words employed in this section are words that remind us of a debate that was at work in Shakespeare's England, a debate that dealt with that which is "owed" and that which is given freely. In Shakespeare's England, the debate between Roman Catholicism and Protestantism raged as both sides fought for a different understanding of law and grace. Christopher Haigh points to the most confrontational differences between Roman Catholicism and Protestantism by explaining that the former is a "Works religion"[6] and the latter is a "Word religion."[7] In the Roman Catholic tradition, a measure of redemptive participation was required of men and women—a participation that had become an integral part of English culture, consisting of generational customs and nationwide traditions. Roman Catholics understood that God wanted them to make proper satisfactions for their sins and take part in earning divine grace by performing good works. These satisfactions, mirrored in Archidamus's desire to satisfy Sicilia, were offered in the form of penance, which could range from fasts to alms giving, a series of prayers, the purchasing of indulgences, the celebration of feasts and festivals, or many other types of offerings.

A Roman Catholic in the Elizabethan Age was familiar with a religious justification that required some form of payment. The Reformation challenged the Roman Catholic traditions of sacrifice and the paying of penances. It was Martin Luther who argued that men and women could not satisfy the demands of God through payment of any kind. According to Luther, justification was not to involve human participation but rather only the work of God himself through the onetime sacrifice of Jesus Christ: "By grace alone (Sola Gratia), through faith alone (Sola Fide), according to scripture alone (Sola Scriptura), for God's glory alone (Soli Deo Gloria)."[8] This sixteenth-century Reformation motto compressed the dramatic turn from human participation into a statement that rejected several hundred years of church tradition. Quoting Walter Benjamin from his text *The Origin of German Tragic Drama*, Jennifer Rust writes, "A melancholic impulse arises in response to the 'empty world' generated by the Reformers' denial of any transcendent value in earthly works and emphasis on salvation through faith alone, a perspective that leads the most sensitive, those who cannot sustain the requisite faith, to view 'the scene of their existence as a rubbish heap of partial, inauthentic actions'"[9] Rust continues in this way by looking at the

structure of "depersonalization" imposed on people of faith by the Reformation "stripping" of custom and participation.[10]

By removing human participation from Christianity, the Reformers toppled religious tradition despite its long history. The Protestant emphasis on the inability of mankind to make a payment or offering of any kind to God resulted in the emphasis on human contrition and humiliation. These alone were the signs of a redeemed soul humbled by the realization of God's goodness and man's baseness. When Archidamus speaks of his kingdom's need for justification, he foreshadows one of the central questions posed by the play: How can a man be redeemed?

Archidamus: Wherein our entertainment shall shame us: we will be justified in our loves . . .
Camillo: . . . You pay a great deal too dear for what's given freely.
(*The Winter's Tale* 1.1.8–9, 17–18)

It was this question that dwelt at the center of the Protestant Reformation.

In the second half of the first scene, the conversation between the two lords shifts to an interesting discussion about the young prince Mamillius, who according to the lords is a "gentleman of the greatest promise" and "a gallant child" (*The Winter's Tale* 1.1.34, 37). The conversation between the two lords takes an interesting yet strange turn as they discuss the impact that Mamillius has had on the people of his country:

Camillo: [Mamillius is] one that, indeed, physics the subject,
makes old hearts fresh: they that went on crutches
ere he was born desire yet their life to see him a man.
Archidamus: Would they else be content to die?
Camillo: Yes; if there were no other excuse why they should
desire to live.
Archidamus: If the king had no son, they would desire to live on
Crutches till he had one.
(*The Winter's Tale* 1.1.39–45)

Though it is not necessary to interpret Mamillius as a Christ figure, the conversation lends itself to a comparison of the image painted of Christ in the Old Testament book of Isaiah. Just as Mamillius is portrayed as a symbol of hope in this scene, so Christ is portrayed in Isaiah: "For a child will be born to us, a son will be given to us; and the government will rest on his shoulders; And his name will be called Wonderful Counselor, Mighty God, Eternal Father, Prince of Peace."[11] The connection to Christ is strengthened by Camillo's reference to people who would long to extend their lives in order to see the prince.

The longing that Camillo describes, and on which Archidamus strangely builds, bears a resemblance to the Roman Catholic feast often called the Purification of the Virgin or Candlemas. This feast celebrated the presentation of Christ at the temple, where, according to the New Testament account, the Christ Child was presented to Simeon the Righteous:

> And behold, there was a man in Jerusalem, whose name was Simeon; this man was just, and feared God, and waited for the consolation of Israel, and the Holy Ghost was upon him. And it was declared to him from God by the Holy Ghost, that he should not see death, before he had seen the Lord's Christ. And he came by the motion of the Spirit into the Temple, and when the parents brought in the child Jesus, to do for him after the custom of the Law, then he took him in his arms, and praised God, and said, Lord, now lettest thou thy servant depart in peace, according to thy word, for mine eyes have seen thy salvation, which thou hast prepared before the face of all people, a light to be revealed to the Gentiles, and the glory of thy people Israel.[12]

The tradition of sacrifice in the Old Testament pointed to a promised Savior, the Prince of Peace who would usher in a new covenant of grace and abolish the Old Testament requirement of sacrifice. While I do not argue that Shakespeare is dramatizing the Christian scriptures, he is indeed working with some of the controversial religious issues of his day. The major voices of the Protestant Reformation sought to emphasize mankind's depravity and his desperate need for justification. The Reformers further emphasized mankind's inability to offer an adequate sacrifice or to take part in its own redemption. From

Archidamus's concern over his justification to Camillo's praise of the long-awaited prince, the opening scene of *The Winter's Tale* is dominated by two key themes: justification and redemption. Julia Lupton claims that the themes introduced by Shakespeare at the beginning of *The Winter's Tale* allow him to create "a stony world of law unredeemed by grace."[13] It is in this stony world and within this "child's tale" that Shakespeare gives life to what was certainly one of the most powerful philosophical-religious shifts of the preceding century. Describing the relationship between Leontes and Hermione in *The Winter's Tale*, Stephen Greenblatt writes, "There is here, as so often in the ordinary conversation of husbands and wives, at once nothing and everything going on."[14] The same conclusion may be drawn about *The Winter's Tale* as a whole, set before us as a "tale," a child's story of "sprites and goblins," yet at the same time suggesting deep spiritual meaning—"at once nothing and everything going on."[15]

In *Spiritual Shakespeares*, Ewan Fernie argues that spirituality in Shakespeare is most often associated with "ideas of emancipation and an alternative world."[16] It is this kind of spirituality, one involving the emancipation of Leontes in *The Winter's Tale*, that may indeed be the central issue at play. In his important work of comparison between *Hamlet* and *The Winter's Tale*, David Lee Miller affirms this claim: "If *Hamlet* is deeply marked by the son's need to reform his mother . . . *The Winter's Tale* is just as deeply marked by the wish to redeem its murderous patriarch."[17] The humiliation of Leontes offers a picture of spiritual redemption. While I appreciate the excellent work that Ewan Fernie, among others,[18] is creating through a philosophical and spiritual approach to Shakespeare's works, it is my intent to employ Fernie's work as a place of departure, a springboard into a more specific historical-religious analysis. I hope to use his new and compelling philosophical and spiritual approaches to uncover the inner workings of the religious and doctrinal influences within *The Winter's Tale*. From Reformation doctrine, Shakespeare  gleans the concept of redemptive humiliation, a concept that transcends restrictive denominational categorizing. The spirituality of *The Winter's Tale* is most poignantly illustrated in Leontes's humiliation, for in this humiliation Shakespeare preserves what Kiernan Ryan explains as "everything that confounds common sense."[19] How can it be that a man is lifted up by being brought to his knees? When is a man given true sight through the confirmation of his blindness? This is the paradox of the Reformation as explained most powerfully in the writings of Martin Luther.

In addition to the redemptive humiliation experienced by King Leontes, the Roman Catholic understanding of repentance and its accompanying traditions of penance are rejected. The play supports the fact that the king is redeemed long before he is attacked by the priestly Paulina, who demands that he suffer and pay for that which is given freely. The conversation in the opening passage of *The Winter's Tale*, as previously mentioned, is heavy laden with religious language and particularly the language of Martin Luther's Reformation platform. In a tract analyzing the Psalms, Luther writes, "Since of ourselves we are nothing but have everything from God, it is easy to see that we can give Him nothing; neither can we repay Him for His grace. He demands nothing from us. The only thing left, therefore, is for us to praise and thank Him."[20] In *The Winter's Tale*, Camillo scolds Archidamus, "You pay a great deal too dear for what's given freely" (*The Winter's Tale* 1.1.16). Archidamus's desire to pay for a gift is a struggle of pride, pointing to one of the key elements of the Reformation debate. Luther in particular focuses much criticism on the traditional Roman Catholic understanding of repentance. Luther continues in this way: "Furthermore, in the New Testament the offering of thanks is to be the true worship of God, and no works are to count at all. Grace cannot stand it when we want to give to God or establish merit or pay Him with our works. This is the greatest of blasphemies and idolatries and is nothing less than the denial and even ridicule of God."[21] Archidamus understands the traditions of hospitality and just and fair repayment; he does not want to be thought poorly of by Camillo or anyone in Leontes's train. Camillo's rebuke is a Protestant correction; it is representative of the campaign waged by English Protestantism to rid the nation of what Luther called "the greatest of blasphemies."[22] Introduced in what seems a simple discussion of hospitality at the outset of the play, the theme of justification runs a clear course through the remainder of the play.

Reformation scholar Alister McGrath describes Luther's teaching of justification in this way: "[Luther claims that] man must recognize his spiritual weakness and inadequacy, and turn in humility from his attempts at self-justification to ask God for his grace. God treats the humility of faith (humilitas fidei) as the precondition necessary for justification under the terms of the pactum."[23] McGrath's statement is helpful in that it describes the religious shift required by the Reformation.

The recognition of spiritual weakness and inadequacy is a call for the humiliation of the redeemed. "Humility of faith"[24] as a precondition of salvation is an affirmation of the vital role of humiliation in the life of the would-be redeemed. Without humiliation, there is no redemption. In *Will in the World*, Stephen Greenblatt makes an interesting statement about Shakespeare's handling of the concept of restoration in *The Winter's Tale*: "The emotion of restoration is powerfully present—the sense that what was seemingly irrevocably lost has  been reclaimed against all hope and expectation—but the recovery is never quite what it seems: the past that is recovered turns out to be an invention or a delusion or, in the worst case, an intensification of loss."[25] Greenblatt recognizes something curious about Shakespeare's handling of restoration in *The Winter's Tale*. It is a restoration that comes at the cost of traditional belief, a difficult tearing away of that which was known and understood. Richard Hooker describes the tearing away from tradition in very simple terms, claiming that the Reformation removed the Roman Catholic tradition of sacrifice so "[Christians] have properly now no sacrifice."[26] Clear support for the denunciation of Roman Catholic "corporal" sacrifice is also found in the Geneva translation of the New Testament, especially in Hebrews 13:15 and its accompanying note:

> *Let us therefore by him offer the sacrifice of praise always to God, that is, the fruit of the lips, which confess his Name.*
>
>> Margin note: Now that those corporal sacrifices are taken away, he teacheth us that the true sacrifices of confession remain, which consist partly in giving of thanks, and partly in liberality, with which sacrifices indeed God is now delighted.[27]

The Reformation doctrine of substitution undermines the Roman Catholic doctrine of sacrifice and participation. As proposed by the Reformers, the sacrificial work of Christ renders any and all participation by men and women unnecessary and even, according to Martin Luther, blasphemous.[28] John Calvin affirms Luther's insistence on the rejection of personal sacrifice and describes Christ's work of substitution in this manner: "Our filthiness deserves that God should hold it in abhorrence, and that all the angels should spit upon us; but Christ, in order to present us pure and unspotted in presence of the Father, resolved to be spat upon, and to be dishonored by every kind of reproaches."[29] In *The Renaissance Bible*, Debora Shuger presents an interesting commentary on this passage from Calvin. She writes, "Particularly in Calvin, Christ's suffering and humiliation work something like a projective charm, where what happens to Christ will not happen to me. A highly literal version of substitution allows each of Christ's torments to 'undo' a piece of our deserved punishment."[30] The doctrine of substitution and the extent to which the Reformers sought to dismantle the tradition of personal sacrifice within Christianity is significant to our understanding of the religious climate of early modern England. In many ways, the early modern Christian was being encouraged to see him- or herself as a much different person before a much different kind of deity.

As mentioned previously, Eamon Duffy and Christopher Haigh describe the Reformation as a painful stripping away of traditional religious practices from the English people.[31] The Protestant Reformation, according to Duffy, Haigh, and others, is now understood as being just as much a cultural reformation as a religious reformation. It was the traditions and practices of common men and women that were attacked by this new spirituality. Haigh writes, "The theological foundation of works-religion was challenged, and the 'ignorant multitude' mocked for its reliance on artificial aids and external acts . . . The hallowed routines of the religion of doing were forbidden . . . The ordinary way to God was declared closed."[32]

Stephen Greenblatt and Louis Montrose have also weighed in heavily on this account, asserting that by Elizabeth's reign, the Reformers had cleansed the church of a wide array of penitential traditions.[33] The removal of these traditions, asserts Greenblatt and Montrose, left a great vacuum in English life. Each of these critics employs this hypothesis to argue that post-Roman Catholic English culture was desperate to satisfy its need for ritual and penitential tradition. According to Greenblatt, the English found this satisfaction in the theater.[34] In *Shakespeare's Tribe*, Jeffrey Knapp takes an interesting and important step beyond both Montrose and Greenblatt by suggesting that the church played a key role in investing the Shakespearean theater with religious purpose.[35] Knapp draws on critics Paul Whitfield White and Debora Shuger, who argue convincingly for a theory that claims that the subject of Shakespeare's theater was largely influenced by the powerful religious controversy of his day. White writes that Reformed doctrine must have had a strong impact on the "composition, performance, and reception" of plays because "Reformation orthodoxy was, by the midpoint of Elizabeth's reign, not merely the official doctrine of the national church but internalized as a major feature of the national consciousness."[36] Shuger argues in like manner: "If it is not plausible to read Shakespeare's plays as Christian allegories, neither is it likely that the popular drama of a religiously saturated culture could, by a secular miracle, have extricated itself from the theocentric orientation informing the discourses of politics, gender, social order, and history [at the time]."[37]

Among many others, the traditions of pilgrimage, indulgence, and penance were an integral part of English religious life, offering the medieval Roman Catholic an opportunity to "please" God and to "work out" his or her salvation.[38] These traditions and their place in culture made up in large part the religious psyche of the early modern Christian. This was a Christian who had the opportunity to enter the eternal realm by performing simple religious duties, a fact that placed a measure of value on the spiritual exercises of men and women. When the Reformers took center stage in the religious forum, it was this participation in the salvific process that was attacked most vehemently. In the face of a more optimistic view of man's ability to do proper penance, the Reformers stressed the depraved state of mankind and therefore man's inability to perform works that were pleasing to God. The Reformation emphasis on man's depravity placed a new importance on the humiliation of the sinner. It was this humiliation that led toward what the Reformers considered a proper and ideal view of self.

In *The Winter's Tale*, Shakespeare poses Leontes as a Reformation saint, one who experiences true redemption through a process of violent and painful humiliation. This humiliation, one that brings Leontes to his knees, allows the king to recognize his depraved condition and to find himself redeemed by God. After commissioning Hermione the task of convincing Polixenes to extend his stay in Sicilia, Leontes is suddenly disturbed by a violent sense of jealousy. Leontes praises Hermione for having spoken well enough to convince Polixenes to stay, claiming that there was only one other time that she had spoken "to better purpose" (*The Winter's Tale* 1.2.88). Hermione's response to Leontes, though she speaks in jest, offers an interesting bit of foreshadowing:

> **Hermione:** My last good deed was to entreat his stay:
> What was my first? It has an elder sister,
> Or I mistake you: O, would her name were Grace!
> (*The Winter's Tale* 1.2.96–98)

In a play that is dominated by themes of law and grace, things owed and things paid, Hermione's cry for "Grace" cannot go unnoticed. When Leontes tells her that her first "good deed" was confessing her love for him, Hermione credits divine grace:

> **Leontes:** Why, that was when
> Three crabbed months had sour'd themselves to death,
> Ere I could make thee open thy white hand,
> And clap thyself my love; then didst thou utter
> "I am yours for ever."
> **Hermione:** 'Tis Grace indeed.
> Why lo you now; I have spoke to th' purpose twice:
> The one, for ever earn'd a royal husband;
> Th' other, for some while a friend. [Giving her hand to Polixenes]
> (*The Winter's Tale* 1.2.102–8)

In this passage, Hermione confirms that her good deed was inspired by grace, an understanding that lines up with the Reformation view of good works and deeds. Reformation theology asserts that all good works are inspired by Providence and it is by the hand of God that men and women choose to do good deeds.[39] This interchange also reveals much about the relationship between Hermione and Leontes.

Stephen Greenblatt comments on this exchange, noting that it is "powerfully convincing in its suggestion of entangled love, tightly coiled tension, and playfulness."[40] It is the tension in this scene—"the slightly edgy intimacy"[41] that Greenblatt notes—that elicits what many have called an unexpected rage from Leontes. On one level, I agree with R. A. Foakes and others when they claim that Leontes's reaction is wild and unreasonable: "It is true that an actor playing Leontes could show incipient signs of passion before this point, but there is nothing in the text to warrant it. It seems rather that Shakespeare deliberately made Leontes blaze out unexpectedly in a concern precisely to leave aside or ignore questions of motive or possible explanations for his behavior."[42] Janet Adelman also claims that his jealousy is unexpected: "Leontes' jealousy erupts out of nowhere and breaks his world apart, as it breaks the syntax and rhythms of his own speeches apart; in the violence and obscurity of its expression, it draws the audience into its own sphere, causing us to snatch at nothings, to reconstruct the world (as Leontes himself does) in a reassuringly intelligible image."[43] A close reading of this spousal exchange will, however, introduce some fairly strong justification for Leontes's initial reaction.

In this exchange, we see Leontes humble himself in the way he describes his courtship of Hermione. Leontes describes her as having forced him to wait three difficult months and to work for her hand in marriage. Leontes's courtship of Hermione did not involve his sweeping her off of her feet or any courageous act of heroism on his part. Leontes describes the courtship as one in which he was forced to beg for her hand, wait sourly, and clasp for her affection. Although Hermione admits to having earned a "royal husband" (*The Winter's Tale* 1.2.104), this admission is once again soured by her quick reference to the winning of Polixenes's friendship. The latter admission, coupled by Hermione's touching of Polixenes's hand, may provide justification enough for the audience to allow for Leontes's jealousy. Even the mere physical touch between Hermione and Polixenes, depending on how it was staged, could justify a jealous reaction from the king. Additionally, Hermione betrays a quick wit and a flirtatious edge in her baiting of Polixenes. When Leontes invites her to help him convince Polixenes to stay, she begins with a rebuke:

Hermione: I had thought, sir, to have held my peace until
You had drawn oaths from him not to stay. You, sir,
Charge him too coldly.

(*The Winter's Tale* 1.2.28–30)

Although Leontes affirms her statement with a "Well said, Hermione" (*The Winter's Tale* 1.2.33), it may in fact be that Leontes found some initial embarrassment in Hermione's approach and then further embarrassment in her use of very physical language:

Hermione: a lady's Verily's
As potent as a lord's. Will you go yet?
Force me to keep you as a prisoner,
Not like a guest . . . How say you?
My prisoner? or my guest?

(*The Winter's Tale* 1.2.50–55)

Hermione takes control of the situation with such command that it is not surprising that Leontes finds fault with her. She takes Polixenes as her guest who she will draw away to question, "Of my lord's tricks, and yours, when you were boys" (*The Winter's Tale* 1.2.61) and to hear stories about when Polixenes and Leontes have acted rebelliously:

Polixenes: we knew not
The doctrine of ill-doing, nor dream'd
That any did . . .

Hermione: By this we gather
You have tripp'd since . . . Yet go on;
Th' offences we have made you do, we'll answer,
If you first sinn'd with us, and that with us
You did continue fault, and that you slipp'd not
With any but with us.

(*The Winter's Tale* 1.2.69–70, 75, 82–86)

Hermione is employing the language of infidelity and thereby questioning Polixenes about his sexual exploits as a youth. Leontes interrupts the conversation in an awkward manner, which suggests that he is disturbed by the direction of the conversation.

Janet Adelman suggests that Hermione's pregnant body adds tension to this scene, drawing a connection between Leontes's boyhood lusts and his wife's sexualized figure.[44] This added tension, according to Adelman, is far too much for Leontes to bear, thus leading him to a place where he must, as Adelman writes, "reconstruct the world . . . in a reassuringly intelligible image."[45]

To add to the discomfort of the exchange, Hermione gives her hand to Polixenes in a manner that further disturbs Leontes. This offering of her hand may have been the final offense. Leontes makes much of this touching, and it would be a mistake for the reader to underestimate the power of the affection that Shakespeare stages between Polixenes and Hermione: "Paddling palms . . . pinching fingers" (*The Winter's Tale* 1.2.115); "Still virginalling / Upon his palm!" (*The Winter's Tale* 1.2.125); "Affection! thy intention stabs the centre" (*The Winter's Tale* 1.2.138); "How she holds up the neb, the bill to him! / And arms her with the boldness of a wife / To her allowing husband!" (*The Winter's Tale* 1.2.182–85). Can all this jealousy be considered mere madness? Does Shakespeare remove the Iago tempter from this play to isolate the madness in Leontes, or does he want his audience to see Leontes as an everyman, tempted by jealous thoughts and vulnerable to his own imagination?

As a man infected with sin and unable to make accurate decisions and judgments, Leontes rushes forward in jealous rage, all the while believing himself wise. As an everyman struggling with jealousy and pride, Leontes seeks to justify his position with Camillo. With a clear mind, unclouded by passion and fear, Camillo speaks the truth to Leontes's deaf ears:

Camillo: You never spoke what did become you less
Than this; which to reiterate were sin
As deep as that, though true.
Leontes: Is whispering nothing?
Is leaning cheek to cheek? Is meeting noses?
Kissing with inside lip? . . . horsing foot on foot?
Skulking in corners? Wishing clocks more swift? . . .
. . . is this nothing?
Why then the world, and all that's in't, is nothing . . .
Camillo: . . . Good my lord, be cur'd

Of this diseas'd opinion, and betimes,
For 'tis most dangerous.
(*The Winter's Tale* 1.2.282–89, 293, 297–99)

The king is presented as being tragically unaware of his ignorance, unaware that he himself is blinded by his own pride and insecurity. He is, as Camillo states, diseased and much like the sick man Luther writes of in his *Lectures on Romans*. In his character Camillo, Shakespeare creates another rejected physician.[46] Leontes is confronted by both Camillo and Paulina regarding his sickness, yet the king finds it far too easy to cast his trusted advisors off.

Leontes's rejection of his advisors resembles King Lear's rejection of Cordelia and Kent, revealing him to be another king who is clearly lacking self-knowledge and the accompanying ability to see his own sickness. Leontes is quick to dismiss Camillo's logical pleadings as ignorant and naïve and even swifter to dismiss Paulina as a foolish, nagging woman. Paulina expresses her desire to the guards who seek to keep her away from Leontes, "I come to bring him sleep . . . / with words as medicinal as true" (*The Winter's Tale* 2.3.34, 37), and she continues,

Paulina: Good my liege, I come,—
And, I beseech you hear me, who professes
Myself your loyal servant, your physician . . .
(*The Winter's Tale* 2.3.53–55)

In *King Lear*, Shakespeare employs the same reference through Kent, whose passionate devotion to Lear is clear to all but the king himself:

Kent: My life I never held but as a pawn
To wage against thine enemies, ne'er fear to lose it,
Thy safety being the motive.
Lear: Out of my sight!
Kent: See better, Lear, and let me still remain
The true blank of thine eye . . .
Lear: O vassal! Miscreant!
Kent: . . . Do, kill thy physician, and thy fee bestow
Upon the foul disease.
(*King Lear* 1.1.156–60, 162, 164–65)

Ignoring the prognosis of his would-be physicians, Leontes follows the model set out by Martin Luther of the unrepentant sinner.

Like Luther's sinner, Leontes refuses to admit his sickness and in turn accuses Camillo, Paulina, and his lords of treason (*The Winter's Tale* 2.3.72). Overcome by pride, Leontes abuses Camillo in this way:

> **Leontes:** It is: you lie, you lie:
> I say thou liest, Camillo, and I hate thee,
> Pronounce thee a gross lout, a mindless slave,
> Or else a hovering temporizer . . .
> (*The Winter's Tale* 1.2.298–302)

In his essay "'Standing in Rich Place': The Importance of Context in *The Winter's Tale*," Maurice Hunt claims that Leontes's statements above are the most "vivid example of despotic speech in Shakespeare's non-tragic drama."[47] Leontes's pride and murderous rage cause him to abuse his faithful servant Camillo, who under great pressure refuses to aid Leontes in his desperate desire to be justified. Leontes continues to reject the counsel of his aides and trusted servants, even going so far as to reject the decision of the Oracle:

> **Leontes:** There is no truth at all i' th' Oracle:
> The sessions shall proceed: this is mere falsehood.
> (*The Winter's Tale* 3.2.140–41)

At this final word, Leontes reaches his greatest point of arrogance and is swiftly cut down by what turns out to be a sovereign act of grace. David Lee Miller compares the humiliation of Leontes with the humiliation of Gertrude in *Hamlet*. As one of the most powerful actions in each play, the redemptions of these two characters seem to overtake much of the plot lines and nearly all the plays' concerns. While Miller does not recognize the impact of Luther's writing on Shakespeare's plays, he is certainly responding to the Reformation ties that are evident in each play's structure, leading him to confess that "in *Hamlet* and *The Winter's Tale* Shakespeare is responding as powerfully to the Reformation . . . as he is to classical epic or popular romance."[48]

In *The Winter's Tale*, Leontes is humbled by an act of the gods, and his restoration is disturbingly swift. Though he must wait sixteen years to be reunited with his wife and daughter, Leontes's moral and spiritual health is restored with an immediacy that is distinctly Lutheran, as he does not require any offering of penance or purchase of indulgence. In just moments, Leontes moves from a bold dismissal of the Oracle—"There is no truth at all i' th' Oracle" (*The Winter's Tale* 3.2.140)—to the following humiliating confession:

Leontes: I have too much believ'd mine own suspicion . . .
. . . Apollo, pardon
My great profaneness 'gainst thine Oracle!
I'll reconcile me to Polixenes,
New woo my queen, recall the good Camillo,
Whom I proclaim a man of truth, of mercy . . .
. . . how he glisters
Thorough my rust! and how his piety
Does my deeds make the blacker!
(*The Winter's Tale* 3.2.151, 153–57, 170–72)

While Louis L. Martz credits Paulina with the true reformation of the king, arguing that Paulina's words lead Leontes toward "a scene that may be called a restoration of faith,"[49] it is unclear what in fact Martz considers the powerful moment of repentance in act 3, scene 2. It is actually here, in this very scene and long before the resurrection of Hermione, that Leontes is redeemed. If we fail to recognize this pivotal moment in the play, we will certainly miss the significance of Paulina's continued abuse of Leontes long after his repentance and reformation. Martz calls Paulina "a bitter reminder of the evil that Leontes has done,"[50] and while this is true, Paulina's reminder signifies far more.

Leontes's swift repentance is a radical rejection of the traditional Roman Catholic doctrine of penance. While Leontes is still on his knees confessing that he "too much believ'd [his] own suspicion" (*The Winter's Tale* 3.2.151), Paulina takes on an interesting persona that stays with her until the close of the play. Paulina's immediate reaction to Leontes's repentance is of particular interest as it bears no grace and demands far more than Leontes can give. My criticism of Paulina opposes a critical tradition that tends to view Paulina as a lovely miracle worker,[51] and yet, if viewed through a historically sensitive lens, Paulina must be understood as a figure of harsh legalism. Paulina speaks the truth of the law to Leontes and makes demands of him that he cannot possibly meet. Luther's description of the law is insightful as we analyze the character of Paulina. Luther writes, "He who masters the art of exact distinction between the Law and the Gospel should be called a real theologian. These two must be kept apart. The function of the Law is to frighten men and drive them to despair, especially the coarse and secure sinners, until they realize their inability to meet the demands of the Law or to obtain grace."[52] Because Paulina rejects Leontes's repentance, it is clear that she speaks the law, yet within the context of the play, her words seem mistimed and misplaced, for Leontes is already a repentant sinner, no longer in need of the harsh law but requiring the hope of grace:

> **Paulina:** O thou tyrant!
> Do not repent these things, for they are heavier
> Than all thy woes can stir: therefore betake thee
> To nothing but despair. A thousand knees
> Ten thousand years together, naked, fasting,
> Upon a barren mountain, and still winter
> In storm perpetual, could not move the gods
> To look that way thou wert.
>
> (*The Winter's Tale* 3.2.207–13)

It is interesting that Leontes, although he admits to deserving the blame and damnation that Paulina delivers, is never required to perform any acts of penance, purchase indulgences, or follow priest ordered forms of purgation. His repentance is a result of what the Reformers had begun to call a work of the Holy Spirit. John Calvin explains it this way: "Man is not possessed of free-will for good works, unless he be assisted by grace."[53] Leontes's ability to repent is granted him, according to Reformation theology, by divine grace. Following Leontes's redemption, he determines to reconcile himself to Polixenes, to "new woo" (*The Winter's Tale* 3.2.155–56) the queen, and to apologize to Camillo for the wrongs he dealt him. These good works, according to Calvin and consistent with the larger body of Reformation theology, are evidence of a redeemed soul that is being aided by divine grace.[54]

Paulina is staged as Shakespeare's priest; she thereby conforms to the standards of works religion and acts as a foil to the Reformation theme of grace woven into the play. Within such a religiously saturated culture, Shakespeare's use of a Roman Catholic foil would most certainly have been appreciated. According to Huston Diehl, it was very common for characters to be used in this fashion: "The religious practices of Elizabethan England may well have predisposed Shakespeare's audiences to interpret the characters portrayed on stage as lively images of virtue and vice, their stories as manifestations of divine will. And Shakespeare's representational theater may well have thrived in an early Protestant culture that was hostile to other forms of human artifice because it directed its spectators' attention to human characters played by human actors—the living images of God—rather than to the imaginary and erroneous, ornamental and lifeless images made by the hands of men."[55] In Paulina, we have an image of Roman Catholic ritual, and in her role, we witness a commitment to the eradicated doctrine of penance. In the shadow of Reformation doctrine, Paulina is an overbearing priest demanding what is unnecessary and irresponsible from Leontes. Her demands are irresponsible because they are misplaced and mistimed, capable as Robert Burton writes, of driving the redeemed into "religious melancholy."[56] John Calvin and Martin Luther were equally concerned with what they believed was the Roman Catholic tendency of demanding the impossible and unnecessary from penitent Christians.[57]

In pure Lutheran fashion, Leontes is confronted by God, brought from a station of pride and arrogance, and powerfully humiliated. Through this divine interaction, Leontes is given the grace to see his great sin and to repent. Leontes's sudden repentance, if interpreted in light of the most prominent religious debate of Shakespeare's age, must be understood as the most powerful and perhaps the most disturbing action of the play. G. Wilson Knight describes Leontes's miraculous repentance in this manner: "No dramatic incident in Shakespeare falls with so shattering an impact, no reversal is more poignant than when, after a moment's dazedness, Leontes' whole soul-direction changes."[58] A change in soul-direction, according to Reformation theologians, is credited exclusively to an act of divine intervention. Reformation theologian and pastor William Perkins explains that any movement toward God or change in soul-direction in this manner is wholly contingent on the grace of God: "When God receiues any man into couenant of eternall life, it proceeds not of any dignitie in the man whom God calleth, but from his mercie and alone good pleasure. . . . As for the opinion of them that say, that foreseene faith and good workes are the cause that mooued God to chose men to saluation, it is friulous."[59] Joel Beeke writes extensively on Perkins's notion of grace, further explaining that without God's grace, "man cannot fulfill God's demands, whereas with it, man finds his will renewed through the Holy Spirit to the point that he is capable  of choosing repentance."[60] By Reformation standards, Leontes's ability to repent and the resultant moral clarity he experiences are clear indications that he has been redeemed.

It is significant that Paulina continues to badger Leontes long after his repentance. With a miraculous humility, Leontes absorbs Paulina's damning rebuke; he is clearly mindful of his sin, yet he does not give in to the despair she seems to wish for him. Paulina's damnation of Leontes is of particular interest in that it continually seeks to demand his allegiance. Paulina acts in a manner that is consistent with Luther's view of the Roman Catholic clergy of his day: "Therefore it was the height not only of insanity but of wickedness when the monks were so zealous in enlisting the youth of both sexes in the monasteries for their religious and, as they called them, 'holy' orders, as a sure state of salvation; and then, once they were enlisted, they commanded them to doubt the grace of God."[61] Susan Snyder, in her study of despair in the Renaissance, draws together the dominant Reformation understanding of despair:

> Calvin joins Luther in identifying Catholicism with the old law. Papist churches are "synagogues of the devil," and the schoolmen are "the Pharisees of our day." Roman practice conceals God's mercy, "which alone can calm the terrors of the conscience" (*Inst., III, II, 15*). For Calvin, Catholic ceremonialism is a kind of Judaism. The conditions of the rites are impossible to fulfill (for example, complete confession and perfect contrition for penance). Thus they lead either to despair or hypocrisy. The Catholics, like the Jews, are vainglorious: they arrogate God's decisions to themselves, deciding who shall be

> saved (*Inst., III, 22.4*) . . . In the people of the law, pride and despair are inextricably combined.[62]

Luther's teaching on the oppression of the pope closely resembles Shakespeare's characterization of Paulina. Paulina is not a Pauline figure as argued by G. Wilson Knight, Velma Richmond, Maurice Hunt, and others, but rather a foil to Pauline literature.[63] In his essay "Standing in Rich Place," Hunt writes, "Given her name, Paulina's harsh but purifying words evoke the image of Pauline Christianity. She is the blessed thorn in the King's flesh. The Pauline notion of mortification and renewal provides a setting for Leontes' self-abasement and inner struggles."[64]

It was Luther's reading of Pauline literature that motivated him to compose his Ninety-five Theses and to speak out against the Roman Catholic Church. It was the Pauline epistles in fact, and the Reformer's focus on them, that started the Protestant Reformation. While Hunt's essay provides some compelling insight into Protestant redemption, his failure to approach Pauline Christianity with an eye for Reformation doctrine keeps him from fully understanding what Shakespeare seems to be doing through Paulina. A Protestant reading of Pauline theology would negate any and all need for the ongoing mortification and humiliation of a man who has expressed sincere repentance. Leontes' confession in act 3 reveals his brokenness: "Apollo's angry, and the heavens themselves / Do strike at my injustice" (*The Winter's Tale* 3.2.146–47). The king is not coerced into a humble position, and Paulina does not lead him to repentance.

While his research appears flawed in parts, Hunt accurately spells out the phases of Protestant redemption, the spelling out of which proves very effective for my analysis—"a plunge into depravity and ignorance, a great spiritual crisis, conversion, heart's sorrow and repentance, and receptive faith"[65]—but he fails to carefully consider Leontes's journey in light of these phases. Leontes plunges into a state of great humiliation upon giving in to his ferocious jealousy. René Girard describes Leontes's jealous rage as a sudden transformation into a "wild beast."[66] Girard writes convincingly about the great depravity that resides in Leontes, claiming that Leontes is "an Othello without his Iago, a Claudio without his Don John."[67] Leontes plunges into ignorance by claiming to have an impeccable discernment; able to sense when someone is untrue:

Leontes: Dost think I am so muddy, so unsettled,
To appoint myself in this vexation . . .
Without ripe moving to 't? Would I do this?
Could man so blench?
(*The Winter's Tale* 1.2.325–26, 332–33)

Leontes's overconfidence is his greatest error, and it keeps him from correcting his path by hearing wise council. Leontes's great spiritual crisis comes when he rejects the Oracle's pronouncement, after which Mamillius is pronounced dead and Hermione unconscious. Leontes's conversion and repentance come immediately after his crisis, and they are full of passion and intensity. The audience is given  no reason to believe that Leontes is merely putting on a show of grief in the repenting scene rather than expressing some strong desires for reform that are evidence of true conversion.

Leontes's heart's sorrow is unmistakable, and one would wonder how Hunt and others have missed the fact that Leontes arrives at this place of true salvation not by an act of human coercion but by "a divinity that shapes" his ends.[68] This divinity, an Apollo of Reformation making perhaps, is a divinity that is staged as one who values humiliation above participation. The final stage of Protestant redemption is receptive faith, a stage that we witness in Leontes as he humbly accepts the refining abuse that the gods see fit to pour out on him through Paulina. Evidence of Leontes's receptive faith may also be in the promise he makes, of his own accord, to regularly visit the tomb of his wife and son (*The Winter's Tale* 3.2.236).

Paulina's abuse of Leontes is an additional aspect of the play that we can more fully appreciate with an understanding of Reformation theology.

Paulina: If, one by one, you wedded all the world,
Or from the all that are took something good,
To make a perfect woman, she you kill'd
Would be unparallel'd.

Leontes: I think so. Kill'd!
She I kill'd! I did so: but thou strik'st me
Sorely, to say I did: it is as bitter
Upon thy tongue as in my thought. Now, good now,
Say so but seldom.

(*The Winter's Tale* 5.1.13–19)

Sixteen years after Leontes is humbled by Apollo, we find Paulina still abusing the king.

From her early damnation of his prayers, "Do not repent these things, for they are heavier / Than all thy woes can stir" (*The Winter's Tale* 3.2.208–9), to her final abuse of him in her gallery, Paulina is an image of judgment that must serve to counter the theme of grace that colors the final act of this play. Of this final scene, Richard Wilson writes the following: "At the end of *The Winter's Tale* Paulina marches Leontes on an exhausting tour of her art gallery, which seems like a reprise of the penance he has paid at the tomb of his wife and son ever since he promised, sixteen years before, that 'Once a day I'll visit / The chapel where they lie, / And tears shed there shall be my recreation'" (*The Winter's Tale* 3.2.236).[69] Shakespeare stages Paulina as a characterization of the Roman Catholic Church. The "exhausting tour" that Wilson refers to may in fact serve to suggest an additional connection between Paulina and the Roman Catholic Church. It is in this gallery—a place associated above all with images and icons—that Paulina has clearly invested much of her time. In the gallery, Paulina continues her demand for penance and her pursuit of legalistic constraints—"Give me the office / To choose you a queen" (*The Winter's Tale* 5.1.77–78)—which positions her as a clear foil to the grace-declaring theologians of the Reformation. Luther was often criticized for what his opponents believed was an overemphasis on the grace of God. He was harshly critiqued for statements like the following: "But what does the wisdom of the Holy Spirit teach us? It maintains that God is not the kind of God who wants to frighten the frightened or break the broken even more, but one who loves the broken, afflicted, and humble, who expects and hears the sighs and voices of the wretched."[70]

In addition to Paulina's legalism, her resurrection of Hermione is in fact very similar to the staged miracles of the Roman Catholic

Church. These staged acts would draw money from men and women, promising everything from a shorter purgatory for loved ones to guaranteed salvation for sinners, yet according to Luther, they only offered bondage to a system of legalism:

> So it is certain that false signs will happen in Christendom and that the false Christians will look upon them as true and genuine signs. This has really been happening in the papacy, though in Turkey, too, there are many such priests and special saints. You can read about this in the books and legends, especially in what the monks have written. They are all crawling with miracles, though they were really nothing but lies and rascalities. How they have made fools of the people nowadays with all those pilgrimages to the Grym Valley, to the Oak, or to Trier![71]

Dennis Taylor makes note of the very Roman Catholic nature of Hermione's resurrection, calling the episode a "simulation of a Catholic miracle."[72] Paulina's incessant desire for control is also evident in her commanding of Hermione. Is it possible that Paulina has kept Hermione under her control by a similar legalistic oppression for all these years? Though in some ways Paulina's staged miracle of resurrection resembles the miracle plays of Roman Catholic indulgence salesmen, as well as the Roman Catholic doctrine of transubstantiation, the more interesting fact is that Shakespeare juxtaposes the tradition of Roman Catholic penance through Paulina's character—namely, through her demand for Leontes to work for his salvation.

The humiliation of Leontes, a redemptive experience orchestrated by the gods, lies at the heart of *The Winter's Tale*. The significance of this redemptive humiliation is best understood through the lens of Reformation doctrine. It is through this lens that we make sense of Leontes's swift and radical change of heart, and his subsequent humility and clarity of thought. It is through this lens that we can better appreciate the Roman Catholic foil that Shakespeare creates through the priestly Paulina. By employing such a foil, Shakespeare forces us to consider the powerful and disruptive invasion of Word religion on a landscape formerly dominated by the traditional Roman Catholic understanding of Works religion.

Chapter 7
Cymbeline

> . . . wipe thine eyes.
> Some falls are means the happier to arise
> (*Cymbeline* 4.2.405–6)[1]

In chapter 6, we examined the humiliation that led to the cooling of Leontes's jealous rage. In this final chapter, we examine *Cymbeline*, wherein the humiliation of Posthumus results in a similar cooling, as well as a miraculous clearing of vision. In Shakespeare's *Cymbeline*, Posthumus displays a tragic moral blindness. Posthumus's inability to see and judge properly leads him to make several horrifying decisions that have the potential to destroy his own life and the lives of many others. The struggle to see clearly, one of the central themes of the play, is described by Innogen in this way: "Our very eyes / Are sometimes, like our judgments, blind" (*Cymbeline* 4.2.301–2).[2] While Posthumus is guilty of great evil and at times takes on the role of the play's villain, his life is spared and his soul redeemed by a miraculous series of events. The nature of Posthumus's redemption is of great importance, requiring that he suffer through an experience of humiliation modeled after a Reformation understanding of salvation. This chapter is about the influence of the Reformation, and particularly the writings of Martin Luther, on Shakespeare's delicately constructed *Cymbeline*. Additionally, this chapter will focus on the depravity of Posthumus and the nature of his powerful redemption. It is weak logic and poor discernment that draw Posthumus into a fog of violent jealousy from which he is rescued by a process of redemptive humiliation.

Through a study of the redemptive humiliation at work in *Cymbeline*, we see morally blind characters receive vision with which they are able to make good decisions and heal broken relationships. In this chapter, I hope to avoid common misreadings and misinterpretations of *Cymbeline*[3] while bringing new understanding of the depth of Posthumus's character and his experience in the play. Posthumus is not simply ignorant or merely misinterpreting signs and signals. Posthumus is, rather, morally and spiritually depraved. He swiftly becomes an antagonizing force within the play, and it is clear that he must be redeemed. In his work on the Nativity in *Cymbeline*, Robin Moffet briefly describes Posthumus's condition as a tragic "bondage of sin."[4] Moffet's conclusion is supported by Posthumus's confession: "My conscience, thou art fetter'd / More than my shanks and wrists" (*Cymbeline* 5.4.11–12). This confession of bondage is also reminiscent of Martin Luther's famous text published in 1525, *The Bondage of the Will*. It was in this text that the Reformer attacked Erasmus's position on grace and works, arguing that man is unable to bring himself to God. Peggy Simonds describes Posthumus's experience in the play as a refinement through a "fire of suffering."[5] At the beginning of the play, Posthumus is stumbling in a fog of misunderstanding and making morally base decisions. In *Cymbeline*, the issue of moral vision becomes important as the characters make life-and-death judgments about the integrity of loved ones. Geoffrey Hill is correct when he describes *Cymbeline* as "a study of situation, relationship, environment, and climate of opinion."[6] A character's moral vision affects his ability to make good decisions, and the actions that follow these decisions lie at the forefront of this play. Richard Harp describes the regaining of a character's moral vision in this way: "Indeed, since fortune / destiny / fate is the instrument of providence it seems to be true in [Shakespeare's late plays] that the more radically one experiences the turns of fortune's wheel, the better he will be able to see beyond to providence."[7] Harp's study recognizes the important "personal" nature of providential involvement in the late plays, his work carefully identifying the redeeming strokes of fortune that bring about restored vision.[8] The strong redemptive theme at work invites one to consider the historical context of the play, standing at the moment when the Old Testament gives way to the New.[9] While I do not explore the implications of the birth of Christ in this work, it is worth noting the great redemptive promise associated with this event.[10] Robin Moffet and Robert Miola contend that Shakespeare intends for *Cymbeline* to symbolize the movement from a pagan world to a Christian world. Although I have great respect for the work of Moffet and Miola, I do not agree that the play offers enough compelling evidence for this claim. The birth of Christ does indeed line up with Cymbeline's reign, but absolutely nothing is made of this event in the play. This leads me to believe that Shakespeare was not as much concerned about the ushering in of a new Christian era as he was about the nature of redemption newly and powerfully portrayed in Reformation literature.

Posthumus's moral blindness is first evidenced, as Ruth Nevo claims, when he allows himself to be separated from Innogen, leaving her "in virtual imprisonment in Britain."[11] As he leaves Britain, the only fight we witness from Posthumus is one in which he "rather play'd than fought" with Cloten.[12] Posthumus's moral depravity is further witnessed through his dealings with Iachimo and through the shallow faith he reveals to Innogen. Through his dealings with Iachimo, Posthumus takes on a most disturbing role of pimp, offering Innogen's "dearest bodily part" to the seductive influences of his rival (*Cymbeline* 1.5.158). Prior to striking the horrible wager with Iachimo, Posthumus is revealed by the Frenchman as a man of poor judgment. The Frenchman reveals the fact that this is not the first time Posthumus has entered into a debate over the issue of Innogen's chastity:

> **Frenchman:** . . . this gentleman at that time
> vouching—and upon warrant of bloody
> affirmation—his [Innogen] to be more fair, virtuous,
> wise,
> chaste, constant-qualified and less attemptable
> than any the rarest of our ladies in France.
> (*Cymbeline* 1.4.375–79)

The Frenchman's comment is important in that it reveals the fact that Posthumus is concerned about Innogen's virtue. His great concern reveals what proves to be a deep insecurity, and as his history contests, this insecurity has the potential of drawing Posthumus into a violent rage. Posthumus reveals far too much enthusiasm about winning a ridiculous argument over the chastity of the women in his country. Worse yet, the bet falls onto his wife, and Posthumus allows Innogen to become the guinea pig in this horrifying test. While there seems no fit climate for this kind of exchange, the fact that Posthumus enters the wager for a second time is certain evidence of his moral depravity. His poor judgment is further highlighted by the Frenchman's ability to recognize the debate over female chastity as something "slight and trivial" (*Cymbeline* 1.4.361):

> **Frenchman:** Sir, you o'er-rate my poor kindness: I was glad I
> did atone my countryman and you; it had been pity
> you should have been put together with so mortal a
> purpose as then each bore, upon importance of so
> slight and trivial a nature.
>
> (*Cymbeline* 1.4.357–61)

Posthumus, still convinced of the nobility of the cause, corrects the Frenchman, claiming that the "quarrel was not altogether slight" (*Cymbeline* 1.4.366). It is on this cue that the cunning Iachimo seizes an opportunity to take advantage of Posthumus's poor moral vision. Shakespeare stages this scene in a way in which Posthumus cannot win, for in the end he commands Iachimo to exercise "free entertainment" with Innogen (*Cymbeline* 1.5.163). In spite of all this, John Alvis and others contend that Posthumus "represents the plight of the good man in a bad regime."[13] Alvis further declares, "No reliable observer has anything to say against [Posthumus'] character."[14] Whether or not his bride proves faithful, Posthumus must be recognized as the villain in this exchange by setting his wife up for a violent encounter with a stranger:

> **Iachimo:** I will lay you ten thousand ducats to your
> ring that, commend me to the court where your
> lady is, with no more advantage than the opportunity
> of a second conference, and I will bring from
> thence that honour of hers which you imagine so
> reserved.
>
> **Posthumus:** I will wage against your gold, gold to it.
> My ring I hold dear as my finger; 'tis part of it.

Iachimo: . . . If I bring you no sufficient
testimony that I have enjoyed the dearest
bodily part of your mistress, my ten thousand
ducats are yours; so is your diamond too. If I come
off and leave her in such honour as you have trust
in, she your jewel, this your jewel, and my gold are
yours, provided I have your commendation for my
more free entertainment.
Posthumus: I embrace these conditions.

(*Cymbeline* 1.4.134–64)

Iachimo's encounter with Innogen is important in that it helps to expose more of Posthumus's depravity. Where Posthumus fails miserably, Innogen succeeds brilliantly. The exchange that most clearly displays Innogen's moral fortitude begins with Iachimo's cunning scheme to stir up jealousy in her mind:

Iachimo: —to be partner'd
With tomboys hired with that self-exhibition
Which your own coffers yield! with diseased ventures
That play with all infirmities for gold
Which rottenness can lend nature! such boil'd stuff
As well might poison poison! Be revenged;
Or she that bore you was no queen, and you
Recoil from your great stock.

(*Cymbeline* 1.6.747–54)

Seeking to dismantle Innogen's high opinion of Posthumus, Iachimo begins by claiming that Posthumus is not depressed about his banishment. Instead, Iachimo claims that Posthumus is running about the town, investing in all kinds of "diseased ventures" and finding great pleasure in all kinds of disreputable places (*Cymbeline* 1.6.146). Innogen's response reveals a great sense of discernment, claiming that she must protect her heart from the things she hears:

Innogen: Revenged!
How should I be revenged? If this be true,—
As I have such a heart that both mine ears

Must not in haste abuse—if it be true,
How should I be revenged?

(*Cymbeline* 1.6.153–57)

The context within which she frames her question must lead the reader to assume that Innogen's tone is not desperate and that she is not actually seeking Iachimo's counsel. Innogen is shocked and appalled by Iachimo's suggestion of revenge, an interpretation that is supported by her swift dismissal of Iachimo in the very next exchange. While Innogen may not have been anticipating his sexual advance, she was determined to proceed slowly and thoughtfully, being careful not to allow the poisonous news to affect her heart and thereby keep her from seeing the truth:

Iachimo: Revenge it.
I dedicate myself to your sweet pleasure,
More noble than that runagate to your bed,
And will continue fast to your affection,
Still close as sure.
Innogen: What, ho, Pisanio!
Iachimo: Let me my service tender on your lips.
Innogen: Away! I do condemn mine ears that have
So long attended thee. If thou wert honourable,
Thou wouldst have told this tale for virtue, not
For such an end thou seek'st,—as base as strange.
Thou wrong'st a gentleman, who is as far
From thy report as thou from honour, and
Solicit'st here a lady that disdains
Thee and the devil alike. What ho, Pisanio!

(*Cymbeline* 1.6.160–81)

The moment she discerns that Iachimo is a villain, Innogen cries out for Pisanio. Her heart is unaffected by the news he has brought, and her deep faith in Posthumus is kept intact. Innogen clearly seeks to protect the faith she has built up in Posthumus, not allowing the poisonous gossip of a stranger to disrupt her trust. The juxtaposition of Innogen's character and Posthumus's character serves to expose her husband's weak moral vision.

Innogen's clear vision, illustrated by her ability to detect and deconstruct Iachimo's lies, provides an important contrast to Posthumus's blindness. The ease with which Posthumus is deceived by Iachimo is ridiculous, the foolishness all the more exposed by Philario's scolding. It only takes Iachimo a few moments to dismantle the weak trust Posthumus has in Innogen. After Iachimo describes the roof of Innogen's bedchamber, Posthumus cries out in a great distress, "This is her honour?" (*Cymbeline* 2.4.115). He is drawn into a rage of murderous proportions much like that of Othello. The Moor is drawn into tight bonds of jealousy, casting off his commitment to Desdemona and vowing for her blood when he hears that she has given Cassio his handkerchief. Othello cries, "O that the Slave had forty thousand lives: / One is too poore, too weake for my revenge."[15] Like Othello, Posthumus is easily convinced of his beloved's dishonor when Iachimo reveals that he has procured Innogen's bracelet. It is this evidence and Iachimo's simple suggestions that reveal Posthumus's shallow faith in Innogen. Even with the guidance of Philario, who seeks to shake Posthumus from investing in Iachimo's tale too readily, Posthumus allows his heart to be "in haste" abused by the poisonous news (*Cymbeline* 1.6.155)[16]:

Philario: Have patience, sir,
And take your ring again; 'tis not yet won:
It may be probable she lost it; or
Who knows if one of her women, being corrupted,
Hath stol'n it from her?

(*Cymbeline* 2.4.143–47)

This exchange is constructed to reveal Posthumus's lack of patience, his inability to discern the probable, and his near-fatal gullibility. Later in the play, Posthumus's poor discernment will plague him once again when, like Othello, he receives a spotted handkerchief. Philario continues to warn Posthumus but is cut off before he can rally his friend's crumbling faith:

Philario: Sir, be patient:
This is not strong enough to be believed
Of one persuaded well of—

(*Cymbeline* 2.4.164–66)

As Philario tries to claim, and as is clearly revealed, Posthumus is not "persuaded well of" Innogen's love, nor is he equipped with the proper moral vision to navigate his way through this situation (*Cymbeline* 2.4.166). Thomas Betteridge notes that the importance of Philario's interjection in this scene is that it gives an additional opportunity for Posthumus to draw back from the brink of disaster. This kind of mind-clearing opportunity is not afforded to Othello, who is drawn into such a delirium that he loses consciousness under the influence of Iago's deceit. Posthumus, even after a strong and clear warning from Philario, does not "pull back from the brink,"[17] as Betteridge writes, but he chooses a course in which he "accepts the commodification of Innogen."[18] I disagree with Glenn Arbery, who suggests that Shakespeare stages Iachimo as a destroyer of faith, a villain for whom victory is not "actual enjoyment of Imogen, then, but this destruction of faith, which takes the form of physical revulsion and which leads to Posthumus' design on Imogen's life."[19] It seems to me, rather, that Shakespeare purposefully handicaps Iachimo's villainous skill so as to place the focus of the blame on Posthumus. While the audience marvels at the masterful quality of Iago's evil in *Othello*, in *Cymbeline* the audience must scoff at the fragility of Posthumus's faith and discernment.[20] Lacking Iago's malice and demonic manipulation, Iachimo is clearly playing a game with Posthumus. This simple game yields the same result as Iago's masterful plotting, a comparison that Shakespeare makes more powerful by having both Othello and Posthumus vow to tear their wives to pieces.[21]

From Philario's insistence that the "government of patience" does not rule over Posthumus's mind to Pisanio's recognition of a "strange infection" within Posthumus's ear, a great gentleman is humiliated before his peers and servants (*Cymbeline* 2.4.192; 3.2.3). In the opening scene of act 5, we witness Posthumus's humbling confession and the beginning of new vision. Upon receipt of a cloth that was meant to bear witness to Pisanio's murder of Innogen, Posthumus's pride is broken, and his confession reveals new insight and wisdom:

Posthumus: Yea, bloody cloth, I'll keep thee, for I wish'd
Thou shouldst be colour'd thus. You married ones,

If each of you should take this course, how many
Must murder wives much better than themselves
For wrying but a little! O Pisanio!
Every good servant does not all commands:
No bond but to do just ones. Gods! if you
Should have ta'en vengeance on my faults, I never
Had lived to put on this: so had you saved
The noble Innogen to repent, and struck
Me, wretch more worth your vengeance.
(*Cymbeline* 5.1.1–11)

Although he is once again guilty of trusting weak evidence, it is clear that Posthumus has moved from a place of arrogant blindness to a place of greater moral clarity. While his discernment is still impoverished, in this passage it is evident that Posthumus recognizes the humble state of mankind, confessing that he is not fit to judge or to deal out such violent penalties for sin. It is my contention that Posthumus's movement from murderous jealousy to humble contrition is in fact the most miraculous action of the play. Even before he understands Innogen to be innocent of infidelity, Posthumus begins to see with a divine sense of clarity. Though he is not guilty of the sexual sin and infidelity he suspects of Innogen, his recognition of the culpability of all mankind is a recognition that Reformation theologians would claim could only be arrived at by a divine encounter. In *The Book of Homilies*, a volume of sermons officially sanctioned by both Edward VI and Elizabeth I, the editors describe the importance of the type of recognition that Posthumus experiences: "Let vs also knowledge the exceeding mercy of GOD towards vs, and confesse, that as of our selues commeth all euill and damnation: so likewise of him commeth all goodnesse and saluation, as GOD himselfe sayth by the Prophet Osee, O Israel, thy destruction commeth of thy selfe, but in me only is thy helpe and comfort" (Hos. 13:9).[22] Posthumus follows his confession by stripping himself of the trappings of a gentleman and by taking on the form of a peasant:

Posthumus: That, Britain, I have kill'd thy mistress; peace!
I'll give no wound to thee. Therefore, good heavens,
Hear patiently my purpose: I'll disrobe me

> Of these Italian weeds and suit myself
> As does a Briton peasant: so I'll fight
> Against the part I come with; so I'll die
> For thee, O Innogen, even for whom my life
> Is every breath a death; and thus, unknown,
> Pitied nor hated, to the face of peril
> Myself I'll dedicate.
>
> (*Cymbeline* 5.1.20–29)

Posthumus vows to give his life for Innogen and sacrifice himself for the welfare of Britain. It is in this moment that Posthumus's faith in Innogen is restored and he is redeemed. Harold Goddard claims that it is here that Posthumus "discards his Italian weeds forever."[23] Finally abandoning his reckless view of women,[24] Posthumus sees himself as one who is neither pitied nor hated and whose life must be lived for another. Peter Platt calls this an "astonishing soliloquy,"[25] for before knowing that Innogen is innocent, Posthumus is "able to call her noble."[26] This scene is reminiscent of *King Lear*. It is at Lear's most humbling moment that his great kingly robes are torn from his body, and he cries out in anguish:

> **Lear:** Thou must be patient. We came crying hither:
> Thou knowst the first time that we smell the air
> We wawl and cry. I will preach to thee: mark me.
> **Gloucester:** Alack, alack the day!
> **Lear:** When we are born we cry that we are come
> To this great stage of fools.
>
> (*Cymbeline* 4.6.174–79)

Posthumus and Lear share a common understanding of their place before men and before the gods. It is their common moral blindness that lands Posthumus and Lear in such humbling positions, and yet each is redeemed through the experience. Both are lowered from places of royalty and power, influence and prestige, to be faced with the humbling recognition of their own vulnerability.

After fighting on behalf of Britain, Posthumus turns himself in to the British forces. Thinking him a Roman, the soldiers throw Posthumus into prison and sentence him to death by hanging. While bound in prison, Posthumus has an experience with the divine. His humble prayer is followed and perhaps rewarded by a supernatural visitation that confirms his proper posture before God. Posthumus prays:

Posthumus: Is't enough I am sorry?
So children temporal fathers do appease;
Gods are more full of mercy. Must I repent?
I cannot do it better than in gyves,
Desired more than constrain'd: to satisfy,
If of my freedom 'tis the main part, take
No stricter render of me than my all.
I know you are more clement than vile men,
Who of their broken debtors take a third,
A sixth, a tenth, letting them thrive again
On their abatement: that's not my desire:
For Innogen's dear life take mine . . .

(*Cymbeline* 5.4.13–24)

Posthumus questions the nature of repentance and reveals a profound understanding of divine grace and mercy. His question, "Is't enough I am sorry?" (*Cymbeline* 5.4.13), puts him in a place beside some of the most famous Reformation thinkers. It was the nature of grace and mercy that Luther sought to clarify, particularly the New Testament doctrine surrounding repentance that he found in Paul's letter to the Romans. Paul writes with much passion, echoing some of the same concerns that Posthumus voices in this scene. Paul writes, "For what I am doing, I do not understand; for I am not practicing what I would like to do, but I am doing the very thing I hate . . . For the good that I want, I do not do, but I practice the very evil that I do not want . . . Wretched man that I am! Who will set me free from the body of this death?"[27] Paul explains that it is through the death of Christ and his own symbolic death to sin that he is saved. Posthumus's insistence that his death will make things right strikes an interesting parallel with the words of Paul's New Testament letter: "What shall we say then? Are we to continue in sin so that grace may increase? May it never be . . . all of us who have been baptized into Christ Jesus have been baptized into his death . . . therefore we have been buried with him through baptism into death, so that as Christ was raised from the dead through the glory of the Father, so we too might walk in newness of life."[28] Posthumus's insistence that his death and what he calls the sacrifice of his freedom bears a strong resemblance to the insistence that Paul makes regarding the death of sinful men. Although Posthumus expresses the belief that he must make a literal sacrifice—a remnant of Roman Catholic works theology, perhaps—the sacrifice that is ultimately demanded of him is symbolic, much like the death described by Paul. Posthumus's sacrifice is of a spiritual nature, one that he makes through an experience of redemptive humiliation. Posthumus is brought to a place of humility where he is able to recognize his great sin and shame. Though the importance of humility before God was emphasized by all the major Protestant Reformers, the sixteenth-century English Reformer William Perkins became famous for his own story of humiliation, in which he describes how God "initiated" the kind of conviction that "stripped away his pride."[29] Following this Reformation model, Posthumus is humiliated and thereby recognizes that he deserves death and damnation, and yet it is on recognition of this fact that he is redeemed. Posthumus is clearly emptied of pride, an act for which Jupiter takes full responsibility:

> **Jupiter:** No more, you petty spirits of region low,
> Offend our hearing! Hush! How dare you ghosts
> Accuse the Thunderer, whose bolt, you know,
> Sky-planted, batters all rebelling coasts.
> . . . Be not with mortal accidents oppressed.
> No care of yours it is; you know 'tis ours.
> Whom best I love I cross, to make my gift,
> The more delayed, delighted. Be content.
> (*Cymbeline* 5.4.95–98, 101–4)

Jupiter's explanation is far too closely tied to a Reformation understanding of salvation to be ignored.[30] Taking full control of the salvation of men, Jupiter confesses to crossing men for the purpose of saving them. It was this shift of responsibility and control that the Reformers made much of. With the emphasis taken off of the works of men, the Reformers insisted that God alone could save.

Because of the depravity of mankind, individuals were unable to save themselves or to navigate themselves toward the path of salvation. Therefore it was in God's power to save men and women, and as stated by Jupiter, the method always involved bringing men and women into a proper understanding of self, others, and the divine. This process required what the Reformers described as a redemptive humiliation, a moment when a man or woman was able to see their great need for a redeemer. Calvin describes redemption coming on a man or woman in this way:

> Yet, when that light of divine providence has once shone upon a godly man, he is then relieved and set free not only from the extreme anxiety and fear that were pressing him before, but from every care. For as he justly dreads fortune, so he fearlessly dares commit himself to God. His solace, I say, is to know that his Heavenly Father so holds all things in his power, so rules by his authority and will, so governs by his wisdom, that nothing can befall except he determine it. Moreover, it comforts him to know that he has been received into God's safekeeping and entrusted to the care of his angels, and that neither water, nor fire, nor iron can harm him, except in so far as it pleases God as governor to give them occasion.[31]

Ironically, Posthumus seems to understand the nature of grace and mercy far better than his parents as they are portrayed in the dream. In this dream, Posthumus's family begs and pleads for Jupiter's mercy, not knowing that he crosses those he loves and therefore humiliates those he chooses to redeem. In *Acts and Monuments*, John Foxe describes what he believes to be the nature of God and divine correction. Foxe's description is compatible with the kind of god that Shakespeare stages in Jupiter. Foxe provides three examples of God's "scourging of his favorites to enable them to suffer so as to achieve wisdom."[32] Posthumus dares not plead with Jupiter for mercy, for he is convinced that he deserves nothing but death. It is this posture, this clear view of self, that sets Posthumus up as an ideal Reformation saint. Finally "relieved and set free . . . from every care,"[33] as stated by Calvin, Posthumus bears the markings of one who has been redeemed.

The transformation we witness in Posthumus is clearly remarkable—something Shakespeare would certainly not have wanted his audience to miss. Jupiter's engagement with Posthumus's family in many ways serves to highlight Posthumus's newfound nobility and honor. While Posthumus's parents plead for his life, he offers his up. While Posthumus's parents seem nervous about the mercilessness of the divine, Posthumus confesses a great confidence in the mercy of God. The interaction with Jupiter, woven with Reformation theology, confirms Posthumus's clarity of vision and his restored connection with the divine. In an essay that confers great importance on the nature of Posthumus's sleep, Margaret Jones-Davies marks this exchange as one that "awakens Posthumus to faith."[34] While Ros King argues that Jupiter rejects the petitions of Posthumus's family because the god considers them "miserable worms who should not be disturbing his godhead,"[35] she misses a rich connection to Reformation theology in this passage. Richard Harp comes closer to the mark in his analysis of Boethius's philosophy within *Cymbeline*, writing that Shakespeare's Jupiter foretells "how suffering may lead to a good end."[36] While Harp locates the divine element, he and Ros King overlook the personal nature of Jupiter's rebuke. In what appears to be a strongly Reformational context, Jupiter offers Posthumus's family an assurance that he is in control and that they have nothing to fear. Shakespeare makes a sharp diversion from a traditional view of the gods, who are shown more often as uncaring and uninterested in the affairs of men. In this play, however, Shakespeare stages Jupiter as a compassionate deity, claiming to discipline those he loves. The nature of Jupiter's personality seems to be modeled after a Reformation reading of the Old and New Testaments.

In the Old Testament, we witness the scolding of Job. In the biblical story extensively employed by Luther to explain the nature of salvation and the process of redemption, God appears before Job in much the same way that Jupiter appears before Posthumus and his family. God answers Job's complaints out of a whirlwind and a violent storm, scolding him with these words:

> Who is this that darkens counsel
> By words without knowledge?
> . . . Where were you when I laid the foundation of the earth!

> Tell Me, if you have understanding . . .
> Have you ever in your life commanded the morning,
> And caused the dawn to know its place . . .
> Who has given to Me that I should repay him?
> Whatever is under the whole heaven is Mine.
> I will not keep silence concerning [My creation].[37]

Luther writes extensively about Job and the humiliation he suffers: "The example of Job in his humiliation and affliction teaches the same. For in this wonderful manner the Lord treats His saint (Ps. 4:3), namely, when we think that it is all over with us, He embraces and kisses us as His dearest sons."[38] There is violence in the words of Jupiter and the Christian God, yet both deities discipline their subjects with a promise of redemption. In perfect Reformation form, Jupiter demands that his subjects come to a place of proper perspective, understanding that he is great and glorious and that they are humble and low. In the passage in Job, we find a similar divine injunction, demanding proper respect from Job. God's questioning of Job results in his humiliation, allowing him to understand his place in the universe more clearly.

In the New Testament, we find an injunction against anxiety, delivered by Jesus, that bears a strong resemblance to Jupiter's injunction in *Cymbeline*. The tone Jesus takes in this passage is one that certainly humbled those whom he addressed: "And which of you by worrying can add a single hour to his life's span? If then you cannot do even a very little thing, why do you worry about other matters? Consider the lilies, how they grow: they neither toil nor spin; but I tell you, not even Solomon in all his glory clothed himself like one of these . . . you men of little faith . . . do not keep worrying . . . your Father knows that you need these things . . . Do not be afraid, little flock."[39] Martin Luther comments on the themes in this passage, his objective to cause men to acknowledge the power and presence of God in human affairs. His concern is focused on the correction of what he believed was a false understanding of God's mercy and strength, a strength that Jupiter exclaims to those that clearly doubt him and fear disaster. Luther writes:

> [God] demonstrated how he has laid up for us at all times a sufficient store of food and clothing, even before we ask him for it. All we need to do is to work and avoid idleness; then we shall certainly be fed and clothed. But a pitiful unbelief refuses to admit this. The unbeliever sees, comprehends, and feels all the same that even if he worries himself to death over it, he can neither produce nor maintain a single grain of wheat in the field. He knows too that even though all his storehouses were full to overflowing, he could not make use of a single morsel or thread unless God sustains him in life and health and preserves to him his possessions. Yet this has no effect upon him.[40]

As one who has been redeemed, Posthumus has the clarity of mind to understand the nature of the divine. He seems to understand, as Hamlet boldly confesses, that "there's a divinity that shapes our ends."[41] Posthumus's moral clarity is witnessed by the gaoler in act 5 when he claims, "Your death has eyes in's head" (*Cymbeline* 5.4.177–78). In terms of moral and emotional vision, this exchange between Posthumus and the gaoler is of great importance:

> **Gaoler:** You must either
> be directed by some that take upon them to
> know, or to take upon yourself that which I am
> sure you do not know, or jump the after-inquiry
> on your own peril . . .
>
> (*Cymbeline* 5.4.183–86)

The gaoler recognizes the strength of vision in Posthumus, who confesses to know where his eternal destiny lies. Robin Moffet claims that Posthumus, after "reaching an ultimate point of destitution . . . finds his life worthless and desperate until he has offered it to the gods."[42] With Posthumus's new spiritual vision, he bears a great confidence about his eternal destiny. He responds in this way:

> **Posthumus:** I tell thee, fellow, there are none
> Want eyes to direct them the way I am going, but
> Such as wink and will not use them.
>
> (*Cymbeline* 5.4.189–91)

In this passage, Shakespeare employs "wink" in such a way as to describe those who close their eyes to danger and fearfully or ignorantly refuse to look on that which is dreadful and threatening. Posthumus claims to be able to look boldly at death, to see it and approach it with the confidence of the redeemed. The gaoler is clearly not accustomed to this kind of boldness, nor to what appears a peaceful resignation to the will of the gods:

> **Gaoler:** What an infinite mock is this, that a man
> should have the best use of eyes to see the way of blindness! I am sure hanging's the way of winking.
> (*Cymbeline* 5.4.192–94)

After Posthumus is released from prison, he is brought before the king. Posthumus humbles himself here, confessing that he is guilty of crimes against Innogen: "Ay me, most credulous fool, / Egregious murderer, thief" (*Cymbeline* 5.5.247–48). Posthumus admits that he deserves to be executed, declaring "Every villain / Be called Posthumus Leonatus" (*Cymbeline* 5.5.260–61).

Posthumus is humbled for his poor moral vision, and the events that bring him to his knees are the very events that lead to his ultimate redemption. This process is identified by Peggy Simonds as a key component of Renaissance tragicomedy. She writes, "Tragicomedy dramatizes personal reform and a redeeming act of faith as part of a spiritual initiation rite . . . reform then becomes the primary motif of the tragicomedy . . . [before one is redeemed] one must die to the sensory world . . . In Christian terms, the old Adam must first die so that the new or redeemed Adam may be born."[43] While Simonds's argument is worth consideration as it deals with the death of pride and arrogance, she fails to recognize the strains of Martin Luther's theology in Shakespeare's text and the vital role humiliation plays in the redemption of Posthumus. Simonds borrows heavily from Arthur Kirsch's work in the area of Christian redemption, but each critic fails to make the key connections between the theology of the Protestant Reformation and Shakespeare's redemptive theme. Simonds joins J. P. Brockbank, Robin Moffet, Homer Swander, and Howard Felperin by arguing that in *Cymbeline* the world of the play "is undergoing a psychological and spiritual preparation for the birth of the Good Shepherd or Christ."[44] It would be more accurate to claim, however, that the play is a reenactment of the Reformation theory of redemption. Posthumus suffers through humiliating events, and through this pain, he receives new life and therefore new vision. As a man who displays great moral blindness at the beginning of the play, Posthumus is reduced to humble questioning and a healthy sense of dependence. It is the redemptive humiliation of Reformation theology that has bled into the fabric of Shakespeare's *Cymbeline*, thereby giving this tragicomedy greater historical and theological power.

Conclusion

In a contemporary context, humiliation is equated with an attack on one's dignity. In its Reformation context, however, a startling majority of Shakespeare's tragedies and late plays reveal humiliation as an elevating experience. The humiliation of Gertrude allows the queen the opportunity to find reconciliation with her much-troubled son, Hamlet. Prospero's humiliation serves to correct his misplaced priorities, a correction that prepares him for his reinstatement as Duke of Milan. For Lear, humiliation draws him out of his narcissistic slumber, helping him finally "see better."[1] This new vision gives Lear the ability to recognize the great love Cordelia has for him. In *Henry VIII*, humiliation sets Cardinal Wolsey on a new path, away from the lust for recognition and toward reconciliation and reformation. Humiliation saves Leontes in *The Winter's Tale* from further acts of violence, ultimately allowing for the reunion of his family. Posthumus, after being painfully humiliated in *Cymbeline*, is given a new vision of grace for himself and others. This new reliance on grace, one must conclude, will result in a reformation of his relationship with Innogen. As the curtain falls on *Othello*, though the stage is strewn with dead bodies, the great general takes his last breath with full assurance of the truth. Having stumbled through the play in a deadly fog, Othello emerges in the end as his best self, cognizant of his frailties and yet also aware that he had been in possession of the truest of loves.

In a truly Reformed context, the negative consequences of humiliation must be recognized as insignificant compared to the less ephemeral and more eternal consequences of such an experience. In strong agreement about the necessity of redemptive humiliation,

Reformation theologians of the fifteenth and sixteenth centuries make it very clear that men and women must recognize their lowly state before a most high God; this recognition must come before they can experience redemption. Luther, Calvin, and Hooker each write about the clarity, both natural and supernatural, that humans experience when they are in proper posture before God. For the great majority of Reformers this proper posture is acquired or proven not through external works but by an internal work of the heart. This internal work is achieved when a man or woman experiences humiliation. In his commentary on Galatians, Luther writes that we must not "trust in our own righteousness" and that we must recognize the "uncleanness of the flesh."[2] This humbling recognition causes us not to work for salvation but rather to "hang our heads"[3] and give up all faith in our own ability to redeem ourselves. This kind of humiliation, declares Luther, causes a man or woman to seek God in faith. In the opening pages of *The Institutes of the Christian Religion*, Calvin explains that redemptive humiliation, "our feeling of ignorance, vanity, want, weakness, in short, depravity and corruption,"[4] miraculously leads us to adopt a proper view of ourselves and of God. Similarly, Hooker, in his *Laws of Ecclesiastical Polity*, explains the necessity of a humble posture by declaring that "[God] is above, and we upon earth; therefore it behoveth our words to be wary and few."[5]

Although they enjoy the natural benefits of redemptive humiliation, some more briefly than others, many of Shakespeare's humiliated characters are not aware of their spiritual redemption. Shakespeare draws his audience into the performance by making them the only people in the theater who know that the humiliated characters are redeemed. Aware of the religious controversy that swirled around his playhouse, Shakespeare works with the knowledge he knows his audience possesses. By such subtle means, Shakespeare creates an entire theater full of actors. The audience-turned-players, it seems, are employed to use their theological knowledge, and perhaps their preferences and prejudices, to engage in the action of the play. Touching on some of the most personal and also very public issues of his day, Shakespeare works with the unsettling religious issues of his time.

One of the most unsettling issues at the center of the Protestant–Roman Catholic debate involved a simple question:

How was a man or woman to be saved? As it involved the stripping of altars and the removal of a long tradition of religious customs and rites, the Reformation challenged the ways by which men and women could approach God. Christopher Haigh's description of the brutal transitioning from Roman Catholic to Protestant governance in the sixteenth and seventeenth centuries is especially important for my thesis. Haigh contends that Protestantism challenged the foundations of "works-religion," mocking those who, with simple-minded devotion, maintained adherence to Roman Catholicism.[6] The "hallowed routines" of the Catholic faith, being forbidden by the new Protestant authority, caused great cultural and religious strife.[7] It is such strife that Shakespeare seeks to touch in his tragedies and late plays, most notably by engaging such controversial Reformation views as the depravity of man and redemptive humiliation.

Roman Catholic theology most certainly declared that man was a sinful being, a recognition that made the payment of penance a very necessary part of the redemptive process. The notion that a man or woman could perform such acts of penance in order to earn redemption, however, was based on a view of the partial depravity of mankind. Partial depravity assumed that a man could perform good works, which would garner the pleasure and approval of God, thereby allowing a man to earn, at least in part, his salvation. The major Reformers, especially Martin Luther, attacked the notion that there was anything a man or woman could do to earn salvation. This controversial teaching is described in much recent criticism as having caused great tension in the early modern era.[8] Within this difficult shift in understanding, one that Haigh describes as a movement from "works religion" to "word religion,"[9] is the concept of humiliation. A confidence in works, long promoted by Roman Catholicism, is subjected to profound humiliation, whereby all confidence in the flesh is destroyed. On corporate and very private levels, men and women of Roman Catholic belief are asked to give up confidence in their works of righteousness and to recognize their total depravity. This demand, made by Protestantism, is a demand for the humiliation of the Christian. Painful as this demand may be, the Reformers explain that there are promises attached to the humiliation.

One of the promises that the major Reformation theologians claimed was attached to humiliation is clarity of vision. This clarity of vision provides the depraved man or woman with the miraculous ability to rise from crippling misunderstandings that are related to one's self-knowledge and to one's knowledge of others. The new vision promised by Reformers also bears with it a vital spiritual component, granting the newly humiliated an improved vision of the divine. Luther employs the metaphor of a sick man, equating the sick man's condition to that of a man who has a depraved soul. In this metaphor, the man who fails to recognize his sickness blames his doctor, claiming that the doctor is a fraud and not worthy of his professional title. Luther also tells the story of a sick man who accepts the doctor's diagnosis, a position that requires humility yet ultimately results in his ability to move toward health, for this man will obey the doctor and agree to the suggested remedy. Calvin explains that a man cannot hope to be able to see and understand things of a spiritual nature without the special intervention of God in his life. He would certainly argue that, like the sick man, the depraved man can only wait on God in a most humble posture if he hopes to be redeemed. Calvin cites the observation of Solomon: "The hearing ear, and the seeing eye, the Lord hath made even both of them."[10] Like Luther and Calvin, Hooker also affirms the clarity that results from the humiliation of a man or woman.

The subtle way in which Shakespeare weaves the powerful theme of redemption into the major tragedies and late plays reveals his true mastery. The strands of Reformation thought, evidenced in each character's experience with redemptive humiliation, are woven into the plays with subtlety. Reformation theologians declared that a man or woman must be broken before he or she could be redeemed. One must indeed have an experience of wonder, through which one acknowledges his or her great spiritual weakness. It is this experience—this humiliation and subsequent redemption—that restores Shakespeare's protagonists to their proper natures, natures that allow them to recognize their places before God and before humanity.

Notes

Introduction

1 Luther, Martin, *Luther's Works*, ed. Hilton C. Oswald (St. Louis: Concordia, 1972). Martin Luther's translation of the Bible (1522), sermons, and biblical commentary; Calvin, John, *Institutes of the Christian Religion* [1536], ed. John T. McNeill, trans. Ford Lewis Battles (Louisville: Westminster John Knox Press, 1960); Hooker, Richard, *The Works of That Learned and Judicious Divine Mr. Richard Hooker: With an Account of His Life and Death by Isaac Walton*, 6th ed., arranged by the Rev. John Keble MA (Oxford: Clarendon Press, 1960).

2 I will be working with the Hilton C. Oswald version of *Luther's Works*, ed. Hilton C. Oswald (Saint Louis: Concordia, 1972). For Luther on damning pride, see his commentary on the Psalms, especially volumes 12–14 (Pss. 51:13, 110:2, 37:1) and volume 25 (Rom. 15:33). I also employ John Calvin's *Institutes of the Christian Religion*. On damning pride, see especially chapters 1–5 for a very close look at Calvin's view. Of Richard Hooker's work, see especially "A Sermon of the Nature of Pride," in *The Works of That Learned and Judicious Divine Mr. Richard Hooker: With an Account of His Life and Death by Isaac Walton*, 6th ed., arranged by the Rev. John Keble MA (Oxford: Clarendon Press, 1874).

3 See essays on this subject by Dutton, Findlay, Miola, Wilson, Duffy, Milward, Kilroy, and others in *Theatre and Religion: Lancastrian Shakespeare*, ed. Richard Dutton, Alison Findlay, and Richard Wilson (Manchester: Manchester University Press, 2003); also Richard Wilson's *Secret Shakespeare: Studies in Theatre, Religion, and Resistance* (Manchester: Manchester University Press, 2004); and essays by David Beauregard and Richard Dutton in *Shakespeare and the Culture of Christianity in Early Modern England*, ed. Dennis Taylor and David Beauregard (New York: Fordham University Press, 2003).

4 Wells, Stanley, *A Dictionary of Shakespeare* (Oxford: Oxford University Press, 1998).

5 Ibid.

6 Both of these texts are employed by Richard Wilson in his "Introduction" to *Theatre and Religion*.

7 Bearman, Robert, "'Was William Shakespeare William Shakeshafte?' Revisited," *Shakespeare Quarterly* 53, no. 1 (2002): 83–94; Bearman, Robert, "John Shakespeare's 'Spiritual Testament': A Reappraisal," *Shakespeare Survey* 56 (2003). Robert Bearman points to an argument made in 1970 by Douglas Hamer. Bearman claims that Hamer's 1970 critical examination of Shakespeare's Lancashire connection has thus far gone unanswered and that Hamer's reservations regarding this connection must be satisfied before confidence can be placed on Shakespeare's Lancashire connection. Hamer claims that the name Shakeshafte was very common in Lancashire, "with a particular concentration in the area where Hoghton family influence was preeminent" (93). Hamer's "reservations concerning the compatibility of William Shakeshafte's age with that of William Shakespeare's also remain unanswered" (93).

8 Wilson, "Introduction," in *Theatre and Religion*, 17.

9 Taylor, Dennis, "Introduction: Shakespeare and the Reformation," in *Shakespeare and the Culture of Christianity in Early Modern England*, ed. Dennis Taylor and David Beauregard (New York: Fordham University Press, 2003), 20.

10 Frye, Roland, *Shakespeare and Christian Doctrine* (Princeton: Princeton University Press, 1963), 89.

11 Diehl, Huston, "Religion and Shakespearean Tragedy," in *The Cambridge Companion to Shakespearean Tragedy*, ed. Claire McEachern (Cambridge: Cambridge University Press, 2002), 91. See also Huston Diehl's *Staging Reform, Reforming the Stage: Protestantism and Popular Theater in Early Modem England* (Ithaca: Cornell University Press, 1997).

12 McEachern, Claire, and Shuger, Debora, *Religion and Culture in Renaissance England* (Cambridge: Cambridge University Press, 1997), 10.

13 Dickens, A. G., *The English Reformation* (London: BT Batsford, 1989), 206.

14 Tjernagel, Neelak S., *Henry VIII and the Lutherans* (St. Louis: Concordia, 1965), 70–72.

15 Starkey, David, *The Reign of Henry VIII: Personalities and Politics* (London: George Philip, 1985), 165.

16 MacCulloch, Diarmaid, "Henry VIII and the Reform of the Church," in *The Reign of Henry VIII: Politics, Policy, and Piety*, ed. Diarmaid MacCulloch (New York: St. Martin's Press, 1995), 180.

17 Dickens, *English Reformation*, 207.

18 Ibid., 339.

19 Shell, Alison, *Catholicism, Controversy and the English Literary Imagination, 1558–1660* (Cambridge: Cambridge University Press, 1999); Haigh,

Christopher, *English Reformations: Religion, Politics, and Society under the Tudors* (Oxford: Clarendon Press, 1993); Duffy, Eamon, *The Stripping of the Altars: Traditional Religion in England 1400–1580* (London: Yale University Press, 1992). Also see essays by Dutton, Wilson, and Findlay in *Region, Religion, and Patronage: Lancastrian Shakespeare* (Manchester: Manchester University Press, 2003).

20 Maas, Korey, Oxford University, personal interview with author, September 6, 2003.

21 Noble, Richmond, *Shakespeare's Biblical Knowledge* (New York: Octagon Books, 1970), 7.

22 Dickens, *English Reformation*, 344.

23 Marx, Steven, *Shakespeare and the Bible* (Oxford: Oxford University Press, 2000), 1.

24 Secor, Philip B., *Richard Hooker Prophet of Anglicanism and Son of Exeter* (London: Burns & Oates, 1999), http://www.exeter-cathedral.org.uk/Clergy/Hooker.html.

25 St. Mary's Drayton Beauchamp is in Hertfordshire, Temple Church is in London, Salisbury Cathedral is in Salisbury, and St. Mary's Bishopsbourne is just outside of Canterbury.

26 McGrade, A. S., "Hooker, Richard (1554–1600)," *Oxford Dictionary of National Biography* (Oxford: Oxford University Press, 2004), http://www.oxforddnb.com/view/article/13696; Kirby, W. J. Torrance, ed., *Richard Hooker and the English Reformation* (Norwell: Kluwer Academic, 2003); MacCulloch, Diarmaid, "Richard Hooker's Reputation," in *English Historical Review*, ed. W. J. T. Kirby (Oxford: Oxford University Press, 2002), cxvii, 473.

27 Frye, *Christian Doctrine*, 88.

28 Luther, *Works*, vol. 25, pp. 202–3.

29 Ibid., 204.

30 *The Catholic Encyclopedia*, ed. Kevin Knight (Denver: New Advent Press, 2012), accessed 17 July 2017, http://www.newadvent.org/cathen/index.html.

31 Luther, *Works*, vol. 10, Psalm 72:5.

32 Ibid.

33 Shakespeare, William, *Pericles*, ed. Germaine Greer and Anthony Burgess (Glasgow: HarperCollins, 1994), 1.1.42. References are to act, scene, and line.

34 Ibid., 1.1.45.

35 Luther, *Works*, vol. 35, p. 173. Luther compares the biblical law to a mirror that shows men and women who they are, depraved and unable to save themselves. Hamlet employs Luther's mirror metaphor in his confrontation with his mother, Gertrude. Hamlet's employment of the mirror resounds powerfully with Pericles's explanation.

36 Shakespeare, *Pericles*, 1.1.47.
37 Ibid., 2.4.9.
38 Ibid., 5.3.96–97.
39 Shakespeare, William, *Hamlet*, ed. Harold Jenkins (London: Thomson Learning, 2003), 3.4.175. References are to act, scene, and line.
40 Ibid., 3.2.389.
41 Shakespeare, William, *The Tempest*, ed. Germaine Greer and Anthony Burgess (Glasgow: HarperCollins, 1994), 1.2.146. References are to act, scene, and line.
42 Ibid., 1.2.63.
43 Holinshed, Raphael, "Chronicles of England, Scotland, and Ireland" (1587), in the Signet Classic edition of *The Famous History of the Life of King Henry VIII*, ed. S. Schoenbaum (New York: Penguin, 2004), 371.
44 Boswell-Stone, W. G., *Shakespeare's Holinshed: The Chronicle and the Historical Plays Compared* (New York: Benjamin Blom, 1966), 482.
45 Shakespeare, William, *Othello*, ed. E. A. J. Honigmann (London: Thomson Learning, 2003), 5.2.347. References are to act, scene, and line.
46 Ibid., 4.1.44.
47 Ibid., 4.1.261, 266.
48 Shakespeare, William, *The Winter's Tale*, ed. J. H. P. Pafford (London: Thomson Learning, 2005), 1.2.297–98. References are to act, scene, and line.
49 Ibid., 1.2.298.
50 Ibid., 3.2.3.

Chapter 1: *Hamlet*

1 Calvin, *Institutes*, vol. 20. Also see Luther, *Works*, vol. 42, pp. 42–43.
2 Ibid., 1:1:1.
3 Bloom, Harold, *Shakespeare: The Invention of the Human* (New York: Riverhead, 1998), 385.
4 Ibid., 714.
5 Taylor, "Introduction," 20; Diehl, "Religion and Shakespearean Tragedy," 91. See also Diehl's *Staging Reform*; McEachern and Shuger, *Religion and Culture*.
6 Melanchthon, Philip, *The Loci Communes 1543*, trans. J. A. O. Preus (St. Louis: Concordia, 1944), 83.
7 Davidson, Clifford, "Dr. Faustus of Wittenberg," *Studies in Philology* 59 (1962): 517.
8 Sohmer, Steve, "Certain Speculations on *Hamlet*, the Calendar, and Martin Luther," *Early Modern Literary Studies* 2, no. 1 (1996), http://purl.oclc.org/emls/02-1/sohmshak.html. Steve Sohmer locates an interesting connection

between Shakespeare's naming of Marcellus and a particular Roman Catholic feast. Roman Catholic history celebrates the life and death of Marcellus the Centurion, a soldier who "converted to Christianity and subsequently refused to engage in violence." The feast of Marcellus the Centurion was the first of a series of feasts that took place in late October every year. The Feast of Marcellus was followed by the vigils of All Hallows' Eve, All Saints' Day, and All Souls' Day. It was during this time of year, from October 30 to November 2, that "spirits of the dead were thought to return to visit their earthly homes." Traditional Roman Catholic belief held that the Feast of Marcellus, in particular, was "associated with the bond between the living and the dead." While these details do not play prominently into my argument here, it is clear that Shakespeare was seeking to draw his audience into thoughts about the living and the dead, the spiritual and the eternal, in his composition of *Hamlet*.

9 Matthew 16:23 (ESV).

10 Although described in a variety of ways, Hamlet's "ability to draw conclusions in regard to the state of his own mind and soul" is found in these and many more: Barker, Francis, "Pre-Pepysian Theatre: A Challenged Spectacle," *The Tremulous Private Body* (Ann Arbor: University of Michigan Press, 1984); Bloom, Harold, ed., *Modern Critical Interpretations: William Shakespeare's Hamlet* (New York: Chelsea House, 1986); Lowell, James Russell, "Shakespeare Once More," in *Major Literary Characters: Hamlet*, ed. Harold Bloom (New York: Chelsea House, 1990); Bloom, Harold, *Hamlet: Poem Unlimited* (New York: Riverhead, 2003).

11 Marlowe, Christopher, *Doctor Faustus*, A- and B-texts, ed. David Bevington and Eric Rasmussen (Oxford: Oxford University Press, 1995). "A surfeit of deadly sin" appears in the A-text (1604) 5.2.11. While there is much debate about the exact publishing date of Marlowe's *Faustus*, I find myself convinced of the 1588 dating by Lisa Hopkins in her text, *Christopher Marlowe: A Literary Life* (Hampshire: Palgrave, 2000).

12 Melanchthon, *Loci Communes*, 82.

13 Davidson, "Dr. Faustus," 517.

14 Jardine, Lisa, *Still Harping on Daughters: Women and Drama in the Age of Shakespeare* (New York: Harvester Press, 1983), 92–93.

15 Jardine, Lisa, "'No Offence I' th' world': *Hamlet* and Unlawful Marriage," in *Critical Essays on Shakespeare's Hamlet*, ed. David Scott Kastan (New York: G. K. Hall & Co., 1995), 93.

16 Curran, John, *Hamlet, Protestantism, and the Mourning of Contingency Not to Be* (Burlington: Ashgate, 2006), 17. Curran follows Calvinist theology to what he sees as its natural conclusion, a conclusion that he believes may have disturbed Shakespeare: If a divinity truly shapes and controls the destiny of mankind, then all of human life is an acting out of empty shows (217–18).

Human action, in this understanding, is worthless "within the relentless and predetermined unfolding of time" (218). As Curran develops his argument, he departs from the mainstream doctrine of the Reformation debate and focuses on Calvin's doctrine of predestination and election. This is a doctrine that the major Reformers did not agree on. Luther, in fact, warned his readers not to engage in speculation about predestination and election in many of his letters and commentaries. Luther warned them "not to make overcurious inquiries into His secret government" (Luther, *Works*, vol. 17, Gen. 43:6). Also see Luther, *Works*, vol. 54, pp. 57, 87, 249; vol. 6, Genesis 32:9.

17 Calvin, *Institutes*, 1.17.3.

18 Ibid., 1.17.4.

19 Ibid.

20 Eliot, T. S., "Hamlet and His Problems" [1950], *Twentieth Century Interpretations of Hamlet*, ed. David Bevington (Englewood Cliffs: Prentice Hall, 1968), 25.

21 Ibid.

22 Ibid.

23 Bloom, *Hamlet: Poem Unlimited*, 59.

24 See Ouditt, Sharon, "Explaining Women's Frailty," review of "A Heart Cleft in Twain: The Dilemma of Shakespeare's Gertrude" by Rebecca Smith, *Hamlet*, ed. Peter J. Smith and Nigel Wood (Buckingham: Open University Press, 1996), 89.

25 See Priestly, J. B., "Characters," *The English Journal* 20, no. 4 (1931): 325–27 for a more complete explanation of this criticism of Bradley. Also see Holland, Norman, "Where Is a Text? A Neurological View," *New Literary History* 33, no. 1 (Winter 2002): 21–38.

26 Bradley, A. C., *Shakespearean Tragedy*, 2nd ed. (London: Macmillan, 1905), 167.

27 Mark 6:34, the Geneva Bible, http://www.genevabible.org/. The accompanying note in the biblical text supports Hamlet's role as prophet and scourge in his mother's life, where true preaching is lacking: "This declareth that there is a horrible disorder among the people, where the true preaching of God's word wanteth."

28 Psalm 51:3, Geneva Bible. The accompanying marginal note for this passage reads as follows: "When thou givest sentence against sinners, they must needs confess thee to be just and themselves sinners." This note stresses the need for man to acknowledge his sin, a command Hamlet takes very seriously as he deals with his mother. His objective is to hold a mirror up to her soul so that she might see the sin in her life and be led to repentance and ultimately salvation.

29 Kastan, David Scott, "Very Like a Whale," *Critical Essays on Shakespeare's Hamlet*, ed. David Scott Kastan (New York: G. K. Hall & Co., 1995), 6.

30 Romans 6:2, Geneva Bible.
31 Ibid., notes 2a, 3c.
32 Romans 7:18, Geneva Bible.
33 Ibid.
34 Romans 7:18, Geneva Bible; see also note 11 under 7:15.
35 Romans 7:24, Geneva Bible, note d.
36 Luther, *Works*, vol. 25.
37 Bradley, *Shakespearean Tragedy*, 110.
38 Foakes, R. A., "Hamlet's Neglect of Revenge," in *Hamlet: New Critical Essays*, ed. Arthur F. Kinney (New York: Routledge, 2002), 95.
39 Ibid.
40 Luther, *Works*, vol. 35, p. 173.
41 Ibid., vol. 39, p. 188.
42 Ibid., vol. 22, John 1:18.
43 See Kelly, Philippa, "Surpassing Glass: Shakespeare's Mirrors," *Early Modern Literary Studies* 8, no. 1 (2002): 2.1–32, 3.
44 "The Council of Trent," *The American Catholic Truth Society*, online document, http://www.americancatholictruthsociety.com/docs/TRENT/trent6.html. Council of Trent, Session VI, January 13, 1547, Chapter XIV, reads as follows: "Hence, it must be taught that the repentance of a Christian after his fall is very different from that at his baptism, and that it includes not only a determination to avoid sins and a hatred of them, or a contrite and humble heart,[85] but also the sacramental confession of those sins, at least in desire, to be made in its season, and sacerdotal absolution, as well as satisfaction by fasts, alms, prayers and other devout exercises of the spiritual life."
45 Luther, *Works*, vol. 25, Romans 15:33.
46 Ibid., vol. 3, Genesis 17:23.
47 Ibid., vol. 25, Romans 15:33.
48 "The Council of Trent," Chapter XV (1546).
49 Luther, *Works*, vol. 48, pp. 281–82.
50 McEachern and Shuger, *Religion and Culture*, 10; Shell, *Catholicism*; Haigh, *English Reformations*; Duffy, *Stripping of the Altars*. Also see essays by Dutton, Wilson, and Findlay in *Region, Religion, and Patronage: Lancastrian Shakespeare* (Manchester: Manchester University Press, 2003).
51 Luther, Martin, "The Day of St. Mary Magdalene," in *Faith and Freedom: An Invitation to the Writings of Martin Luther*, ed. John Thornton and Susan B. Varenne (New York: Vintage Books, 2002), 237–38.
52 Calvin, *Institutes*, 1.18.1.
53 Marlowe, Christopher, *Doctor Faustus*, A-text, ed. David Bevington and Eric Rasmussen (Oxford: Oxford University Press, 1995), 5.1.35–46.
54 Ibid., 5.1.62–65.

55 Romans 7:15, Geneva Bible.
56 Luther, *Works*, vol. 48, pp. 281–82.

Chapter 2: *The Tempest*

1 See Luther's defense of his translation of the Gospels into the language of the masses in any number of his writings, especially Luther, *Works*, vols. 28, 32, 40, 42.
2 Calvin, *Institutes*, 3.3.8; Luther, *Works*, vol. 22, John 3:4.
3 Thomsen, Kerri Lynne, *Disappearing Daughters: Prosperpina and Medea in the Works of Spencer and Shakespeare* (dissertation, University of Massachusetts Amherst, 1994), 45. Kerri Thomsen argues convincingly that Miranda recognizes that the magic is Prospero's, but she also works with the interesting possibility that Miranda may in fact be upset that Prospero has in fact "appropriated the 'feminine tradition' of witchcraft for his own ends."
4 It is worth mentioning here that the act of raising the dead need not be understood as part of "black magic." This miracle is performed by Jesus multiple times in the gospels, and the disciples are actually commanded to perform this act among many other signs and wonders. The Gospel of Matthew records Jesus's command: "Heal the sick, cleanse the lepers, raise the dead, cast out devils: freely ye have received, freely give" (Matt. 10:8, Geneva Bible).
5 Coursen, H. R., *The Tempest: A Guide to the Play* (London: Greenwood Press, 2000), 15.
6 Stetner, S. C. V., and Goodman, O. B., "Lear's Darker Purpose," *Literature and Psychology* 18, no. 2–3 (1968): 82.
7 Ibid., 16.
8 Lisa Hopkins noted in a conversation on August 2, 2007, that Charles V indirectly causes the English Reformation by blocking the divorce of his aunt, Catherine of Aragon. This is an interesting connection that deserves additional attention, especially as it concerns the Reformation connection to Shakespeare's work.
9 Headley, John M., *The Emperor and His Chancellor: A Study of the Imperial Chancellery under Gattinara* (Cambridge: Cambridge University Press, 1983), 74–75.
10 Rodriguez-Salgado, M. J., *The Changing Face of Empire: Charles V, Philip II and Habsburg Authority, 1551–1559* (Cambridge: Cambridge University Press, 1988), 126.
11 Ibid., 129.
12 Ibid.
13 Maltby, William, *The Reign of Charles V* (New York: Palgrave, 2002), 117.

14 Brotton, Jerry, "'This Tunis, Sir, Was Carthage,'" in *Post-Colonial Shakespeares*, ed. Ania Loomba and Martin Orkin (London: Routledge, 1998), 30–31.
15 Luther, *Works*, vol. 52, p. 160.
16 See Coursen, Tempest; also see Mowat, Barbara, "Prospero, Agrippa, and Hocus Pocus" (1981), in *Critical Essays on Shakespeare's The Tempest*, ed. Virginia Mason Vaughan and Alden T. Vaughan (London: Prentice Hall, 1998); Sturgess, Keith, "'A Quaint Device': *The Tempest* at the Blackfriars," in *Critical Essays on Shakespeare's The Tempest*, ed. Virginia Mason Vaughan and Alden T. Vaughan (London: Prentice Hall, 1998); Kastan, David Scott, "'The Duke of Milan and His Brave Son': Dynastic Politics in *The Tempest*," in *Critical Essays on Shakespeare's The Tempest*, ed. Virginia Mason Vaughan and Alden T. Vaughan (London: Prentice Hall, 1998); Hirst, David, *The Tempest: Text and Performance* (London: Macmillan, 1984). David Hirst writes the following: "Shakespeare is strongly influenced by John Dee, and through Prospero makes a strong statement about the superiority of Renaissance values—learning, rediscovery of the art, scientific exploration—over the reactionary attitude which dominated the new century when James I came to the throne" (54).
17 Mowat, "Prospero"; see the quote from "A Letter, Nine Yeeres Since" by John Dee on p. 210.
18 Coursen, *Tempest*, 23.
19 Mowat, "Prospero," 198.
20 Szonyi, Gyorgy E., *John Dee's Occultism: Magical Exaltation through Powerful Signs* (New York: State University of New York Press, 2004), 251–52.
21 Gyorgy Szonyi's 2004 work is the most current on the topic.
22 Szonyi, *John Dee's Occultism*, 24.
23 Ibid., 252.
24 Kastan, "Duke of Milan," 98.
25 Quoted in Kastan, "Duke of Milan," 98.
26 Kastan, "Duke of Milan," 99.
27 Mowat, "Prospero," 208.
28 Empson, William, *Faustus and the Censor: The English Faust-book and Marlowe's Doctor Faustus*, ed. John Henry Jones (Oxford: Blackwell, 1987).
29 Hirst, *Tempest*, 54.
30 Orgel, Stephen, *The Oxford Shakespeare: The Tempest* (Oxford: Clarendon Press, 1987), 110.
31 Greenblatt, Stephen J., *Learning to Curse* (New York: Routledge, 1990), 116.
32 Mowat, "Prospero," 208.
33 See the Old Testament book Job. See also the Genesis account of Jacob in Genesis 32–33.
34 Feuer, Lois, "Happy Families: Repentance and Restoration in *The Tempest* and the Joseph Narrative," *Philological Quarterly* 76, no. 3 and 8 (1997).

35 Luther, *Works*, vol. 22, John 3:4.

36 Ibid., vol. 10, Psalm 36:11.

37 Jinkins, Michael, "Perkins, William (1558–1602)," *Oxford Dictionary of National Biography* (Oxford: Oxford University Press, 2004), http://www.oxforddnb.com/view/article/21973; Davies, Michael, "Falstaff's Lateness: Calvinism and the Protestant Hero in Henry IV," *The Review of English Studies, New Series* 56, no. 225 (Oxford: Oxford University Press, 2005).

38 Quoted in Ann Thomson's *The Art of Suffering and the Impact of Seventeenth-Century Anti-Providential Thought* (London: Ashgate, 2003), 71.

39 Thomsen, *Art of Suffering*, 71.

40 Ibid.

41 Cox, John D., "Recovering Something Christian about *The Tempest*," *Christianity and Literature* 50, no. 1 (2000): 38.

42 Davies, "Falstaff's Lateness," 362.

43 Luther, *Works*, vol. 22, John 3:4.

44 Ibid., vol. 13, Psalm 110:4.

45 Genesis 37:3.

46 Genesis 37:5.

47 Genesis 37:20.

48 Genesis 42:21–24.

49 Feuer, "Happy Families," 5.

50 Luther, *Works*, vol. 6, Genesis 37:10.

51 Bate, Jonathan, "From Myth to Drama," in *Critical Essays on Shakespeare's The Tempest*, ed. Virginia Mason Vaughan and Alden T. Vaughan (London: Prentice Hall, 1998), 48–9.

52 Genesis 43:30.

53 Luther writes:

> By this he teaches that in the world to come the life of the elect and saved will be in heaven and will be a heavenly being and life, where we shall no longer have to work, have toil or trouble, eat, drink, mourn, or be sorrowful, as we must in this world. We shall have an eternal Sabbath and holy day, be eternally satisfied in God, eternally joyful, safe, and free of all sorrow. We shall see God and His work eternally, not hidden behind a veil, as in this life the veil has been drawn over Him, but "with unveiled face" (2 Cor. 3:18) in the revelation. It will not be an earthly, temporal life, but a heavenly, eternal life. (*Works*, vol. 12, Ps. 8:4)

54 Genesis 45:4–8. Luther's comments about Joseph and the process of humiliation relate to Prospero's role as minister:

> Accordingly, Joseph deals rather harshly with his brothers. It is his purpose to urge them on to repentance and the acknowledgment

> of their sinfulnes, to slay their smugness and drive them to despair by threatening death and punishments of every kind. He does not say that they will render satisfaction for sin in this manner, as the papists prattle. No, he wants to arouse grief and contrition and to induce them to seek health and cleansing for themselves . . . Thus God afflicts us with various disasters, not to punish us, although this really is a punishment. But He takes no pleasure in it. What, then, does He mean by sending so many troubles, vexations, sicknesses, etc.? He does this in order that you may be led to a knowledge of your sin. (*Works*, vol. 7, Gen. 42:8)

55 Feuer, "Happy Families," 6.

56 Luther, *Works*, vol. 37, p. 95.

57 Ibid., "The Book of Concord," Smalcald 3, III, 2.

58 Shakespeare, *Othello*, 5.2.300: "Demand me nothing. What you know, you know. / From this time forth I never will speak word."

59 See Hopkins, Lisa, *Beginning Shakespeare* (Manchester: Manchester University Press, 2005), 172.

60 Ibid.

61 Stories about cannibals and such places created a stir in England when, in the early 1600s, the Virginia Company lost a ship destined for the American colonies. The sea venture was separated from the rest of the voyagers and was shipwrecked on Bermuda. It is believed by some that Shakespeare was given permission to read a well-protected letter from one of the members of this vessel, William Strachey. It may have been that some of the details in *The Tempest* were drawn from Strachey's letter. LoMonico, Mike, "Columbus Day," *Folger Shakespeare Library*, accessed 12 July 2017, https://folgereducation.wordpress.com/2009/10/09/columbus-day/.

62 Lupton, Julia Reinhard, "The Minority of Caliban: Thinking with Shakespeare and Locke," in *Thinking with Shakespeare*, ed. Julia Reinhard Lupton (Chicago: University of Chicago Press, 2011), http://www.thinkingwithshakespeare.org/files/MinorityCaliban.pdf, 4.

63 Ibid., 18.

64 In 3.2.85ff., Caliban convinces Stephano to batter Prospero's skull with a log, to "paunch him with a stake," and to "cut his wezand with thy knife" (*The Tempest* 3.2.85–87).

65 Lupton, "Minority," 15.

66 Ibid., 8.

67 Ibid., 2.

68 Orgel, Stephen, "Introduction," *William Shakespeare's The Tempest* (Oxford: Oxford University Press, 1987), 28.

69 Lupton, "Minority," 18. Lupton's handling of the attempted rape is far too mild. See p. 18 for her description.

70 Ibid.

71 Caliban references his imprisonment in the rocks. After this scene, we witness him running freely through the island. Miranda also refers to Caliban's confinement, but at no time in the course of the play do we see Caliban sitting in his rocky prison (*The Tempest* 1.2.361).

72 Skura, Meredith Anne, "Discourse and the Individual: The Case of Colonialism in *The Tempest*" (1989), in *Critical Essays on Shakespeare's The Tempest*, ed. Virginia Mason Vaughan and Alden T. Vaughan (London: Prentice Hall, 1998), 65.

73 Ibid.

74 Fernie, Ewan, "Introduction," in *Spiritual Shakespeares*, ed. Ewan Fernie (New York: Routledge, 2005), 23.

75 Skura, "Discourse," 66.

76 Hunter, Robert Grams, *Shakespeare and the Comedy of Forgiveness* (New York: Columbia University Press, 1965), 241.

77 Luther, *Works*, vol. 26, Galatians 3:22.

78 Greenblatt, *Learning to Curse*, 26.

79 Romans 1:29–32.

80 Luther, *Works*, vols. 20–28.

81 Cox, "Recovering Something Christian," 47.

Chapter 3: *King Lear*

1 Myrick, Kenneth, "Christian Pessimism in *King Lear*," in *Shakespeare 1564–1964*, ed. Edward A. Bloom (Providence: Brown University Press, 1964), 67.

2 Ibid.

3 Myrick, "Christian Pessimism," 66–67.

4 Shakespeare, William, *King Lear*, ed. R. A. Foakes (London: Arden, 1997). All references to *King Lear* in this chapter are to the Arden Edition.

5 Ibid., 2.2.16, notes 16–18.

6 Ibid., 4.6, notes 231–40. Foakes claims that the accent is one of a West Country yokel.

7 Myrick, "Christian Pessimism," 66–67; Jenkins, Gary W., "Smith, Henry (c. 1560–1591)," *Oxford Dictionary of National Biography* (Oxford: Oxford University Press, 2004), http://www.oxforddnb.com/view/article/25811.

8 Ibid., 61.

9 Myrick, "Christian Pessimism," 66–67.

10 Shell, *Catholicism*, 16.

11 Bloom, *The Invention of the Human*, 455.

12 Shakespeare, *King Lear*, 169.

13 Schneider, Ben Ross, Jr., "*King Lear* in Its Own Time: The Difference That Death Makes," *Early Modern Literary Studies* 1, no. 1 (1995): 3.1–49, 24.
14 Luther, *Works*, vol. 47, pp. 5–16, 30–55.
15 Calvin, *Institutes*, 4.20.32.
16 Hooker, *Works*, vol. 1, pp. 144–45, note 3.
17 Diehl, "Religion and Shakespearean Tragedy," 91.
18 Luther, *Works*, vol. 54, p. 346.
19 Ibid., vol. 25, Romans 15:33.
20 See note 1. "Miscreant," *Oxford English Dictionary* (Oxford: Oxford University Press, 2006), accessed 24 August 2007, http://dictionary.oed.com/cgi/entry/00311151?single=1&query_type=word&queryword=miscreant&first=1&max_to_show=10.
21 Luther, *Works*, vol. 25, pp. 202–3.
22 Booth, Stephen, "On the Greatness of *King Lear*," in *Twentieth Century Interpretations of King Lear*, ed. Janet Adelman (Englewood Cliffs: Prentice Hall, 1978), 111.
23 Bickersteth, Geoffrey L., "The Golden World of *King Lear*," annual Shakespeare lecture (London: Geoffrey Cumberlege, 1946), 5.
24 Greenblatt, Stephen, "Shakespeare and the Exorcists," in *Critical Essays on Shakespeare's King Lear*, ed. Jay L. Halio (New York: G. K. Hall & Co., 1996), 110.
25 Luther, *Works*, vols. 52, 58, 59.
26 Calvin, *Institutes*, 36–7.
27 Hooker, *Works*, vol. 3, "A Learned Sermon of the Nature of Pride," pp. 387–88.
28 Targoff, Ramie, *Common Prayer: The Language of Prayer in Early Modern England* (Chicago: University of Chicago Press, 2001), 48.
29 Luther, *Works*, vols. 52, 59.
30 Bickersteth, "Golden World," 23.
31 Luther, *Works*, vols. 52, 59.
32 Buechner, Frederick, *Speak What We Feel* (New York: HarperCollins, 2001), 132.
33 In note 3.7.67–9 of *King Lear*, R. A. Foakes includes a reference to Peter Brooks's 1962 production of the play in which Cornwall gouges out Gloucester's eye with a spur.
34 Tromly, Fred B., "Grief, Authority and the Resistance to Consolation in Shakespeare," in *Speaking Grief in English Literary Culture: Shakespeare to Milton*, ed. Margo Swiss and David A. Kent (Pittsburgh: Duquesne University Press, 2002), 35.
35 Schleiner, Winfried, "Justifying the Unjustifiable: The Dover Cliff Scene in *King Lear*," *Shakespeare Quarterly* 36, no. 3 (1985): 338.
36 Wilson, *Secret Shakespeare*, 285.

37 Miola, Robert, "Jesuit Drama in Early Modern England," in *Theatre and Religion*, 79.

38 Ibid.

39 Luther, Martin, *Tischreden*, vol. 3 (Weimar: Böhlau, 1967), 52–53.

40 Luther, *Works*, vols. 52, 59.

41 Ibid.

42 Aquinas writes the following, describing humiliation as a spiritual discipline employed by a man or woman to gain humility:

> The spontaneous embracing of humiliations is a practice of humility not in any and every case but when it is done for a needful purpose: for humility being a virtue, does nothing indiscreetly. It is then not humility but folly to embrace any and every humiliation: but when virtue calls for a thing to be done it belongs to humility not to shrink from doing it, for instance not to refuse some mean service where charity calls upon you to help your neighbours. . . . Sometimes too, even where our own duty does not require us to embrace humiliations, it is an act of virtue to take them up in order to encourage others by our example more easily to bear what is incumbent on them: for a general will sometimes do the office of a common soldier to encourage the rest. Sometimes again we may make a virtuous use of humiliations as a medicine. Thus if anyone's mind is prone to undue self-exaltation, he may with advantage make a moderate use of humiliations, either self-imposed, or imposed by others, so as to check the elation of his spirit by putting himself on a level with the lowest class of the community in the doing of mean offices.

(*The Catholic Encyclopedia*, online at http://www.newadvent.org/cathen/index.html)

43 A Reformation understanding of humiliation is represented by the following excerpt from Luther, *Works*. Luther's description is far more violent and severe than that found in the teachings of the Roman Catholic Church, especially as proposed by Aquinas. Luther writes:

> But we do not understand, and the reason is that the flesh stands in the way. It cannot endure the mortification of itself and hinders the spirit so that it cannot perceive the boundless love and goodwill of God towards us until it comes forth from this struggle and repels the hindrances of the flesh. But the same things are copiously handed down everywhere in Holy Scripture. For it is stated in Rev. 3:19: "Those whom I love, I reprove and chasten." In Prov. 3:11–12 we read: "My son, do not despise the Lord's discipline or be weary of His reproof, for the Lord reproves him whom He loves, as

> a father the son in whom he delights." These and other statements like them are very striking and memorable. But is it taking delight in a son to strike him with scourges and blows? Scripture certainly teaches this, and experience testifies the same. For those who are good and faithful fathers chastise their sons severely. (*Works*, vol. 6, Gen. 33:1)

44 In the following passage, Luther uses the story of Joseph (Gen. 42) to describe the process of humiliation as one that leads to redemption:

> Accordingly, Joseph deals rather harshly with his brothers. It is his purpose to urge them on to repentance and the acknowledgment of their sinfulness, to slay their smugness and drive them to despair by threatening death and punishments of every kind. He does not say that they will render satisfaction for sin in this manner, as the papists prattle. No, he wants to arouse grief and contrition and to induce them to seek health and cleansing for themselves . . . Thus God afflicts us with various disasters, not to punish us, although this really is a punishment. But He takes no pleasure in it. What, then, does He mean by sending so many troubles, vexations, sicknesses, etc.? He does this in order that you may be led to a knowledge of your sin. (*Works*, vol. 7, Gen. 42:8)

45 Fernie, Ewan, *Shame in Shakespeare* (London: Routledge, 2002), 173.
46 Calvin, *Institutes*, 4.20.32.
47 Myrick, "Christian Pessimism," 62.

Chapter 4: *Henry VIII*

1 Shakespeare, William, *Henry VIII*, ed. S. Schoenbaum (New York: Penguin, 2004). All *Henry VIII* citations are drawn from the Signet Classic Edition.
2 Knecht, R. J., *Renaissance Warrior and Patron: The Reign of Francis I* (Cambridge: Cambridge University Press, 1994), 171. Also see Holinshed's "Chronicles," 371.
3 Jack, Sybil M., "Wolsey, Thomas (1470/71–1530)," *Oxford Dictionary of National Biography* (Oxford: Oxford University Press, 2004), http://www.oxforddnb.com/view/article/29854.
4 Russell, Joycelyne G., *The Field of Cloth of Gold: Men and Manners in 1520* (London: Routledge & Kegan Paul, 1969), 27.
5 Ibid.
6 Knecht, *Renaissance Warrior*, 171, and Russell, *Field of Cloth*, 23–46.
7 Russell, *Field of Cloth*, 49.
8 Ibid., 190.

9 Holinshed, "Chronicles," 373.
10 Russell, *Field of Cloth*, 187.
11 Holinshed, "Chronicles," 371.
12 Pearlman, E., *William Shakespeare: The History Plays*. (New York: Twayne Publishers, 1992), 172.
13 Morley, Carol A., "John Fletcher," Teaching Shakespeare and Early Modern Dramatists, ed. Lisa Hopkins and A. Hiscock (New York: Palgrave Macmillan, 2007), 1.
14 Pearlman, *History Plays, 175.*
15 While Augustine and others wrote extensively on the depravity of man long before Martin Luther, the church of the early modern period had moved well beyond the Augustinian view of man to something far more Pelagian. Pelagianism allowed for a more participatory view of salvation, one in which men were required and therefore deemed able to participate with God in the work of salvation.
16 Shuger, Debora, "Subversive Fathers and Suffering Subjects: Shakespeare and Christianity," in *Religion, Literature, and Politics in Post-Reformation England, 1540–1688*, ed. Donna B. Hamilton and Richard Strier (Cambridge: Cambridge University Press, 1996), 46.
17 Greenblatt, *Will in the World*, 321.
18 Ibid.
19 Fernie, *Shame in Shakespeare*, 183.
20 Ibid., 184.
21 Luther, *Works*, vol. 26, Galatians 1:13.
22 Ibid.
23 Ibid.
24 Augustine, "St. Augustine and the Psalms," trans. Hebgin, Dame Scholastica, and Dame Felicitas Corrigan (London: Newman Press, 1961), 369–70.
25 Bonner, Gerald, "Pelagius (fl. c. 390–418)," *Oxford Dictionary of National Biography* (Oxford: Oxford University Press, 2004), http://www.oxforddnb.com/view/article/21784.
26 Marlowe, Christopher, *The Tragedy of Doctor Faustus*, B-1616, ed. W. W. Greg (Oxford: Clarendon Press, 1950), 1.1.25.
27 Ibid., 1.1.17–22.
28 Ibid., 1.1.46.
29 Ibid., 1.1.80–84.
30 De Lubac, Henri, S. J., *Augustinianism and Modern Thought* (New York: Herder and Herder, 1969), 101.
31 Luther writes:

> For beyond nature, in which glorying about works is implanted, I also acquired the disposition and custom of paying attention to my works and my worthiness. But I know for certain that now one

reading and one Our Father avails more and is more acceptable to God than all those prayers I mumbled for 15 whole years, for I know that I am heard. There is no need of any vigils or of special fasts and of abstinence, for God gave me "a messenger of Satan" (2 Cor. 12:7) together with other difficulties and the crosses of this world which plague me more than all those things. (*Works*, vol. 5, Gen. 29:4)

32 For a more exhaustive definition of Pelagian thought, see Henri de Lubac, *Augustinianism and Modern Thought*, especially pages 3–5 but also continuing through page 100. De Lubac's text does an excellent job of explaining two views of grace and of human depravity. Also see Daniel Stempel's work, "The Silence of Iago," in *PMLA* 84, no. 2 (1969): 252–63. In this article, Stempel claims that Iago is "the spokesman of Jesuit 'Pelagianism'" (256).

33 Hunt, Maurice, *Cymbeline: Constructions of Britain* (London: Ashgate, 2005), 136.

34 Luther, *Works*, Romans 5.

35 Hunt, *Cymbeline*, 134.

36 Luther, *Works*, Matthew 9:20–22. Also quoted in Hunt, *Cymbeline*, 146.

37 Ibid., Galatians 1:13.

38 Fernie, *Shame in Shakespeare*, 184.

39 Luther, *Works*, Isaiah 23:7.

40 Daniell, David, "Shakespeare and the Protestant Mind," in *Shakespeare Survey*, vol. 54, ed. Peter Holland (Cambridge: Cambridge University Press, 2001), 11–12.

41 The Signet Classic edition of *The Famous History of the Life of King Henry VIII*, ed. S. Schoenbaum (New York: Penguin, 2004). According to S. Schoenbaum, the Cavendish text "was utilized by chroniclers from Stowe (1565) onwards" (365).

42 Cavendish, George, *The Life of Cardinal Wolsey* (London: Harding and Lepard, 1827), online *Google Books*, https://books.google.com/books?id=cisIAAAAQAAJ&pg=PA96#v=onepage&q&f=true, 394.

43 Boswell-Stone, *Shakespeare's Holinshed*, 482.

44 Calvin, *Institutes*, 1.1.35.

45 Ibid., 1.1.36–7.

46 Felperin, Howard, "Shakespeare's *Henry VIII*: History as Myth," *Studies in English Literature* 6, no. 2 (1966): 244.

47 Written in 1607.

48 Dekker, Thomas, and Webster, John, "The Famous Historie of Sir Thomas Wyat," in *The Dramatic Works of Thomas Dekker*, ed. Fredson Bowers (Cambridge: Cambridge University Press, 1953), 1.1.1–3, 9–10, 13–19.

49 Ibid., 1.1.9–15.

50 Ibid., 1.2.37–38.
51 Ibid., 1.2.53–54.
52 Ibid., 5.2.50–51.
53 Ibid., 5.2.129–34, 137–40.
54 Felperin, "History as Myth," 244.
55 Haigh, *English Reformations*, 288.
56 Philippians 2:12.
57 Luther, *Works*, Galatians 3:23.
58 Haigh, *English Reformations*; Duffy, *Stripping of the Altars*.
59 Haigh, *English Reformations*, 214.
60 Duffy, Eamon, "Recent Trends in the Study of Christianity in Sixteenth-Century Europe: The English Reformation after Revisionism," *Renaissance Quarterly* 59, no. 3 (2006): 721–22.
61 Haigh, *English Reformations*, 277.
62 Luther, *Works*, Galatians 3:23.
63 Ibid., Matthew 5:14—"Thus God gave the Law to reveal sin and to work wrath (Rom. 4:15). Therefore it is a discipline and a rod, or as Paul says, 'our custodian' (Gal. 3:24), without which the flesh does not understand sin. But God is not accustomed to give grace or to help us unless the folly that is fastened on a boy's back and the wickedness that is in a man's heart are revealed, so that they become fit for grace. He seeks humiliation, contrition, and condemnation unto life. Accordingly, true repentance is not contrition alone; it is also faith, which takes hold of the promise, lest the penitent perish. But these brothers have not yet arrived at perfect knowledge of sin. Therefore Joseph will continue to plague them. They must be put through the mill even more. One must get up and say: 'Everything that is born and lives on earth is useless, it is rotten and corrupt before God.' Thus we condemn the sanctity, wisdom, and worship which the whole world has thought up for itself, apart from the Word of God and without holding to Christ alone, as the devil's invention, which belongs in the abyss of hell."
64 Ibid., Romans 10:9.
65 Ibid., John 1:10.
66 Fernie, "Introduction," 8.
67 Ryan, Kiernan, "'Where Hope Is Coldest': All's Well That Ends Well," in *Spiritual Shakespeares*, ed. Ewan Fernie (London: Routledge, 2005), 37.

Chapter 5: *Othello*

1 Vitkus, Daniel J., "Turning Turk in *Othello*: The Conversion and Damnation of the Moor," *Shakespeare Quarterly* 48, no. 2 (1997): 145–76. Vitkus claims that Othello is portrayed as a monster and as the personification of the fears that surrounded the Elizabethan view of the Turk.

2 Watson, Robert, "*Othello* as Reformation Tragedy," in *The Company of Shakespeare: Essays on English Renaissance Literature in Honor of G. Blakemore Bruster*, ed. Thomas Moisan and Douglas Bruster (London: Associated University Presses, 2002), 66.

3 Shakespeare, *Othello*, 25.

4 Luther, *Works*, vol. 4, Genesis 21:17.

5 Ibid., vol. 26, Galatians 1:15.

6 "The Council of Trent," 14th Session, Chapter I.

7 Luther, *Works*, vol. 30, 1 John 2:19.

8 Calvin, *Institutes*, 3.4.17.

9 Ibid., 1.1.36–37.

10 Ibid., 1.1.1.

11 Ibid., 1.1.37.

12 Aristotle's *Poetics*, trans. S. H. Butcher, The Internet Classics Archive by Daniel C. Stevenson, http://classics.mit.edu//Aristotle/poetics.html. On hamartia, see I.VI, I.XIV, I.XV; on anagnorisis, see I.XI; on peripeteia, see I.VI.

13 Ibid.

14 Luther, *Works*, vol. 26, p. 126.

15 Ribner, Irving, *Patterns in Shakespearian Tragedy* (London: Methuen & Co Ltd., 1960), 99.

16 Moisan, Thomas, "Repetition and Interrogation in *Othello*," in *The Company of Shakespeare: Essays on English Renaissance Literature in Honor of G. Blakemore Bruster*, eds. Thomas Moisan and Douglas Bruster (London: Associated University Presses, 2002), 66.

17 Moisan, "Repetition and Interrogation," 66; O'Day, Rosemary, "Ascham, Roger (1514/15–1568)," *Oxford Dictionary of National Biography* (Oxford: Oxford University Press, 2004), http://www.oxforddnb.com/view/article/732. John S. Mebane describes Ascham, though briefly, as a champion of chivalry and manners in "'Impious War': Religion and the Ideology of Warfare in Henry V," *Studies in Philology* 104, no. 2 (2007): 250–66. John Carpenter writes the following in his essay, "Placing Thomas Deloney": "Conservative educator Roger Ascham conflates poetic and moralistic perspectives, condemning London shops for being 'so full of lewd and rude rymes,' 'lewd' alluding to moral content and 'rude' applying to formal structure. Ascham reverses the high/low metaphor while maintaining its binary view of cultural placement, claiming that low-grade writers of both 'bookes and balettes make great shew of blossomes and buddes, in whom is neither roote of learning nor frute of wisdome at all' (Elizabethan Critical Essays 1.31). This metaphor is important in that blossoms and buds are

attractive to all: ballads are tempting but dangerous" (*Journal of Narrative Theory* 36, no. 2 [2006]: 125–62, 306). Besides Ascham, important writers who denigrated romance include Vives, Erasmus, Francis Meres, and Thomas Nashe. See Nelson, William, *Fact or Fiction: The Dilemma of the Renaissance Storyteller* (Cambridge: Harvard University Press, 1973).

18 Moisan, "Repetition and Interrogation," 67.

19 Mangan, Michael, *A Preface to Shakespeare's Tragedies* (London: Longman Group, 1991), 152.

20 Bradley, *Shakespearean Tragedy*, 59.

21 Ibid., 61.

22 Ribner, *Shakespearian Tragedy*, 99.

23 Vitkus, "Turning Turk," 145–76. Daniel J. Vitkus claims that Othello's "fear of female sexual instability is linked in the play to racial and cultural anxieties about 'turning Turk'—the fear of a black planet that gripped Europeans in the early modern era as they faced the expansion of the Ottoman power" (146).

24 Loomba, Ania, *Gender, Race, Renaissance Drama* (Manchester: Manchester University Press, 1989), 54.

25 Fernie, *Shame in Shakespeare*, 138.

26 Bloom, *Invention of the Human*, 455.

27 Bradley, *Shakespearean Tragedy*, 59. See Lupton's "Othello Circumcised: Shakespeare and the Pauline Discourse of Nations," *Representations* 57 (1997): 73–89; see also Lupton's "Ethnos and Circumcision in the Pauline Tradition: A Psychoanalytical Exegesis," in *The Psychoanalysis of Race*, ed. Christopher Lane (New York: Columbia University Press, 1998): 193–210, and her essay "Creature Caliban," *Shakespeare Quarterly* 51, no. 1 (2000): 1–23; Sinfield, A., *Faultlines: Cultural Materialism and the Politics of Dissident Reading* (Berkeley: University of California Press, 1992), 33–35. A. C. Bradley's claims about Othello's race are frightening: "If the reader has even chanced to see an African violently excited, he may have been startled to observe how completely at a loss he was to interpret those bodily expressions of passion which in a fellow-countryman he understands at once, and in a European foreigner with somewhat less certainty" (59). Julia Lupton takes a different course, seeking to make a connection between Othello's racial and religious identity. Lupton makes some interesting points about Othello's ethnicity in her essay "Creature Caliban." In this essay, she suggests that Caliban "might appear to be a sorry cousin of Othello" (6). Sinfield describes Othello as a black barbarian suffering under racial discrimination, this being the major thrust of the play.

28 Lupton, "Othello Circumcised," 79.

29 Sohmer, Steve, "The 'Double Time' Crux in *Othello* Solved," *English Literary Renaissance*, 32, no. 2 (2002): 214–38; Gilbert, Anthony, "*Othello*, the

Baroque, and Religious Mentalities," *Early Modern Literary Studies* 7, no. 2 (2001): 3.1–21, http://purl.oclc.org/emls/07-2/gilboth.htm. By asserting that Shakespeare "repeatedly associated pilgrimage with his Catholic characters" (224), Steve Sohmer builds a case for a Roman Catholic Othello. Sohmer also describes Iago as a Roman Catholic figure, a "repository of the rival doctrine of merit" (236). Anthony Gilbert describes Othello as a Roman Catholic who is tempted by a Protestant Iago to distrust all things Roman Catholic (3).

30 Luther, *Works*, vol. 26, p. 10.

31 Calvin, *Institutes*, 4.10.1.

32 Luther, *Works*, vol. 22, pp. 51–52.

33 Matthew 23:15, 24, Geneva Bible.

34 Moisan, "Repetition and Interrogation," 57.

35 Ibid., 58.

36 Luther, *Works*, vol. 22, p. 264.

37 Calvin, *Institutes*, 3.12.6.

38 Philippians 3:7–9, Geneva Bible.

39 Braden, Gordon, *Renaissance Tragedy and the Senecan Tradition* (New Haven: Yale University Press, 1985), 176–77.

40 Luther, *Works*, vol. 22, p. 144.

41 Elliot, G. R., *The Flaming Minister* (Durham, NC: Duke University Press, 1953), 236.

42 Ibid., 238.

43 Matthew 13:46, Geneva Bible.

44 Cruden, Alexander, *A Complete Concordance to the Holy Scriptures of the Old and New Testaments* (Hartford: S. S. Scranton & Company, 1899), 432.

45 Matthew 7:6, Geneva Bible.

46 In his forthcoming book, *Laughing and Weeping in Early Modern Theatres*, Matthew Steggle includes the following account of the powerful affect that Desdemona's gaze had on one early modern audience:

> Other descriptions draw attention to the boy-actor playing a woman as a figure particularly likely to induce audience weeping. One example of this is the eye-witness account of a touring performance of Othello at Oxford in 1610, written in Latin by the academic Henry Jackson. Normally considered of interest for its description of a boy-actor at work, it also contains within it the unexamined assumption that a performance at a theatre has moved its audience to tears:
>
> In the last few days the King's Actors have been here. They performed, with the greatest applause, in a full theatre . . . they also had tragedies, which they performed with decorum and skill. In them, not just in their speaking, but also in their action, they moved tears

> [lachrymas movebant] . . . Desdemona, when dead, was even more moving than when alive, lying on the bed imploring the pity of the spectators even with her expression.

Steggle, Matthew, *Laughing and Weeping in Early Modern Theatres: Studies in Performance and Early Modern Drama Studies* (Aldershot: Ashgate, 2007). Steggle cites the passage above from Salgado, Gāmini, *Eyewitneses of Shakespeare:* First Hand Accounts of Performances, 1590–1890 (New York: Barnes & Noble, 1975), 30. This is Steggle's translation.

47 Fernie, Ewan, "Shame in *Othello*," *The Cambridge Quarterly* 28, no. 1 (1999): 172.

48 Luke 22:48, Geneva Bible.

49 Acts 1:18, Geneva Bible.

50 Shakespeare, *Othello*, 342–43.

51 Fernie, "Shame in *Othello*," 172.

52 Calvin, *Institutes*, 1.1.1.

53 Luther, *Works*, vol. 25, Romans 15:33.

54 Shakespeare, *Othello*, ed. Edward Pechter (New York: W. W. Norton & Company, 2004), 98.

55 Matthew 4:8, Geneva Bible.

56 Matthew 16:21–23, 26, Geneva Bible.

57 See St. John-Stevas, Norman, *Life, Death and the Law* (New York: World Publishing Company, 1964), 232–46. Also see Carlo Leget's "Authority and Plausibility: Aquinas on Suicide," in *Aquinas as Authority*, ed. Paul van Geest, Harm Goris, Carlo Leget (Leuven: Peeters, 2002), 279. In this work, Leget claims that both Augustine's and Aquinas's teachings on suicide were upheld by the Roman Catholic Church until the late eighteenth century. These teachings required "severe and cruel punishments" for those who commit suicide and their families (279). Aquinas claimed that suicide was "a sin against three laws: natural law, moral law, and divine law" (279).

58 Gilbert, "Religious Mentalities," 7. Gilbert claims that Othello's suicide is honorable and compares it to a soldier's death.

59 This notion further supported by Edward Hubler's work, "The Damnation of Othello: Some Limitations on the Christian View of the Play," *Shakespeare Quarterly* 9, no. 3 (1958): 295–300. Hubler claims that "Shakespeare's audience, a diverse collection of people, was [not] as orthodox as we are told" (299). Hubler contends that the Shakespeare's audience would have been divided in its understanding of suicide. Hubler describes the early modern period as "a time of curiosity and questioning and doubting the ultimate value of things in which one believed" (299). Vitkus, in "Turning Turk," argues for the damnation of Othello. Vitkus's analysis fails to take into consideration the differences between Roman Catholic doctrine and Protestant doctrine. First, in regard to suicide, Vitkus makes the inaccurate claim that all Christians in the early modern era understood suicide as "a faithless act of despair, bringing certain damnation" (175). In fact, suicide was not understood as an unpardonable sin by either Martin Luther or John Calvin. See note 58 in "Turning Turk" for more on the Protestant understanding of suicide as established by Martin Luther and John Calvin. Although John Donne's *Biathanatos* was not published until after his death in 1647, he wrote the text in 1607 and 1608. In this work, John Donne examines the moral implications of suicide and criticizes Aquinas's claim that suicide violates the laws of nature. Donne also argues that the Bible does not condemn suicide and that God may allow suicide for purposes related to His glorification. See "John Donne: *Biathanatos*," in *Garland English Texts*, no. 1, ed. Stephen Orgel (New York: Garland Publishing, 1982). Also see Siemens, R. G., "'I Haue Often Such a Sickly Inclination': Biography and the Critical Interpretation of Donne's Suicide Tract, *Biathanatos*," *Early Modern Literary Studies* Special Issue 7 (2001): 10.1–26, http://purl.oclc.org/emls/si-07/siemens.htm. Also see David Colclough's "Donne, John (1572–1631)," *Oxford Dictionary of National Biography* (Oxford: Oxford University Press, 2004), http://www.oxforddnb.com/view/article/7819. Vitkus also confuses the Reformation and Roman Catholic doctrines of justification. By claiming that Othello "is 'doubly damned' for backsliding" (176), Vitkus unknowingly employs a Roman Catholic understanding of justification, for according to Reformation theology, there are no sins outside of blasphemy of the Holy Spirit that a person can commit that will earn them certain damnation.

60 Gilbert's contention turns the argument into a confusion of the Roman Catholic doctrine of works. Does Othello's noble heart and unselfish intention earn him salvation and thereby trump his sin of suicide? While Gilbert seeks to separate himself from a Roman Catholic reading of the play, his ultimate conclusion and his confusion of doctrine results in his return to a reading that is largely Roman Catholic in nature.

61 Luther, *Works*, vol. 54, p. 29. John Calvin's teachings on suicide are similar to Luther's. Calvin claims that a person who commits suicide has been defeated by the schemes of the devil. See Jeffrey R. Watt's "Calvin on Suicide," *Church History* 66, no. 3 (1997): 463–76. In Calvin's commentary on Matthew, he opposes the Roman Catholic teaching on suicide, declaring that the only "unpardonable sin" is to "blaspheme against the Holy Spirit." Calvin explains that this sin is of a specific nature, not including sins of malice such as murder or self-mutilation. Calvin writes:

> We do not maintain, that those persons are said to pour contempt on the Spirit of God, who oppose his grace and power by hardened malice; and farther we maintain, that this kind of sacrilege is committed only when we knowingly endeavor to extinguish the Spirit who dwells in us . . . This passage refutes also the error of those

> who imagine that every sin which is voluntary, or which is committed in opposition to the conscience, is unpardonable. On the contrary, Paul expressly limits that sin to the First Table of the Law; and our Lord not less plainly applies the word blasphemy to a single description of sin, and at the same time shows, that it is of a kind which is directly opposed to the glory of God. "Que c'est un peche qui battaille directement contre la gloire de Dieu;"—"that it is a sin which fights directly against the glory of God."

Calvin, *Commentary on a Harmony of the Evangelists, Matthew, Mark, and Luke*, vol. 2, trans. Rev. William Pringle (Grand Rapids: Baker Books, 2003); Matthew 12:31, note 31.

62 See Luther, *Works*, vol. 26, Galatians 3; vol. 28, 1 Timothy 1; vol. 54.

63 Ibid.

Chapter 6: *The Winter's Tale*

1 See Knight's "Great Creating Nature," in *Modern Critical Interpretations*, ed. Harold Bloom (New York: Chelsea House, 1987). I agree with G. Wilson Knight when he describes *The Winter's Tale* as a play in which "Orthodox tradition is used, but it does not direct; a pagan naturalism is used too. The Bible has been an influence; so have classical myth and Renaissance pastoral; but the greatest influence was Life itself, that creating and protecting deity whose superhuman presence and powers the drama labours to define" (45). Though I agree that there are many influences and many ideas at work within this play, I feel strongly that there is a directing theology that governs this very spiritual text. The approach I take to the play will not negate the fact that Shakespeare works with classical myth and Renaissance pastoral or rule out the possibility that Shakespeare employs pagan naturalism alongside biblical themes. The approach I use in this essay is of a largely historical flavor. Shakespeare weaves the theology of the Protestant Reformers into *The Winter's Tale*.

2 Alpers, Paul, *What Is Pastoral?* (Chicago: University of Chicago Press, 1996), 221; Hatten, Robert S., "Shubert's Pastoral: The Piano Sonata in G Major, D894," in *Shubert the Progressive: History, Performance, Practice, Analysis*, ed. Brian Newbould (Aldershot: Ashgate, 2003), 151. Hatten's work focuses on the evolution of the pastoral in music, but he makes some very interesting comparisons with the same in literature.

3 Girard, René, "The Crime and Conversion of Leontes in *The Winter's Tale*," *Religion and Literature* 22, no. 2–3 (1990): 193ff.; Martz, Louis L., "Shakespeare's Humanist Enterprise: *The Winter's Tale*," in *Modern Critical Interpretations*, ed. Harold Bloom (New York: Chelsea House, 1987);

Hunt, Maurice, "'Standing in Rich Place': The Importance of Context in *The Winter's Tale*," in *Rocky Mountain Review of Language and Literature* 38, no. 1–2, 1984; Knapp, Jeffrey, *Shakespeare's Tribe: Church, Nation, and Theater in Renaissance England* (Chicago: University of Chicago Press, 2002), see Appendix 2 "Autolycus."

4 Cicero, Marcus Tullius, *De Officiis*, book 1:50, trans. Walter Miller (Cambridge: Harvard University Press, 1913), http://www.constitution.org/rom/de_officiis.htm.

5 Ibid., book 1:43, 44, 54.

6 Haigh, *English Reformations*, 287–88.

7 Ibid.

8 Luther, *Works*, vol. 4, pp. 41, 44, 52. Also see Brenda Jung's "A Time for Truth: 15th Anniversary Issue," in *Modern Reformation* 16, no. 1 (2007): 20.

9 Rust, Jennifer, "Wittenberg and Melancholic Allegory," in *Shakespeare and the Culture of Christianity in Early Modern England*, ed. Dennis Taylor and David Beauregard (New York: Fordham University Press, 2003), 266–67.

10 Ibid., 267.

11 Isaiah 9:6. All biblical references drawn from a modern translation of the Geneva Bible. Bible Gateway, *The Geneva Bible* [1599] (Tolle Lege Press), accessed 17 July 2017, www.biblegateway.com/passage/?search=Genesis+1&version=GNV.

12 Luke 2:25–32.

13 Lupton, Julia Reinhard, *Afterlives of the Saints: Hagiography, Typology, and Renaissance Literature* (Stanford: Stanford University Press, 1996), 186.

14 Greenblatt, Stephen, *Will in the World: How Shakespeare Became Shakespeare* (New York: W. W. Norton & Company, 2004), 131.

15 Ibid.

16 Fernie, Ewan, "Shakespeare, Spirituality, and Contemporary Criticism," in *Spiritual Shakespeares*, ed. Ewan Fernie (London: Routledge, 2005), 8.

17 Miller, David Lee, *Dreams of the Burning Child* (Ithaca: Cornell University Press, 2003), 118.

18 See Fernie, Ewan, ed., *Spiritual Shakespeares* (London: Routledge, 2005) for a collection of essays including work by Kiernan Ryan, David Ruiter, Lisa Freinkel, Richard Kearney, and others.

19 Ryan, "Where Hope Is Coldest," 37.

20 Luther, *Works*, vol. 14, Psalm 118:1.

21 Ibid.

22 Ibid.

23 McGrath, Alister, *Iustitia Dei: A History of the Christian Doctrine of Justification* (Cambridge: Cambridge University Press, 1986), 5.

24 Ibid.

25 Greenblatt, *Will in the World*, 84.

26 Hooker, Richard, *Ecclesiastical Polity*, ed. John Keble, 5.78.3, note 1 (Oxford: Clarendon Press, 1876), accessed 17 July 2017, http://anglicanhistory.org/hooker/.

27 Hebrews 13:15, marginal note, Geneva Bible.

28 Luther, *Works*, Psalm 118:1.

29 Calvin, *Commentary on a Harmony*, Matthew 27:27.

30 Shuger, Debora, *The Renaissance Bible: Scholarship, Sacrifice, and Subjectivity* (Berkeley: University of California Press, 1994), 96.

31 See also Jensen, Phebe, "Singing Psalms to Horn-pipes: Festivity, Iconoclasm, and Catholicism in *The Winter's Tale*," *Shakespeare Quarterly* 55, no. 3 (2004): 305.

32 Haigh, *English Reformations*, 288.

33 For Louis Montrose, see *The Purpose of Playing: Shakespeare and the Cultural Politics of the Elizabethan Theatre* (Chicago: University of Chicago Press, 1996), 30–32. For Stephen Greenblatt, see *Shakespearean Negotiations: The Circulation of Social Energy in Renaissance England* (Berkeley: University of California Press, 1988), 125–27.

34 Greenblatt, *Negotiations*, 125–27.

35 Knapp, *Shakespeare's Tribe*, 8.

36 Quoted from Knapp, *Shakespeare's Tribe*, 8.

37 Ibid. Originally in Debora Shuger's "Subversive Fathers," 46.

38 Philippians 2:12.

39 In Calvin's *Institutes*, the Reformer quotes the words of Bernard, affirming the way in which men and women perform good works: "The testimony of conscience, which Paul calls 'the rejoicing' of believers, I believe to consist in three things. It is necessary, first of all, to believe that you cannot have remission of sins except by the indulgence of God; secondly, that you cannot have any good work at all unless he also give it; lastly, that you cannot by any works merit eternal life unless it also be freely given" (Calvin, *Institutes*, 1.2.41).

In regard to mankind's dependence upon God for good works, *The Book of Homilies* includes the following:

> Our Sauiour Christ sayth, There is none good, but GOD (Mark 10.18, Luke 18.19): and that we can doe nothing that is good without him, nor no man can come to the father but by him (John 15.5, 14.6) . . . In the meane season, yea, and at all times let vs learne to know our selues, our frailty and weakenesse, without any craking or boasting of our owne good deedes and merits. Let vs also knowledge the exceeding mercy of GOD towards vs, and confesse, that as of our selues commeth all euill and damnation: so likewise of him commeth all goodnesse and saluation.

"Homily on the Misery of Mankind," in *The First Book of Homilies*, ed. Ian Lancashire (Toronto: University of Toronto, 1994), accessed 17 July 2017, http://www.anglicanlibrary.org/homilies/bk1hom02.htm.

Luther writes simply: "there is no 'congruity' or work performed before grace" (*Works*, Galatians 2:17).

40 Greenblatt, *Will in the World*, 132.

41 Ibid.

42 Foakes, Reginald A., *Shakespeare: The Dark Comedies to the Last Plays: From Satire to Celebration* (London: Routledge, 2005), 66.

43 Adelman, Janet, *Suffocating Mothers: Fantasies of Maternal Origin in Shakespeare's Plays, Hamlet to The Tempest* (New York: Routledge, 1992), 222.

44 In *Suffocating Mothers*, Janet Adelman suggests that it is Hermione's pregnant body, a symbol of female sexuality, that interrupts and thereby disrupts the peaceful relations between the two men. Adelman writes: "Hermione's entrance—perhaps literally between the two kings?—disrupts this male haven. The visual impact of her pregnant body inevitably focuses attention on her, reminding the audience of what has been missing from the gentlemen's conversation; and her body immediately becomes the site of longing and terror, its very presence disruptive of male bonds and male identity" (220).

Adelman continues by making a connection between Hermione's pregnant body and sexual temptation. Polixenes begins this conversation by disclosing the fact that he and Leontes were tempted with sexual sin as young men: "Polixenes may call Hermione 'most sacred lady,' but he makes her body the locus and the sign of division and original sin, as Hermione is quick to note (1.2.80–82). Moreover, her visible pregnancy stages the submerged logic of his account of original sin: temptations have been born to us, her presence suggests, because we have been born to them, acquiring original sin at the site of origin" (221).

45 Adelman, *Suffocating Mothers*, 220.

46 Luther, *Works*, Romans 15:33.

47 Hunt, "Standing in Rich Place" 21.

48 Miller, *Dreams of the Burning Child*, 10.

49 Martz, "Shakespeare's Humanist Enterprise" 137.

50 Ibid.

51 Knight, "Great Creating Nature," 26; Hunt, "Standing in Rich Place"; Richmond, Velma Bourgeois, *Shakespeare, Catholicism, and Romance* (New York: Continuum, 2000); Adelman, *Suffocating Mothers*. Adelman praises Paulina as an agent of restoration (235). See Mary Nichols's "*The Winter's Tale*: The Triumph of Comedy over Tragedy," *Interpretation* 9, no. 2 (1981): 169; Jensen, "Singing Psalms to Horn-pipes," 279.

52 Luther, *Works*, John 7:38.

53 Calvin, *Institutes*, 2.2.6.

54 In a sermon by Richard Hooker published in 1612, the Reformer stated: "We are not dust and ashes but worse, our minds from the highest to the lowest are not right . . . not capable of that blessedness which we naturally seek but subject to that which we most abhor anguish tribulation death woe endless misery." See paragraph 4. Hooker, Richard, "A Learned Sermon of the Nature of Pride," in *The Works of That Learned and Judicious Divine Mr. Richard Hooker with an Account of His Life and Death by Isaac Walton*, vol. 3, arranged by the Rev. John Keble MA, 7th edition revised by the Very Rev. R. W. Church and the Rev. F. Paget (Oxford: Clarendon Press, 1888), accessed 17 July 2017, http://oll.libertyfund.org/titles/hooker-the-works-of-richard-hooker-vol-3/simple.

Luther writes, "I answer that the whole task of the apostle and of his Lord is to humiliate the proud and to bring them to a realization of this condition, to teach them that they need grace, to destroy their own righteousness so that in humility they will seek Christ and confess that they are sinners and thus receive grace and be saved" (*Works*, Rom. 15:33).

55 Diehl, *Staging Reform*, 88.

56 From Robert Burton's *The Anatomy of Melancholy* as quoted in Susan Snyder's "The Left Hand of God: Despair in Medieval and Renaissance Tradition," *Studies in the Renaissance* 12 (1965): 30.

57 Snyder, "Left Hand of God," 33.

58 Knight, "Great Creating Nature," 25.

59 Perkins, William, *The Work of William Perkins*, vol. 3 (1607), *The Courtenay Library of Reformation Classics* (Abingdon: Sutton Courtenay Press, 1970), 87.

60 Beeke, Joel R., "William Perkins on Predestination and Preaching," in *A Puritan's Mind*, ed. C. Matthew McMahon, http://www.apuritansmind.com/puritan-favorites/william-perkins/perkins-on-predestination-and-preaching/, *Works*, 1:70 (1607).

61 Luther, *Works*, Galatians 4:7.

62 Snyder, "Left Hand of God," 32–33.

63 Knight, "Great Creating Nature," 26; Hunt, "Standing in Rich Place"; Richmond, *Shakespeare, Catholicism, and Romance*; Adelman, *Suffocating Mothers*.

64 Hunt, "Standing in Rich Place," 24.

65 Ibid.

66 Girard, "Crime and Conversion," 194.

67 Ibid., 202.

68 Shakespeare, *Hamlet*, 5.2.10.

69 Wilson, *Secret Shakespeare*, 246.

70 Luther, *Works*, Psalm 51:18.
71 Ibid.
72 Taylor, "Introduction," 17.

Chapter 7: *Cymbeline*

1 Shakespeare, William, *Cymbeline*, ed. Barbara A. Mowat and Paul Werstine (New York: Washington Square Press, 2003). All cited material from *Cymbeline* comes from the Folger Edition.
2 See Alison Thorne's "'To Write and Read / Be Henceforth Trecherous': *Cymbeline* and the Problem of Interpretation," in *Shakespeare's Late Plays: New Readings*, ed. Jennifer Richards and James Knowles (Edinburgh: Edinburgh University Press, 1999). Following the editors of the Oxford and Norton editions, Alison Thorne, Stephen Greenblatt, and other prominent critics, I have chosen to employ this spelling of the heroine's name. This spelling, writes Thorne, "recall[s] the legendary first queen of Britain" (178).
3 For a cross section of authors who have played prominently into this notion, see Peter G. Platt's *Reason Diminished: Shakespeare and the Marvelous* (Lincoln: University of Nebraska Press, 1997), 140. Also see Frank Kermode's "*Cymbeline*," *William Shakespeare: The Final Plays* (London: Longmans, Green & Co., 1963), 19–29; Meredith Skura's "Interpreting Posthumus' Dream from Above and Below: Families, Psychoanalysis, and Literary Critics," in *Representing Shakespeare: New Psychoanalytic Essays*, ed. Murray M. Schwartz and Coppélia Kahn (Baltimore: Johns Hopkins University Press, 1980), 203–16; Leah Marcus's *Puzzling Shakespeare: Local Reading and Its Discontents* (Berkeley: University of California Press, 1988); and Peggy Munoz Simonds's *Myth, Emblem, and Music in Shakespeare's Cymbeline: An Iconographic Reconstruction* (Newark: University of Delaware Press, 1992).
4 Moffet, Robin, "*Cymbeline* and the Nativity," *Shakespeare Quarterly* 13, no. 2 (1962): 214.
5 Simonds, *Myth, Emblem, and Music*, 296.
6 Hill, Geoffrey, "The True Conduct of Human Judgment," in *The Morality of Art*, ed. D. W. Jefferson (London: Routledge & Kegan Paul, 1969), 30.
7 Harp, Richard, "Providence in Shakespeare's Late Plays," in *Shakespeare's Last Plays: Essays in Literature and Politics*, ed. Stephen W. Smith and Travis Curtright (Lanham: Lexington Books, 2002), 22.
8 Harp's work identifies the prominent role of Providence in the play, a role that fits well with the Reformation strokes identified within this chapter. See page 30 of Harp's "Providence."
9 The approximate historical date of the action of *Cymbeline* is AD 40. See Malcolm Todd's "Cunobelinus (d. c. AD 40)," *Oxford Dictionary of National*

Biography (Oxford: Oxford University Press, 2004), http://www.oxforddnb.com/view/article/6939. I am also indebted to Lisa Hopkins for her insightful comments on the matter.

10 Moffet, "*Cymbeline* and the Nativity," 207–18; Miola, Robert, "*Cymbeline*: Shakespeare's Valediction to Rome," in *Roman Images: Selected Papers from the English Institute, 1982*, ed. Annabel Patterson (Baltimore: John's Hopkins University Press, 1984), 52–54.

11 Nevo, Ruth, "*Cymbeline*: The Rescue of the King," in *New Casebooks: Shakespeare's Romances*, ed. Alison Thorne (New York: Palgrave Macmillan, 2003), 96.

12 Shakespeare, *Cymbeline*, 1.1. 201.

13 Alvis, John E., "*Cymbeline* in Context: The Regime Issue," in *Shakespeare's Last Plays: Essays in Literature and Politics*, ed. Stephen W. Smith and Travis Curtright (New York: Lexington Books, 2002), 41.

14 Ibid., 42.

15 Shakespeare, *Othello*, 3.3.445–46.

16 This reference is drawn from Innogen's conversation with Iachimo, where she states with great conviction that she must not act on any rash emotion. Where Innogen is successful at guarding her heart, Posthumus fails miserably.

17 Betteridge, Thomas, *Shakespearean Fantasy and Politics* (Hertfordshire: University of Hertfordshire Press, 2005), 171.

18 Ibid.

19 Arbery, Glenn C., "The Displaced Nativity in *Cymbeline*," in *Shakespeare's Last Plays: Essays in Literature and Politics*, ed. Stephen W. Smith and Travis Curtright (Lanham: Lexington Books, 2002), 164.

20 Harold Bloom in *Invention of the Human* makes an interesting observation about Iago's genius: "We cannot arrive at a just estimate of Othello if we underestimate Iago, who would be formidable enough to undo most of us if he emerged out of his play into our lives . . . Othello is a great soul hopelessly outclassed in intellect and drive by Iago" (438).

21 In Shakespeare, *Othello*, 4.1.196, and in Shakespeare, *Cymbeline*, 2.4.147.

22 "Homily on the Misery of Mankind."

23 Goddard, Harold, "*Cymbeline*," in *Shakespeare's Romances*, ed. Harold Bloom (Philadelphia: Chelsea House Publications, 2000), 85.

24 In act 2, scene 5, Posthumus delivers his infamous criticism of women.

25 Platt, *Reason Diminished*, 147.

26 Ibid.

27 Romans 7:15, 19, 24.

28 Romans 6:1–4.

29 Beeke, "William Perkins."

30 That Jupiter/ Jove may indeed be understood as referring to the Christian God is based on the fact that the name of the Christian God could not be spoken on the English stage during the early seventeenth century. A more complete argument focusing on this topic can be found in Simonds's work *Myth, Emblem, and Music.* In this work, Simonds points out that during the seventeenth century, Jove/ Jupiter was a "standard English euphemism for the deity" (294).

31 Calvin, *Institutes*, 1.17.11.

32 Quoted from Lila Geller's "*Cymbeline* and the Imagery of Covenant Theology," *Studies in English Literature, 1500–1900* 20, no. 2 (1980): 245.

33 Calvin, *Institutes*, 1.17.11.

34 Jones-Davies, Margaret, "*Cymbeline* and the Sleep of Faith," in *Theatre and Religion*, 197.

35 Ibid.

36 Harp, "Providence," 19.

37 Job 38:1–2, 4, 12.

38 Luther, *Works*, Genesis 33:1.

39 Luke 12:25–27, 28b, 30b.

40 Luther, *Works*, vol. 45, p. 480.

41 Shakespeare, *Hamlet*, 5.2.10.

42 Moffet, "*Cymbeline* and the Nativity," 211, 209.

43 Simonds, *Myth, Emblem, and Music*, 31, 35, 48.

44 Ibid., 36.

Conclusion

1 *King Lear*, ed. R. A. Foakes. (London: Arden, 1997), 1.1.159. References are to act, scene, and line.

2 Luther, *Works*, vol. 27, Galatians 1:1.

3 Ibid.

4 Calvin, *Institutes*, 1.1.1.

5 Hooker, Richard, *Laws of Ecclesiastical Polity*, 6th ed. (Oxford: Oxford University Press, 2014), 1.2.2, p. 201.

6 Haigh, *English Reformations*, 288.

7 Ibid.

8 See Haigh, *English Reformations*, and Duffy, *Stripping of the Altars*. Also see Lisa Freinkel's work *Reading Shakespeare's Will: The Theology of Figure from Augustine to the Sonnets* (New York: Columbia University Press, 2002), 121. Luther's controversial teaching on human depravity and the sin that separates man from God is described with great accuracy by Lisa Freinkel. She writes, "Luther argues that the flesh is not simply the corporeal self but the human as creature in distinction from the Creator. Carnality in this light goes far beyond concupiscence, far beyond the corporeal, to include intangibles like our reason, our intentions, and our desires . . . for Luther the opposition between flesh and spirit is absolute: it is the opposition of

Creator to creature and of infinite commandment to finite capacity" (121). Freinkel goes on to describe the great tension caused by Luther's teaching on works and faith, the former "which can never achieve salvation" (123).

9 Haigh, *English Reformations*, 288.

10 Calvin, *Institutes*, 2.4.7.

About the Author

John J. Norton is full professor and chair of the English department at Concordia University Irvine. His career as a Shakespeare scholar began at Sheffield Hallam University under the tutelage of Lisa Hopkins (*Shakespeare on the Edge: Border-Crossing in the Tragedies and the Henriad* and *Beginning Shakespeare*). Norton has researched Shakespeare's cultural influence all over the world, from Beijing, China, to Kolkata, India, to Kigali, Rwanda, to Leipzig, Germany. Norton enjoys research and uncovering new insight in the great Shakespeare canon as well as enticing undergraduates at Concordia University to read and appreciate the great Bard.

Made in the USA
San Bernardino, CA
03 January 2019